DEEP DELTA JUSTICE

DEEP DELTA JUSTICE

A BLACK TEEN, HIS LAWYER, AND THEIR GROUNDBREAKING BATTLE FOR CIVIL RIGHTS IN THE SOUTH

MATTHEW VAN METER

Little, Brown and Company
New York Boston London

Little, Brown and Company
Hachette Book Group
1290 Avenue of the Americas, New York, NY 10104
littlebrown.com

First Edition May 2020

Little, Brown and Company is a division of Hachette Book Group, Inc. The Little, Brown name and logo are trademarks of Hachette Book Group, Inc.

The publisher is not responsible for websites (or their content) that are not owned by the publisher.

The Hachette Speakers Bureau provides a wide range of authors for speaking events. To find out more, go to hachettespeakersbureau.com or call (866) 376–6591.

Map by John Barnett

ISBN 978-0-316-43503-1
LCCN 2020930302

10 9 8 7 6 5 4 3 2 1

LSC-C

Printed in the United States of America

For C., even so.

Contents

Prologue—Down the Road   3

1—A Dirty Storm   7

2—The Boss   19

3—What Is Ours   29

4—Contact   40

5—Going to War   48

6—Determination and Unity   59

7—Dire Straits   64

8—Cruelty   71

9—Klantown, USA   78

10—The Case for the Prosecution   86

11—The Case for the Defense   96

12—Investigation   101

13—Trouble   107

14—No Error of Law   111

15—The Chief Engineer   117

16—Bailing Out   122

17—Where Is Your Law?   128

18—Absent and Unrepresented   133

19—The Fruits of Benevolence   137

20—Losing Everything   143

CONTENTS

21—Having a Field Day   149

22—Flambeaux   159

23—Suppression   169

24—The Facts of This Case   179

25—If It Ain't True, It Oughta Be   185

26—First and Foremost   194

27—Workhorse   200

28—Profound Judgment   204

29—Tranquility   209

30—A Clean Storm   218

Epilogue   223

Afterword   227

Acknowledgments   233

Notes   237

Sources   267

Index   277

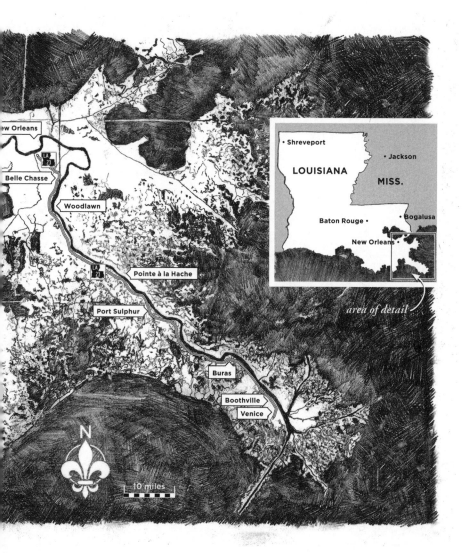

New Orleans

Belle Chasse

Woodlawn

Pointe à la Hache

Port Sulphur

Buras

Boothville
Venice

N

10 miles

Shreveport

Jackson

LOUISIANA

MISS.

Baton Rouge

Bogalusa

New Orleans

area of detail

DEEP DELTA JUSTICE

Prologue—Down the Road

THE EARLY AFTERNOON of October 18, 1966, was a picture of ideal fall in southern Louisiana. Songbirds and waterfowl navigated invisible eddies, while from across the levee came the diesel-engine throb of ships making their way down the last few miles of the Mississippi River.

Two black boys trudged out of Boothville-Venice High School. Bert Grant and Bernard St. Ann were cousins, and they stuck together for safety. On the first day of school that year, they had been among seventy-eight black students who had walked through an angry throng of white neighbors to break segregation's stranglehold on their school district.

Both boys were in seventh grade, although someone watching them make their way home from school that day might have said they didn't look like it. Grant was confident and athletic, and he towered over St. Ann, who was small and timid despite being two years older.

As they approached the Little Fish barroom, they heard voices behind them, laughing and egging one another on.

"Hey!" shouted one voice, over the others. "What's y'all's names?"

Grant and St. Ann walked faster. The laughter grew.

"I said, what's you all's names?"

Grant turned and saw four white boys. He recognized a couple of them; they had jumped him that day in the bathroom. He didn't know what to do. St. Ann slunk behind him. The white boys were crossing the road towards them and smirking.

———

Gary Duncan was exhausted. After a long week working a tugboat on the Mississippi River, he had jumped straight into his car, not even bothering to change out of his uniform. He had gotten off work at noon, and he wanted to go on up to New Orleans to visit his wife, who had just given birth to their first child. But he hadn't wanted to make the trip without a spare tire, so he was driving back to Boothville-Venice with his cousin, which was not what he wanted to be doing.

As he passed the Little Fish bar, Gary saw six boys gathered up on the far side of the highway, four white and two black. He recognized the black boys as his nephew Bert and cousin Bernard. Something wasn't right. He stopped the car and backed up to them.

Gary took stock of the scene. At nineteen, he wasn't much older than the boys he was looking at. Until just a few years ago, he had been in school himself—the "Negro school" a ways up the road.

The six boys parted slightly as his car pulled up, and Gary could see that none of them had been fighting. Still, he didn't like that Bert and Bernard were outnumbered, and he couldn't imagine that the interaction was friendly. Bernard had spit on his shirt and looked shaken. Gary got out of the car.

"What's wrong, Bert?" he asked.

"These boys want to fight us," replied his nephew.

"No," countered one of the white boys. "We just want to know their name."

"Well, don't you suppose you could ask him his name?" Gary said to the boy. He waved Bert and Bernard towards the car: "Come on, y'all get in the car."

As his nephew and cousin walked behind him, Gary turned to the curly-haired white boy who glared defiantly as the others standing around him averted their eyes. He recognized Herman Landry. He *knew* the Landrys, so he was shocked to see the anger in this child's eyes.

"Do you want to know my name?" Gary said, an edge creeping into his voice.

"Sure."

"Can you read?"

"Yeah."

Gary stepped towards the boy and looked down at him—Landry was a foot shorter than he was. He pointed to the embroidered name tag on his green uniform and asked flatly, "You still want to know it?"

Landry did not look, but spat, "Yeah."

Gary stood for a second, his finger still touching the stitched letters on his breast. Landry met his gaze with hard eyes. Neither one spoke a word as the tension between them quivered and then slackened. Gary turned back to his car, which Bert and Bernard were climbing into.

He heard Landry's voice whisper low behind him.

"He's a real smart nigger, ain't he?"

Blood surged in Gary's head, and he spun around. "What did you say?"

"You're a smart nigger, ain't you?"

Gary squared himself to Landry and then took a breath.

"You best run along home now," he said, reaching out to the boy's arm in a gesture that was both conciliatory and final—the conversation was over.

———

The moment that Gary's hand came into contact with Landry's arm marked the beginning of one of the most important—and improbable—criminal cases in American history. Gary's gesture that day would put a crack in the dam that strained to hold back racial strife in his community. And, just as surprisingly, it would help dismantle the infrastructure of white supremacy that had strangled that community for centuries.

The next two years would contain a life's worth of plot twists for Gary. His legal odyssey would take him from his tiny hometown to the Supreme Court of the United States; at stake would be the function of civil rights lawyers in the South and the fundamental right to a trial by jury.

———

Gary and Landry locked eyes for a moment as they touched. Then the boy withdrew his arm as if bitten by a snake, and Gary turned and strode back to the car.

As he was walking away, he heard Landry mutter, "My people can put you in jail for that."

Gary, ignoring the threat, drove back down the road.

1—A Dirty Storm

> graves at my command
> Have wak'd their sleepers, op'd, and let 'em forth
> By my so potent Art.
> —Shakespeare, *The Tempest*

THERE ARE TWO kinds of storms, they say, in Plaquemines Parish, Louisiana: there are clean storms, and there are dirty storms. Hurricane Betsy was a dirty storm.

———

On an August day in 1965, the astronauts of Gemini V sped at fifteen thousand miles per hour, a hundred and fifty miles above the tangled deltas of southern Louisiana.

"It sure is a pretty day down over the Caribbean here," said astronaut Gordon Cooper. Below the capsule, the sea sparkled, dappled with puffy cumulus clouds that, the astronauts noticed, gathered into a colossal gyre—a storm.

"That's Betsy," mission control informed them. The tropical depression—which drew in the moist summer air as a drain draws in water—appeared to stretch at least a hundred miles in each direction from its central eye. As they spun away on their ninety-minute orbit, the astronauts could see pulses of lightning illuminating the dark clouds from within.[1]

A few days later, Gemini V hurtled down through the atmosphere, cutting a fiery path from Louisiana to a quiet patch in the Atlantic. Mission control cut the flight short when Betsy, now a tropical storm and rapidly intensifying, lurched north towards the planned splashdown site off the coast of Florida.[2]

Directly below Gemini V as it went into radio blackout for reentry, Gary Duncan was getting ready for church, unaware of the historic spaceflight ending above his head. Big and athletic, with umber-colored skin and huge hands abraded to a leathery toughness from thousands of hours at sea, he wasn't scared of hurricanes.

Gary lived with his family on a narrow plot of land in Boothville, Louisiana, that backed up to the river levee, a grassy berm of earth that kept the Mississippi River from overtopping its banks. Across the road, barely a hundred yards from the house, was the back levee, which protected the habitable land from the wild marsh beyond.

You might hear the Duncans before you saw them. Boisterous and argumentative by nature, the children argued and ribbed one another about everything from scriptural interpretation to the proper use of filé in gumbo. Their parents, Lambert and Mazie, smiled and tried to tune out the cacophony. Both mother and father worked compulsively; they were makers of things. Lambert made extravagant home improvements by hand when he wasn't taking a job on one of his two boats, and Mazie stayed up long after the others had gone to bed, chewing tobacco at the sewing machine as she made clothes for the family.[3]

Of eight siblings, Gary was the baby, and the one thing they all could agree on was that he was spoiled—they knew it because they did the spoiling. Impish and restless, Gary was always sneaking out and causing trouble, but it was part of the pact with his siblings that they would protect him from whipping, even if it meant taking one themselves.

He was only eighteen, but Gary had already spent much of his life on the water. He didn't even remember the first time he had set foot on a boat. He had started trawling for shrimp with his brothers when he was twelve years old, so by the time he first took the helm of a boat, he knew every pass and bay and bayou in Plaquemines Parish, his home.

Plaquemines Parish—Louisiana counties are called parishes—is the end of the road. It sits at the extreme end of the Mississippi River, southeast of New Orleans, almost entirely surrounded by the Gulf of Mexico.

The river built Gary Duncan's world, and the river defined it. Every granule of earth that made up Plaquemines (pronounced "PLACK-uh-mens" or "PLACK-mins") had been carried by water from the Great Plains or the Appalachians or the Rockies and deposited in the Gulf, eventually building a delta in the shape of a bird's foot. From its source, in Minnesota, to its mouth, near Boothville, the Mississippi River carved a 2,300-mile path through the interior of the United States, forming the third-most-populous river basin in the world. The mouth of the Mississippi in Plaquemines was the anchor of a vast expanse of marshland that stretched from the Everglades to Mexico.

The marsh had always drawn people to Plaquemines. Only 5 percent of the land in the parish lay between the levees and could be built on.* The rest was wetlands, fretted with bayous and great fields of grass that overflowed with life. There were even settlements out there, tiny clutches of wooden shacks built on stilts and accessible only by boat, where people subsisted on what they could shoot or trap or catch in a net.[4]

But for most of the parish's twenty-four thousand residents, life existed on the narrow ribbon of land between the levees. Everything in Plaquemines Parish was either "up the road" or "down the road."† The road was State Highway 23, and it was the spine of the west bank, winding seventy miles south from New Orleans. Only one town, with the aspirational name of Venice, sat farther down the road than Boothville. From there, the thin ribbon of land on the west bank of the Mississippi dissipated into the Gulf.

---

* Today, the percentage of habitable land in Plaquemines is quite a bit greater than it was in 1965, but only because the total landmass of the parish has shrunk enormously. A complex set of factors, including rising sea levels and saltwater intrusion, has led to the Louisiana marsh disappearing at an average rate of more than a football field per hour. Much of the land that comprised the Plaquemines of Gary's youth is now open water.

† These are also place names. "Up the Road," used as a location rather than a direction, always means Jefferson Parish and New Orleans. "Down the Road," or just "DTR," refers to Plaquemines.

A few miles up the road was Buras, a boomtown fueled by thousands of high-paying jobs in the offshore oil industry.[5]

Hard work was deep in the culture of Plaquemines. Almost as early as Gary Duncan could remember, he had been working. After school in the winter, he had clipped and packed oranges or worked in the bean fields and gardens. He ran cattle on the levee. And if he wasn't working agriculture, he was on a boat. He was so young when he got his first job that his mother had to sign a release before he could be hired. All of the Duncan boys were raised to be independent, both personally and financially, and they taught one another the skills they needed.[6]

There were just so many ways to make money in Plaquemines Parish. Work was freedom and security. Work provided for the family and allowed for leisure. Since the 1930s, the oil industry had dominated. There was so much work available with oil companies that a lifelong Plaquemines resident remembers newcomers in suits walking down the shoulder of Highway 23 with briefcases, striding right into the oil-field offices, so sure were they that a job was waiting for them. Men worked in the fields in dozens of roles, each paying well enough to support a family. Many of them roughnecked on the offshore rigs that had sprung up along the continental shelf. The work was hard, and it was dangerous ("If you didn't get burned up in a fire, you got blowed up by an explosion," said one man who worked at Chevron), but it paid better than almost anything else a man could do with a high-school education.[7]

But the oil fields offered jobs only to white workers, so black men did what everybody in Plaquemines had always done: they worked the land and they worked the water. There was gardening, tugboats, domestic work, seafood processing, tending and harvesting citrus, and the beginnings of a charter fishing business. There was trapping, Plaquemines Parish's oldest industry (at one time, Louisiana produced more furs than any other state). Most of all, in Boothville, there was trawling. Gary worked as a deckhand on his brothers' shrimp boats and learned that, by getting up early and finding the right spots, a man could make almost as much money shrimping as in the oil fields, though the job was seasonal and came with no benefits.

The water provided a good living to black people in Boothville; there was no wealth, but they owned their own houses and cars and boats.[8]

But just as it made the parish, the water also threatened it. Hurricanes and floods had killed thousands in Plaquemines over the years. Until the 1920s, the only real protection came from the landscape itself—the river built up a small natural levee, and the marshland absorbed the force of incoming storm surge. When those barriers were overcome, whole communities had been wiped out in a matter of hours.[9]

But as Hurricane Betsy made its way north from the Caribbean and began to threaten the Gulf, few in Plaquemines Parish were really worried. Since 1928, when the Army Corps of Engineers had built the Mississippi levee system— the world's largest—no storm had breached those massive defenses.[10]

But no one had expected Betsy to grow so large or move so fast.

———

A hurricane is essentially a jet engine. It sucks in air and, using the combustive fuel of warm ocean water, energizes that air with heat and moisture, sending it spinning into the sky as soaring, puffy clouds. But as the clouds tower higher and the pressure beneath the uplifted air gets lower, the center of the system collapses, hurtling back to the surface of the ocean, where it becomes yet more charged with heat and moisture and is catapulted aloft again to repeat the cycle. As the system grows, it rotates and pulls in still more air to feed itself.

Betsy paused in the Atlantic, gathering fuel from the warm sea, spinning faster and growing. When it lurched towards Florida, its eye was sixty miles across, the largest ever photographed. Miami residents had less than twenty-four hours to evacuate. Some were still stuck in traffic when the storm surge trapped them in their cars.[11]

In Plaquemines, the first sign of danger came when three thousand roughnecks were brought in from the offshore oil rigs. Perhaps spooked by the reports of Betsy's assault on Florida, the oil companies swiftly sent their people to land. Two days later, the evacuation order came.

Evacuating Plaquemines was uniquely challenging: the parish was a giant bottleneck, and even a well-organized exodus would leave thousands of residents waiting in line on the highway, where they were vulnerable.

But no one worried too much. For people in Plaquemines, leaving was a hassle and an expense, but they had weathered hurricanes before. Finding shelter was a part of life, a familiar inconvenience.[12]

———

Boothville awoke at five in the morning on September 9 as patrol cars rolled slowly down the highway, blaring the evacuation order from loudspeakers. A light rain was soaking into the soil—Betsy's eye was still hundreds of miles away, but ribbons of rain clouds lashed away at the storm's fringe.[13]

The Duncans began packing at once, except for Gary and two of his brothers, Mancil and Calvin, who said they would stay behind to close up the house. Then they planned to head to the Venice Marina to ride out the storm. It sounded like fun. They would take Lambert's dog and pick up some wine and a few friends, and they could enjoy the impromptu day off from the safest place: on the water. Calvin was captain of a big two-engine tugboat, the *Sea Master,* which would bob right over the storm surge, they reasoned.

Their mother was not pleased. The family was going up to New Orleans, and she did not like the idea of leaving three of her four sons in harm's way. But they had ridden out storms before, and anyway she knew they were past the age when a mother's insistence had power, so she climbed into the car and joined the line of sleepy families making their way up Highway 23 in the dark.

Gary piled his brothers, two friends, and the dog into his car and drove down to the marina, passing over The Jump, as locals called the last of the huge Army Corps of Engineers levees. Beyond The Jump, the land was precarious, though a network of breakwaters offered some protection. Gary's convoy was joined at the dock by many others, some intent on staying with their boats, some just sick of waiting in line on the highway. A couple of sheriff deputies were at The Jump, pleading with residents to turn around and go up the road to safety. They were ignored.[14]

The Duncan boys loaded food and booze onto the *Sea Master* and, for good measure, tied their father's boats and Calvin's skiff to the big tug. There were already two or three hundred people on boats spread out in the harbor. Some families without other accommodation caught rides to the marina and boarded a steel-hulled sand dredge that, while clammy and uncomfortable, was like a floating bomb shelter.[15]

Gary parked his car on a high spot on the levee and returned to the little flotilla. In the tight cabin, he cracked open a beer and waited. Darkness fell, and the rumble of rain on the cockpit roof grew until it sounded like a continuous roll of thunder. Above that low, wet sound came another: a high whistling that was rounded out by a low tone you could feel in your chest, like the deep bass notes of an organ.[16]

Gary knew the sounds of a hurricane, but this howling was like nothing he had heard before. A rhythmic knocking sound reverberated through the cabin, and Gary jumped up. He exchanged a glance with his brothers, and he knew they all worried about the same thing: that a steel barge had come free and would smash the smaller boats to pieces.

Gary looked out the window and saw Calvin's skiff crashing against one of Lambert's tugs, rubbing off the paint and sending little slivers of wood flying. He started praying that the skiff would sink.

He could see the water level rising. First, the marshland dropped out of sight, then the pastures began to disappear, and then the bushes and shrubs, until only trees were visible. Muddy water gushed through a channel up the road from them, roiling back into the marina in a visible current. The *Sea Master* rose with all the boats, but the storm was not yet halfway over, and already the Gulf was spilling in.

As the water covered everything around them, the brothers' prayers were answered, and Calvin's skiff sank before it could beat a hole in the hull of their father's boat. They wished, though, that they had had the presence of mind to bring Gary's portable radio with them. Without it, they had no way of knowing how others were faring or how long the storm might last. But it was back in his car, a hundred yards or more away, an impossible distance to travel in these fatal conditions.

Late at night, Gary felt the wind and rain diminish. Betsy's eye had passed over Venice, he knew, and it occurred to him that he had a window of time to run and get his radio. He raced from the cabin and into the eerie silence. Storm surge had submerged all of the land except for a skinny band of levee, and Gary ran out along it towards his car. It was dark, but he knew the marina well, almost by feel, and he wasted no time—the calm of the eye would not last for long.

He saw with relief that the car was safe and dry where he had left it. He grabbed the radio and set out again for the *Sea Master*, threading his way back over the levee in the darkness.

All at once, Gary heard an unearthly, apocalyptic noise. The force of the wind hit him like a solid object, knocking him off his feet and back towards the surging water. With a blow that emptied his lungs, he was flung against something massive and pinned there. Pain shot up from his back, and he felt behind him the featureless hull of a barge. Trapped by the wind, he could barely open his eyes against the droplets of rain that stung like hailstones and battered his face and chest. He dropped low and painstakingly crawled back towards his brothers.[17]

On either side of him was a hellscape. Lumber and boat parts bobbed among loose skiffs, and barges skidded up and over the buildings. Cows windmilled their legs in a vain attempt to right themselves before they drowned.[18]

Somehow Gary had made it back to the *Sea Master*, and somehow he had managed to hold on to the radio. For several long hours, the sound of wind and water filled the brothers' skulls until, at last, the storm had passed.

The Duncans waited until the first soft light began to glow in the east, and then they set out along the levee for Gary's car. It had stayed mercifully dry, and they rolled along slowly, weaving between barges and piles of debris that had washed up in the night. They figured that once they reached The Jump, the driving would get easier. Experiencing some storm surge was an expected, even routine part of riding out a hurricane in Venice Marina, and one needed only go up the road as far as the massive river levees to reach safety. When they came around the final turn, though, the Duncan brothers stopped.

In the weak light, all they could see in every direction was water and trash: trash in the canals and in the bayous, trash up in the trees and on the roof of the marina. Oil drums, shotguns, pieces of boats, boards, roofing, trailers, people's homes and possessions—all mixed in with organic detritus: mud, branches, grass, carcasses. A tugboat, intact, rested atop the firehouse as if deliberately placed there by a giant. Dead cattle carved slow circles in the water. Only the very top of the levee protruded above the water, and it was covered with boats and clusters of livestock that snorted and paced nervously among the thronging fire ants and snakes. The snakes—they had never seen so many snakes.[19]

The Duncans stared for a moment at the seemingly endless body of water that had appeared overnight on top of their homes, and then they turned around and made their way back to the *Sea Master*. There was nowhere else to go.

Later in the day, Gary, Calvin, and Mancil commandeered a small skiff to motor up the road towards home. The water was most of the way up the walls, so Gary had to swim through a broken window to get inside. There was nothing to be done with the floating debris and furniture, but he swam over to the front door and reached up over the casing. With some relief, he felt his guns there—a shotgun and a .22 rifle—where he kept them. He took them down and swam carefully back to the skiff.

Calvin went to his house, which had shifted off its blocks and tilted to one side. The building was a mess, but he was overjoyed to find his beloved chihuahua floating on a sofa in the living room. There was nothing left to do there, and none of the brothers dared think too much about the destruction of their houses as they returned to Venice.[20]

———

The water would not leave. Plaquemines Parish was almost completely inundated, and the water that had overtopped the levees was now stuck there. In a satellite picture of the bird-foot delta taken after Betsy, Venice had disappeared entirely.[21]

One of the few places that escaped the flood was Belle Chasse, a small town all the way up the road, not far from New Orleans. Refugees were taken to the high ground of Belle Chasse schools. Like the schools themselves, the shelters were segregated: white residents went to an all-white school, black residents to an all-black school. In all, fifteen hundred Plaquemines residents, about half of them black, were crammed into the school buildings, where the Red Cross made up beds and served sandwiches.[22]

———

A few days later, when it was clear that the water was not going to recede and the debris that clogged the channel would not clear out, the brothers at last untied themselves from the other boats and pulled the *Sea Master* out into the Mississippi. As they went, they picked up a dozen people, rescuing friends and family from the levee or the rooftops where they stood, waving and calling for help.

They approached New Orleans and realized that they did not know how to find their family. It was clear that the city had been flooded, too. Hundreds of boats were traversing the city, its streets changed to canals, picking up refugees and corpses as they went. Through the chaos, the Duncan boys piloted the *Sea Master* to the Canal Street ferry landing. There, a crowd of people waited and craned their necks to see which boats were coming upriver. In front of the crowd was a line of body bags.

As he drew near, Gary saw his father. He shouted and waved, and the *Sea Master* pulled up to the landing. The dog leapt into Lambert's arms as the family wept and embraced. After weathering the storm in the city, Mazie and Lambert had come every day to the ferry landing to look for their sons, watching as boats rounded the riverbend and came into view, their hearts rising each time a tugboat appeared only to motor on by.

Gary apologized for the boats left unattended at Venice Marina. "I'm not worried about no boats," Lambert said fiercely, clutching his sons to himself.

———

"Wake up, niggers!"

It was three o'clock in the morning on September 15, and everyone in Scottville School, the all-black school that housed hundreds of Betsy refugees, was asleep.

"Wake up! Wake up! Wake up, you black bastards!"

The voice belonged to Harold Asevedo, known to all as "Dutch." He was a thirty-eight-year-old white man with the physiognomy of a battleship and a temper best left unprovoked. In the dim light, people could make out the shape of a submachine gun in his hands.*

He told the sleepy refugees to prepare themselves to work—men on clearing storm debris, women on cleaning the house of a parish official—and then he stalked out.[23]

When he returned, Asevedo used a metal-tipped club to herd young black men out to the schoolyard. Turning to two teachers, he barked, "You nigger boys get on the bus. You're going to work."

The teachers explained that they were already at work, supervising refugees at the school.

"Damn what you have to do. Get your asses on that bus."

They joined a group of sixty or so other black men on the front lawn as a parish school bus pulled up. A deputy sheriff stepped out of the bus and motioned for the men to board. Just then, the principal of the school strode out onto the lawn, shouting that two of the gathered men were teachers and had other duties.

"The hell with their duties," growled Asevedo. "Alright, niggers, get the hell on the bus."

One of the teachers refused. Asevedo, incensed, grabbed his arm.

"Take your hands off me," said the teacher.

---

* A few years later, Asevedo was asked by a reporter whether he had a machine gun during this incident. He replied, "I've had so many different guns in my hands so many times that I can't remember what gun I was holding at any particular time."

Asevedo did, and then he raised his club to strike him, but the other teacher pulled his colleague away. Then everyone froze.

Behind them they heard a low voice, gravelly from decades of cigar smoking and public speaking. It spoke deliberately and with a menace that was difficult to describe but impossible to miss: "I have two or three hundred of you niggers here at this school, eating my food. And you're getting on this bus."

"Let's just get on the bus," one of the teachers muttered. They did.

The man who had spoken was well known to them. His name was Leander Perez, and in Plaquemines Parish, he was best not ignored.[24]

2—The Boss

I always take the offensive. The defensive ain't worth
a damn.

—Leander H. Perez

I F POLITICS IS a game, Louisiana politics is a blood sport, and Leander
H. Perez was its reigning champion.

Earl Long called Perez "the King." More accurately, lawmakers in Baton
Rouge referred to him as "the third house of the Louisiana legislature."
"Dictator" is the word most often used today by Plaquemines residents of a
certain age. Perez himself preferred—indeed insisted on—being called "the
Judge," although his abortive judicial career spanned just five of his fifty
years in politics. By the time Hurricane Betsy hit in 1965, he was among the
most powerful politicians in the South.

After Betsy, Perez was everywhere. The hurricane struck when he was in
his forty-sixth year of public service and at the height of his powers. He had
spent those years turning the impoverished community of his birth into
one of the wealthiest rural counties in the United States. And he would be
damned if he'd let the forces of nature stand in the way of that progress.

Stocky and athletic, Perez hurled himself bodily at challenges, heedless
of opposition or difficulty. His primary mode of interaction was a frontal
assault, declaiming or cajoling in his gravelly voice and jabbing the air with
a cigar as if it were an appendage.

Eschewing his usual three-piece suit and Panama hat for short sleeves and
a baseball cap, Perez was most often found at his hurricane headquarters in

Belle Chasse. There, he spent his day directing parish officers in recovery efforts or calling politicians, contractors, and oil-company executives. He met with state highway engineers and representatives of industry to be sure that contracts for demolition, cleanup, and reconstruction went to locals.[1]

The scale of the cleanup was daunting. First, there was the water. The levees that had been built to protect the parish now kept the water from flowing back to the Gulf, and drainage was painfully slow. Only after the water had been drained could people begin to clear debris, which was, if anything, a greater challenge. Betsy had dredged up a foul slurry of organic matter and human detritus and slopped it all over the land.[2]

Perez knew intimately the scale of the damage. He had personally overseen most of the development in the first place. "Plaquemines Parish," he wrote in a letter to the US House of Representatives two weeks after Betsy, "constructed a system of modern public schools, auditoriums, drainage plants, and facilities at a cost of at least $15 million financed entirely by the parish. These public facilities were damaged to the extent of at least $2 million."[3]

He wanted far more than a few million dollars, though. He wanted a new $900,000 stormproof telephone system. He wanted new communication towers, urban-style municipal sewerage, bigger levees, public swimming pools and libraries, a $5 million canal to shorten the shipping route between the Gulf and the Port of Plaquemines—he demanded $100 million of repair and development in all, representing almost 1 percent of the entire state's GDP that year.[4]

Perez got most of what he wanted. He spent hours first lobbying and then threatening oil-industry executives until they agreed to hire hundreds of local contractors and pay their own employees to do cleanup work before returning to the oil fields. He cajoled state highway officials into paying millions for road reconstruction and the building of drainage canals and embankments along Plaquemines thoroughfares.

Perez made a great show of refusing federal disaster relief. "We're allergic to federal monies," he declared in early October 1965. Having covered his own costs, he even offered to foot some of the bill for federally funded levees, as long as the feds agreed to use local contractors.[5]

The recovery was indeed miraculous. A month after Betsy, the three upriver schools were ready to open, and they announced that they would take all the students from down the road as well. Within three months, all but one of the schools was operating again. By Thanksgiving, three-quarters of Plaquemines residents had returned to their land. Two weeks later, 95 percent of salvageable homes had been repaired. Perez's improbable phoenix act had succeeded.[6]

That some of the recovery had been completed by forcing black men at gunpoint to work without pay was largely ignored. "It's too bad that…Negroes had to do a little cleanup work," Perez deadpanned to a reporter. The FBI opened an investigation (the topic was described as "Involuntary Servitude and Slavery"). Agents talked to a couple of people and then closed the file. Nothing more was said.[7]

———

Perez was born in 1891 and first came to office twenty-eight years later. At the time, Plaquemines Parish was a backwater: most residents were illiterate, and the levees were so fragile that muskrat holes were a routine cause of collapses. Ships steamed up and down the Mississippi continually, enriching New Orleans but bypassing Plaquemines completely.[8]

The Perezes were a minor political family, and Leander held office first in 1919, when he was appointed to be a local judge. It was an election year, and he was an outsider to the notoriously rough politics of southern Louisiana, where the Democratic Party apparatus was called "the Ring" and operated more like the Mafia than a modern political party.

Unintimidated, Perez took the offensive, cultivating a taste for brutally negative campaign strategies. "Lies!" was the refrain of his speeches. At events all over the parish, he would play on class resentments, declaring before gatherings of rough and unschooled men that the Ring was a collection of self-dealing "gentlemen" who were "deliberate liars" and "old, professional politicians." It was said that Perez slapped a rival candidate in the face; instead of an apology or a denial, he hinted with a smirk that the man had started weeping after being struck. Another enemy, named Estopinal, accused Perez of creating a "deplorable" situation, and Perez embraced the phrase, crowing at an event in Venice that he had indeed made the situation "politically deplorable to the Estopinal family, yes!"[9]

His aggression did not end with his rhetoric or fistfights, though. Perez used his political position to intimidate and even hamstring his enemies. As judge, he indicted opponents on all sorts of violations and initiated lawsuits against members of the Ring—cases over which he would preside, of course. In one trial, he instructed the jury that the defendant was a "damn criminal" and "guilty as hell." (After the acquittal, he dismissed the jurors, reconvened court, and found the man guilty himself.) None of this was legal. Much of it was flagrantly unconstitutional. It didn't matter; although most of these cases disappeared or were dismissed on appeal, Perez had made his point.[10]

More importantly, citizens of Plaquemines seemed to enjoy their brash, outspoken judge. Even the New Orleans papers indicated their approval. His rallies drew large crowds, and his growing base of supporters scoffed at claims that he was unfit for office. Defamation suits flew back and forth between Perez and his opponents, ultimately going nowhere.

In 1923, the Ring teamed up with a group of concerned citizens to try to impeach Perez, a case that wound up before the Louisiana Supreme Court. Perez finally crushed that effort, and his political rivals retreated forever. By the time of the next election, Perez was running unopposed. But Perez never ran for a judgeship again; in his time on the bench, he realized that the role of prosecutor was, in fact, more powerful. His career as district attorney began in 1925, and it was as DA and parish attorney that he would transform Plaquemines.[11]

Perez could barely afford to maintain his family's lifestyle. His wife, Agnes, was the daughter of a New Orleans businessman. She was happy to move to Plaquemines, but Perez had to borrow money from her parents to afford their house. Now they had four children. The salary of a district attorney was less than $6,000,* which even in Plaquemines Parish in the

---

* About $90,000 today.

1920s was hardly a fortune. His was not the sort of foundation on which political dynasties were built.[12]

It is not easy to become a political boss—the maintenance of a machine requires power, which Perez had obtained, and money, which he had not yet.

———

The money, it turned out, was underground. The first petroleum exploration in Plaquemines Parish happened in 1928. No oil was found, but the company paid handsomely for the mineral lease that enabled it to drill. Perez wanted that money.

It was not as simple as that. By law, leases on marshland belonged to state-controlled levee boards, not to local governments. Undeterred, Perez massaged the web of state laws and local ordinances that governed the bayou country, gaining local control of as much state-managed land as he could. His tactics ranged from deceptive to illegal, but in short order Perez seized tens of thousands of acres of state land and waited for businesses to come to him.[13]

By the time the oil companies flooded in—Gulf, Chevron, Shell, Tidewater, Humble, and others—Perez had a near-monopoly on the leases they needed. When those companies found oil, the money started flowing in, too. By Louisiana law, one-eighth of the value of oil discovered on public land was due back to the government as a "royalty." Normally, that royalty went to the state-controlled levee board. But because of Perez's land grab, the royalties in Plaquemines went not to the state, but straight into parish coffers.* By midcentury, the parish was raking in tens of millions of dollars a year from these leases.[14]

---

* Production in Plaquemines peaked at 290 million barrels in 1970 ($115 million in royalties to the parish). Yields plummeted during the energy crisis of the 1970s, but revenues continued to rise with oil prices. In 1980, when production had fallen to 52 million barrels, these royalties yielded more than $140 million to the parish. Today, however, the seemingly endless flow of money has slowed: in 2017, combined oil and gas royalties paid out less than $7 million.

That money was invested in local government. By the time Hurricane Betsy devastated it, Plaquemines Parish had the best infrastructure in the state of Louisiana, the lowest taxes, and the highest high-school graduation rate. The dirt road Perez had grown up on became a four-lane, paved highway with drainage control and a free transit system.

Perez also used the money to provide for his people. Anyone who wanted a job—black or white—got a job, provided that they were not a Perez enemy, and there were few enough of those. The Judge always found something: there were dozens of levee inspectors and road inspectors and facilities inspectors and tariff agents and assistants and assistants to those assistants. A million-dollar hospital was built in Port Sulphur, and the parish ran a fleet of ambulances. The parish even provided municipal water and sewerage, a rarity to this day in rural areas, and a welcome service in a place where the digging of wells and septic systems was often impossible. Well-maintained levees ran up and down the river, and a bridge and toll-free ferry promised safe passage across the Mississippi.

With money had come influence in the state capital, and Perez never missed a legislative session (he even had an office in Baton Rouge, though he never held a job there). When a plucky governor tried to challenge Perez's stranglehold over local politics in 1943, Perez mustered a militia and staged a rebellion that was only quelled when the National Guard marched into the parish—in the middle of World War II.* The so-called Little War is a book in itself, but suffice to say that Perez emerged unscathed.[15]

Armed insurrection aside, life was good in Plaquemines, and Perez wanted everyone to celebrate. The *Manta*, a seventy-foot teak-decked yacht officially purchased "to patrol the waters of Plaquemines against seafood depredation," raced between Venice Marina and a hunting camp at Port Eads, at the mouth of the Mississippi, where Perez would entertain politicians and oil executives. There were free barbecues and picnics, a Parish Fair and Orange Festival, galas thrown by various government agencies with free

---

* Highlights of this fiasco include a declaration of martial law and the erection of a fiery roadblock made of oil-drenched oyster shells.

food and liquor and speeches by politicians. Perez emceed all these events, and still he found time to play a few rounds of poker and dispense advice on local issues—advice that would be gospel truth by the time church let out on Sunday. Everyone agreed that the Judge played a mean hand of poker, although some few grumbled that it was only because everyone let him win.[16]

It turns out that Perez had been playing a different sort of rigged game with the parish's money, too. Just as soon as he started acquiring land and strong-arming oil companies into building public works for his parish, Perez began skimming for himself from every single deal.

The scheme was simple. As parish attorney, he was the contact person for oil companies looking to drill for oil. A representative from an oil company would inquire about a parcel of land, and Perez would ask him to wait until the next council meeting. At the meeting, Perez would tell the council that a "development company" wanted to lease that same parcel for a few pennies per acre; the council always agreed. Then Perez would return to the oil man to say that the land in question was already leased by a development company, but that it could probably be subleased—for a hefty price. He did not tell either the council or the corporations that he operated every one of these development companies.[17]

To this day, it is unclear how many shell companies Perez incorporated or how much money he made from them. They were given innocuous names, like Suburban Coast Realty and Delta Development Company, nominally based in places like Delaware or Michigan, and registered to various Perez lackeys, c/o various post-office boxes. Perez made money coming and going: he was paid attorney fees, commissions, finder's fees, and royalties. By the time the ruse was discovered in 1983, Perez was long dead, and his personal income from the largest shell company was more than $78 million— probably much more. The full extent of his graft will probably never be known.[18]

In truth, few people in Perez's domain seemed to care; they knew he had their backs. Perez made unprecedented demands on the oil industry to secure prosperity for his people and his parish. In order to drill in

Plaquemines, corporations needed to agree to fund public works, hire local people, and, in many cases, provide employees with affordable housing. When the companies tried to circumvent his requirements, Perez was a step ahead of them. Older Plaqueminians still remember how Perez required oil companies to work their employees on a "five-and-two" schedule—five days on, two days off—instead of the more common twenty-one-and-seven. With only two days off, workers would need to move their families into the parish, send their kids to local schools, become members of local churches. For all this, the people of Plaquemines gave Perez their loyalty.*

A 1950 article in the *New Orleans Item* suggested that, where Plaquemines residents had once been kept in the thrall of political bosses because of poverty and illiteracy, they were now just as effectively manipulated by prosperity and education. In the first thirty years of his life in politics, Perez had made himself into an insurgent populist and then an all-powerful political boss, a builder of things. The third phase of his career, the one that would make him famous, came to him from the most disruptive Supreme Court decision in American history.[19]

The actual effect of *Brown v. Board of Education* was limited, but the South reeled in shock nonetheless. It was 1954, and Perez was at the height of his powers. He saw the decision, which ordered the desegregation of public schools, as an affront, a challenge to his authority and worldview. At a dinner that year honoring his thirty-fifth year of public service, Perez stood to announce that he was dedicating the rest of his life to preserving the segregation of the races. He was a man who kept his word, and he embarked on an unparalleled campaign of disinformation, propaganda, community organizing, legislation, litigation, and incitement of violence.[20]

Just two years after *Brown,* Perez was investigated by the FBI—he had

---

* Like many autocrats, Perez was not satisfied with merely overwhelming support. Even when he could have won an honest election easily, he embarked on serial campaigns of intimidation, vote-buying, and outright fraud. In one election, the voter rolls were found to contain Babe Ruth, Charlie Chaplin, and other unlikely residents. In another, Perez's favored candidate for statewide office received 180 percent of the Plaquemines vote. ("The muskrats must be voting," was the line in New Orleans. "If muskrats were voting," noted the *New York Times* dryly, "Negroes were not.")

physically removed a black priest from a Catholic church in Belle Chasse. The case was eventually dropped, but not before the agents wrote a dire letter to J. Edgar Hoover. Leander Perez, they warned, "is a man completely obsessed with his opposition of the Federal Government, the Supreme Court of the United States, and his opposition to any integration of the races." Further, the agents noted, "It is observed that he is completely engrossed in his own ideas and opinions, and anyone or anything that is not in complete agreement with him is either a Communist or a Communist tool."[21]

Before 1954, Perez had not made a special project of stoking racial tensions—they were pre-stoked by his time and milieu—but it had been his longtime hobby to read up on the various pseudoscientific "discoveries" of the nineteenth century. His curiosity did not extend much beyond long-debunked dreck like phrenology and racial hygiene, but within that realm his knowledge was encyclopedic. After *Brown*, what had been a private pursuit became a public passion. He would buttonhole lawmakers and journalists to lecture them about the physical limitations of black cranial capacity or the heritability of immoral child-rearing or any of a dozen other such inanities.[*]

Perez found a mass audience in 1960, when New Orleans became the first big city in the South to desegregate its schools. At a rally against integration, Perez delivered the keynote speech: "Don't wait for your daughters to be raped by these Congolese!" he shouted. "Don't wait until the burr-heads are forced into your schools! Do something about it now!" The next day, a throng of whites stormed city hall. Finding that the mayor was in hiding, the mob ran into the streets of black neighborhoods, assaulting anyone they could find. As a result, 250 men were arrested, nearly all of them black.[22]

Perhaps more importantly, Perez worked behind the scenes to shore up Louisiana's racial hierarchy. All over the country, segregationist lawyers and

---

[*] "His library overflowed with material on the subject," writes his biographer, Glen Jean-sonne. After Perez's death, some boxes of his books were left anonymously on the steps of the New Orleans Public Library, where they were added to the Louisiana Collection. They remain as they were delivered: unsorted and without commentary.

legislators were innovating their way around racial integration. Perez studied their successes and failures; he would ultimately craft the most extensive and imaginative system of racist laws in the South. He penned beefed-up versions of segregationist staples: voter disenfranchisement laws and the like. He pushed some of his pet projects through as well, such as an act that required the labeling of all medical blood supplies by race. But his masterwork was a convoluted system of overlapping regulations and policies that gave local leaders almost unlimited tools for staving off desegregation. In fact, his last stand to preserve Jim Crow would be the greatest of his public works—the one that he was willing to sacrifice anything for, including all the others.

Asked in a 1961 interview about the possibility of eventually desegregating his schools, Perez said flatly, "No, sir. I hope the day will never come. I hope the day—not as long as I live. I hope the day will never come when they attempt to integrate our schools because I swear they'll—it'll never happen. And I'll stake my life on it."[23]

3—What Is Ours

ON THE MORNING of Wednesday, August 29, 1962, a gathering thunderstorm made the air heavy and wet in Buras, just up the road from Boothville. Forty-three children, flanked by nuns, emerged from Mass at Our Lady of Good Harbor, a Spanish-style Catholic church. Thirty-eight of them were white; five were black.

The children clutched their schoolbooks and recited the rosary as they walked, two by two, between the spooky mausoleums of the cemetery and towards Highway 23. The road was lined with cars. Beside the cars stood dozens of white men and women, their neighbors, bearing signs:

> WE PAID FOR THIS SCHOOL AND WE WANT IT BACK
> ALL THE PEOPLE FEEL AS WE DO
> OUR SCHOOL HAS ALWAYS BEEN SEGREGATED
> WE WANT TO KEEP OUR SCHOOL WHITE

And, most commonly, WE ONLY WANT WHAT IS OURS.[1]

Father Chris Schneider, who ran Our Lady of Good Harbor, unlocked the schoolhouse doors and held them open as the first racially integrated class walked into a school in Plaquemines Parish.[2]

For months, Perez had been working to prevent this moment. As the archbishop of New Orleans prepared to desegregate church schools, Perez mounted an investigation into the finances of the archdiocese, declaring his suspicion that the church had fallen under the influence of Communists and Jews. For this, Perez was excommunicated, a move that shocked the Catholic community in New Orleans and earned Perez national notoriety.[3]

Rejection by the Catholic establishment seemed to embolden Perez. "If they think they can send me to hell, I beat them to it and I told them to go to hell!" he declared. If anything, excommunication increased his appeal to segregationists; he used it like an honorific. Within a week, he had founded an organization for segregationist Catholics and joked that he had his own church: the "Perezbyterians."[4]

Still, Our Lady of Good Harbor opened, and a small but integrated group of pupils walked inside. For a moment, it looked as if Perez had lost. But overnight, white parents got phone calls from their bosses and parish officials, who threatened their jobs and businesses. Black parents got the same treatment; at least one of them also got a call from the sheriff, who warned that it might be best to leave town. Schneider, the priest, received bomb threats and a promise that he and the nuns would be tarred and feathered.[5]

The next morning, only twenty-five students showed up, all white. Schneider stood impassively in his black robes at the open schoolhouse door for an hour, waiting for the black students to arrive. They never did. The picketers were triumphant. "They had their day yesterday," said one, referring to the black students, "Now it's our turn."[6]

When Schneider walked through the picket line the following morning, the schoolyard was covered with feathers. He looked at the ground briefly and then gave a simple statement to the waiting reporters: "There is no school today because of numerous threats of physical violence and fear of insufficient police protection."[7]

The picket line turned into a party. Perez rolled up in his Cadillac and joined the celebration, giving a short speech to punctuate the victory. He urged the protesters not to slacken their efforts. "We have never been confronted with a situation where our very church, our religion, your property, has been more basely, outrageously violated," he said.[8]

Our Lady of Good Harbor opened again after Labor Day, but by the end of the week, no children at all were showing up. Still, every morning for the rest of the school year, Schneider unlocked the building and stood beside the entrance for at least half an hour before locking up and leaving. No students ever came, and Schneider was twice awoken by gunshots that shattered windows in his home.

The night before Our Lady of Good Harbor was scheduled to open for the next school year, an explosion blew through the building's ductwork. Flames shot out of the windows and swept through the classrooms. By the time the fire was extinguished, much of the interior was charred, and the walls of one classroom were completely gone.[9]

Someone had poured fifteen gallons of gasoline into the school's ventilation system and lit a fuse. No one was hurt, but the arson attracted attention. A short-lived FBI investigation turned up little more than the empty gas cans, and no one was ever arrested.[10]

Dan Rather, then a young reporter working for CBS, went to Plaquemines to put together an hourlong special. "The Priest and the Politician," as the story was called, ran a few weeks after the attack. In his interview with Rather, Perez was expansive. "I am not against violence as a matter of self-defense," he said, nor was he against any sort of resistance to "unlawful, unchristian, unmoral acts."

Rather asked if Perez would recommend that his people bring violent resistance against any further integration efforts. "I don't have to recommend," Perez stated. "I *know* they'll resist it....I cannot subscribe to the principle of surrender and the brainwash technique of saying, 'It's bound to happen.' So what? Let's just lie down and let it happen? Let them kick our teeth out? Let the American people forget that they are *men?*"[11]

Our Lady of Good Harbor did not reopen. Even when the archdiocese paid for repairs, the parish government refused to issue the necessary permits. For decades after, whites in Buras would lament the school's loss. "What a shame that that school had to close," people would say. "It was such a nice school."[12]

"Plaquemines Parish is in for some bad times," Perez told a reporter on June 29, 1966. "A dark hand from Washington will soon descend," he went on. "The federal government will try to destroy the school system."[13]

Since Perez had won the battle of Our Lady of Good Harbor, no attempt had been made to integrate schools in the parish, public or parochial. But, nationally, leaders of the civil rights movement were beginning to achieve the big victories for which they had suffered so much. When President Johnson signed the Civil Rights Act into law in 1964, Perez felt the ground shifting underfoot. Sure enough, a few weeks after Perez made his statement, it was announced that the Civil Rights Division of the Department of Justice had filed a lawsuit to desegregate all the Plaquemines schools, and Perez was given just five weeks to comply.

Perez had spent years preparing for this moment. He first heard of the lawsuit on June 14, when the parish received a notice from the Civil Rights Division. Perez knew that he needed to move quickly. Given his notoriety, the lawsuit could involve a restraining order to stop him from interfering with desegregation.

First, Perez ordered S. A. Moncla, the superintendent of schools, to withhold contracts from white teachers but to send them as usual to black teachers. This locked the teaching staff at black-only schools into their positions but left white teachers in limbo—they received a short letter explaining that their contracts had been delayed, with no elaboration or explanation. Many people wondered what was going on, but Perez kept silent. The truth was that if he could not save his state-of-the-art school system from racial integration, he would build himself another.[14]

He was not the first to try. Most famously, Prince Edward County, Virginia, which was one of the school districts lumped in with *Brown v. Board of Education,* gave up on public education altogether. Shortly after *Brown* was decided, several all-white private schools were opened by a non-profit organization that was essentially a branch of the government. Once every white child had a guaranteed spot at a private school, the county simply cut all funding to its public schools. Eventually, the Supreme Court ordered the public schools reopened, but for five years there were no schools at all for black residents of Prince Edward.* But even when the

---

* This situation resulted in a cohort of black residents of Prince Edward County who received no formal education, ever.

public schools reopened, few whites attended, and the county was nearly as segregated as it had been before *Brown;* white kids studied in "academies" while black kids languished in underfunded public schools.[15]

Perez was an eager student of Prince Edward County, and he was not alone. All over the South, segregation academies were erected. The Supreme Court had ruled that shuttering an entire public-school system violated the Constitution, but the justices had nothing to say about how well funded the schools that remained needed to be. The Prince Edward model was easy to replicate, at least in theory, and it was also perfectly legal. All it required was money, hard work, and solidarity from whites.

What Perez intended, though, was more sophisticated and more ambitious. Where Prince Edward County had taken years to build its academies, Perez intended to have enough academies for every white parishioner to have a spot by late October, so they could graduate on time in the spring. He also planned an intricate system of state-funded tuition vouchers so that no white student, however poor, would need to attend public school (Virginia had tried to create a voucher system for Prince Edward County, but Perez's was far more robust and innovative). He figured out how to insulate the private schools legally, wrapping them and their funding mechanisms in layers of legal protection and obfuscation. Of all the counties that had followed the Prince Edward model, none had started with so little or intended to build so much, so fast.

In the meantime, Perez quietly oversaw the purchase of prefabricated building parts—concrete partitions, steel panels and supports, ceiling tiles—everything that would be needed for the rapid construction of school buildings. The massive stockpile was hidden on private land around the parish, in case federal investigators started poking around. Within weeks, there was enough material to build four or five large buildings, and the plan was ready for its second phase.

Perez got in with time to spare; he finished his work a week before the Justice Department brought its suit. All of the subterfuge worked: nowhere in the complaint did the government allege that Plaquemines Parish was trying to create a private-school system to circumvent desegregation.

33

Even when he was done and the lawsuit was filed, Perez spoke only in coded language about the academies. At a series of mass meetings in the all-white high schools—not publicly advertised for fear that the FBI would show up—Perez encouraged the white people of the parish to meet the challenge of racial integration in the same way they had responded to Hurricane Betsy: united and ready to build anew what had been destroyed. "There will be no more graduations from the public schools in this parish," Perez lamented, and the next year would be difficult. Still, he promised, it would "work out if they all stuck together."[16]

As flawlessly as his plan had gone so far, Perez's victory must have been bittersweet. Those schools were the greatest symbol of how far Plaquemines Parish had come since the Judge himself had learned to write in a one-room schoolhouse on a dirt road. Now he was ready to destroy his signature achievement for the sake of racial purity.

———

The scene on August 29, 1966, was familiar to all who had witnessed the scene at Our Lady of Good Harbor four years prior: a mob of white people in front of a school, carrying signs. These read, simply, DON'T.[17]

Perez visited a few of the picket lines on registration day. He circulated, shaking hands and offering quiet words of encouragement. He kept his voice down; as predicted, he had been barred from interfering in the orderly desegregation of Plaquemines schools. In fact, the judge had threatened him with contempt after an outburst in court.* But there was little to be done. Perez and his lawyers had successfully drawn the proceedings out for weeks, resulting in crippling delays.

On the courthouse steps, Perez turned to reporters and bemoaned the loss of his constitutionally protected right to speech, but that was all for

---

* The presiding judge was not subtle in his threat: "I wouldn't like to put a man of your years in jail," he said. If Perez was chastened, he didn't show it; a few minutes later, he was accusing the Justice Department of wiretapping the Plaquemines Parish School Board.

show: he had done what he needed to do. By the time Civil Rights Division lawyers discovered his plan to build and finance all-white academies, none of it was traceable to him.

After visiting the picket lines, Perez met with principals, who informed him that very few students of any race had registered—at one school, only two students had arrived, both black; at another, no black students at all showed up, and only twenty of the usual 1,700 whites did. Perez seemed pleased with the result.[18]

That afternoon, Superintendent Moncla announced his resignation. (In fact, it turned out, he had secretly resigned more than a month earlier but had not told anyone, thus maximizing the chaos.) The school board met that evening to select a replacement, and they picked Frank Patti, who supervised child welfare in the parish. It was ironic that, before being tapped to oversee a state-sponsored school boycott, Patti's main responsibility had been to enforce truancy laws.[19]

Claiming that the lawsuit had made timely desegregation impossible, the school board announced a two-week hiatus from classes. It was true that there was not enough time; Perez had made sure of it. By the time the trial was done and the court order was entered, only four days—two of them the weekend—remained before school was supposed to start. When the delay was announced, frustrated lawyers from the Civil Rights Division subpoenaed more than fifty teachers and administrators, hastily convening a hearing on September 7 to try to piece together what was happening in Plaquemines.

The hearing was not illuminating. Perez's lawyer railed at the judge, accusing him of orchestrating a campaign of harassment; the boss, meanwhile, sat in the audience and smirked. Outside the courthouse, a beleaguered Superintendent Patti told reporters that he was under a lot of pressure. Asked where the pressure was coming from, Patti grumbled, "Draw your own conclusions." That evening, he resigned. No replacement was named.[20]

Two days later, every teacher at Woodlawn School, in a Perez stronghold on the east bank, quit. Teachers at Belle Chasse High School, it seemed, were not far behind. Bus drivers went on strike, citing the "emotional distress" of driving mixed-race buses. Just as Perez had planned, the school system was disintegrating.[21]

On September 12, the first day of school, multiracial groups of reporters from as far away as Chicago and New York gathered by the school entrances. FBI agents sat nearby in unmarked cars. Outside Belle Chasse High School, a crowd of white protesters hurled insults and slurs at eighteen black and seventy-two white students who showed up for class. There were few adults present in the building; many of the teachers and all the staff had stayed home. Similar scenes played out at the other high schools on the west bank, Port Sulphur and Boothville-Venice.[22]

At Woodlawn School, thirty-one black students (and no whites) showed up, only to be told by the principal that there were no teachers, no staff, and that she herself was not technically allowed to be there because she had neither a contract nor a boss. Everyone was shooed out of the building, and the doors were locked.[23] The school never reopened.*

Despite the tension, people in the picket lines did not resort to physical violence as had been feared, even expected. Hate boiled over instead in neighboring St. Bernard Parish, which integrated the same day. There, black parents in their cars and black girls on a school bus were attacked by a white mob that broke windshields and hurled rocks, shouting, "Send 'em back to Africa!" and "We want a leader! Give us a Perez!" Two days later, white students tried to burn St. Bernard High School down.[24]

By contrast, integration in Plaquemines seemed uneventful, at least by the standards of the civil rights era. White journalists from big-city newspapers penned short pieces that got buried in the back pages. Out-of-town black reporters, including one from the *Chicago Defender,* the nation's largest and most important black newspaper, came away cautiously optimistic. Local

---

* In 2005, Sara Shreve, a historic preservationist working for FEMA, was in Plaquemines assessing the damage from Hurricanes Katrina and Rita when she stumbled on an Art Deco school building. It was wonderfully preserved, but there was no record of a school anywhere near that location. A parish official told her it wasn't a school at all, but a maintenance building. How strange, Shreve thought—this beautiful school hiding away, full of gravel and backhoes. It was, she learned a decade later, Woodlawn School.

black journalists were less sanguine. *Louisiana Weekly,* the black newspaper in New Orleans, called the boycott "a chronic growth of hate whose evil roots are buried deep in the minds and daily lives of the people of Plaquemines Parish by Leander Perez, the archenemy of integration."[25]

All day, Perez held court from the veranda of his home, puffing thoughtfully on a cigar as he dispensed faux-naïf quips with a wink. "The people of Plaquemines Parish know the national administration has confiscated their schools." He shrugged to reporters. What could he possibly have to do with it?[26]

———

Just because the scene outside Plaquemines public schools failed to devolve into headline-making violence did not mean that integration was peaceful. Despite the boycott, 173 black students showed up for school that week. Once they had passed the hissing, spitting pickets, they entered a hostile environment.

"It was miserable," remembered Lucretia Hunter, who integrated Buras High School. "Nobody prepared us for what we was going to go through." Students in that first integrated class remember the older, athletic boys as protectors. "We stood together in a group. We protected each other," Gregory Bradley, who integrated Belle Chasse High School, recalled years later. Bradley and others remember being escorted to and from school by US Marshals; there was no bus service, so a convoy of carpooling black parents and grandparents would follow the federal agents' cars. Peggy Ragas, who integrated Port Sulphur High School, remembers agents coming to her house and talking to her father, who was a minister, about how to keep everyone safe.[27]

Harassment at school came through hundreds of small acts of violence and humiliation. Some white boys routinely knocked black students' books out of their hands, pointed to the floor, and said, "Nigger, pick up your books." They slammed locker doors on black students. One group of boys put a dead snake in Lucretia Hunter's locker ("Never let them see you sweat," she remembers thinking to herself as she forced herself to calmly get out her books).[28]

For boys especially, physical force was the best way to ensure safety. "You were called 'nigger,' and they told you to go back to where you come from and stuff like that," recalled Harold Jones, who integrated Boothville-Venice High School. "Lunchtime we would all stick together because if you got caught somewhere else, you got beat. After the bell rang, and with the lack of teachers, somebody always got caught over there by himself, and he got beat. That was how it was at Boothville-Venice. A group of guys would come up to you, and you went to fist city."

Conflict spilled from the hallways to the playing fields and beyond. "You were threatened in school, and you were threatened out of school. You'd be walking home, and someone would throw a bottle at you—" Jones paused for a moment in relating his story. "You know, it was far worse than we can sit down here and talk about."[29]

Most black kids didn't want to go to desegregated schools in the first place. They attended because their parents worried that it might be their only chance to go to a better school, because their community had fought for a long time for the right to do so, or because it was the right thing to do. "I was disgusted by Port Sulphur," Reverend Theodore Turner remembered. He stayed at the all-black Sunrise School as long as he could. "I didn't want to integrate. I didn't want to go to school with all these white people."[30]

Black children left their friends and entered an alien society, the boundary demarcated by a picket line of their white neighbors yelling slurs and threats. "[At the all-black schools], you didn't have that tension," recalled Laverne Jones, who went to Buras High School in 1969. "You didn't have to feel like you was walking on eggshells. You didn't have to feel like, 'What's going to happen tomorrow?' You wasn't afraid to go to school the next day."[31]

Even when black students weren't faced with outright harassment, the strictures of Plaquemines Parish reminded them of their place. Carolyn Parker, who went to Buras in 1967, remembers a field trip to Fort Jackson on which she was the only black student. The bus pulled up to the gate at the fort, a local historical site, and was stopped by the guard. His face fell when he saw a black girl on the bus: Fort Jackson was still segregated. He called the parish office to ask what to do. Parker remembers sitting on the bus for what felt like hours, her cheeks burning, before the call finally came back to the guard from parish officials, allowing her onto the grounds of the fort.[32]

More than anything else, it was the day-in, day-out persistence of mistreatment, and its unpredictability, that wore on black students. Lucretia Hunter remembered, "I couldn't learn because I couldn't function. It was hard to be in class when you was worried about what they might do. You never knew how crazy they could get. You always had to watch your back. Every second."[33]

The slow accrual of indignities still marks the memories of integrators. "In school, I built up some hatred," admitted Harold Jones. "I got to the point one time where I didn't think I would ever talk to a white person again." He said that, years later, "I'd run into some of those [white] kids at my sister's bar in Port Sulphur. And I'd see those kids, and it all started coming back. It all started—it built up. It built up. And I let it out."[34]

Slowly, some services returned to Plaquemines public schools as the government won court orders to combat Perez's resistance. School buses, which had sat idle, resumed service in October, though only the oldest buses were back on the road, and their new routes were spectacularly circuitous, managing somehow to buck the linear geography of Plaquemines and snake from levee to levee on the side streets. Bus schedules had pickups set for the early hours of the morning, depositing children at school long before their first classes. Still, they rode.[35]

At first, the bus drivers tried to segregate seating, but they ran into resistance from their newly empowered passengers. "They wanted us to go to the back of the bus," Carolyn Parker recalled. "But we wasn't going to the back. Those days was over."[36]

4—Contact

GARY DUNCAN KNEW and approved of the effort to desegregate Plaquemines schools, but he was too busy to bother much about it. His life had gone pretty well, all things considered, in the year or so since Hurricane Betsy. When the waters finally receded, the Duncans returned to rebuild their homes and fix their boats.

One major aspect of Gary's life had changed, though, between 1965 and 1966. While waiting for the storm surge to drain away from Boothville, he had gone to a party in Pontchartrain Park, a middle-class black neighborhood in the Upper Ninth Ward of New Orleans. There, he met Lynn Lange, and her vivacity and brassiness drew him in. The evening they met, he leaned over to one of his brothers and announced, "That girl, she's gonna be my wife."

A few months later, Lynn and Gary were married, and she soon discovered that she was pregnant. Amid the rebuilding and restoring of their homes, Lambert sat his son down to detail the responsibilities of fatherhood, and, for once, Gary listened—for the most part, anyway.[1]

Lynn was Creole, a racial designation unique to southern Louisiana, and her skin was so light that passing for white was easy.* This put her in the awkward position of being able to walk in the front door of Plaquemines businesses where her husband and in-laws had to go through the back, if they were welcome at all.[2]

---

* Creoles (more accurately, "Creoles of color") were simultaneously in the middle of the black-white spectrum and outside of it, and they often had little in common with the descendants of slaves. Some had ancestors who were free people—in Louisiana, unlike in the rest of the South, the offspring of mixed-race relationships could be legitimized. Many identified primarily as Native American. Most were Catholic. Some Creoles spoke French or one of a variety of unique dialects (which linguists call, as it happens, "creoles"), and many saw themselves as separate from and superior to "Negroes."

Lynn's family was urbane, but they all loved coming down to Plaque-mines, especially Gary's brothers-in-law, who felt like they had gained a house in the country. Lynn mostly stayed with her parents in New Orleans. It was easier that way; there wouldn't be room for her in Boothville until Gary had his own place. So Gary worked almost every day to save up enough money to get them a house or a trailer. He bought a dinky little shrimping boat and dropped an old car engine into it, so he would trawl on his days off from working as crew on tugboats and crew boats serving the offshore oil industry. He was making $250* a month, which was decent enough money for a young man.[3]

Their daughter, Geralyn, was born on October 2, 1966, a few weeks after Gary's nineteenth birthday. Gary went up to New Orleans to see Lynn and the baby anytime he could, which is what he was doing on October 19, when he spotted four white boys and two black boys—his nephew and cousin—on the shoulder of Highway 23.

Gary knew that tensions were high between blacks and whites in the parish, and he knew that black students felt threatened and unwelcome at the white schools. He imagined that there were fights, that the black students were called all sorts of words in an attempt to belittle them and break their equanimity. But Gary didn't worry about fistfights; that seemed like a natural way for boys to sort out their differences, and that was how men in Plaquemines Parish always were. No, it wasn't the students Gary was worried about; it was their parents. So he might have driven on past his nephew and cousin, had the white men not been watching.

Across the street from the group of boys was a group of white men standing in front of a stubby, prefabricated building that was still under construction. Gary instantly knew that something was wrong, and he felt an overwhelming instinct to intercede. He got out of the car and approached the six boys.[4]

---

* About $2,000 today.

Parnell "Bud" Latham watched the entire interaction from across the road. As president of the Boothville-Venice Private School Association, he was attuned to the ever-present threat of racial "trouble" that could at any time erupt among people whose emotions were rubbed raw by desegregation. At the moment, he was overseeing the final construction of Seaway Academy, the elementary and middle school that was being rushed forward to meet Perez's demanding schedule. In fact, the door he was standing by was the entrance to the academy itself.

Latham was just glad that he happened to be outside to witness the altercation. From across Highway 23, he could not hear what anyone was saying, but he grew concerned as the big black man loomed over fourteen-year-old Herman Landry.

"Hey!" he hollered. "Get away!"[5]

The black man looked at him, strode back to his car, and sped away down the road.

Latham knew just what to do. He rushed out to the boys and told them that he was going to call the police. They should stay right there, he said; he was going to make this right. As he jogged back to Seaway Academy, his mind churned.

It was fear of racial violence in Plaquemines that drove Latham to lead the push for a private school in Boothville; it drove him to work nights and weekends and days off to ensure that Seaway Academy was constructed as quickly as possible. Every day that white and black students attended Boothville-Venice High School together was a day with the specter of "trouble": bullying, malingering, miscegenation, gang rape, and riots. He had read in the *Gazette* about the horrors of race mixing in Washington, DC, and Chicago, and he was afraid. When Bud Latham thought he saw a grown black man striking a white child, it was the first blow in the coming race war.[6]

———

Deputy F. J. Smith was at home writing an accident report when he got the call from headquarters telling him to phone Bud Latham at Seaway

Academy. He did, and Latham narrated the incident. As Latham described the assailant—black man, green uniform, brown Chevy—Smith knew right away that it was Gary Duncan.[7]

The man who would arrest Gary Duncan was thirty-three and a native of Venice. He had known the Duncans his whole life and liked them. Lambert was recognized as a dignified and hardworking member of the community, Mazie as a generous soul, and the children as polite and law-abiding—save for a speeding ticket here or there for the boys, but that was hardly unusual in Plaquemines Parish. As Latham described the "disturbance" on Highway 23, Smith listened but felt a little skeptical. He patrolled a community that he loved and called home, and he tried not to be involved in the politics of Perez's racial crusade one way or another. Latham, on the other hand, was from Mississippi. It was said that outsiders were especially susceptible to Perez, and Latham had made himself a political figure with this private-school business. For his part, Smith saw no problem with sending his nine-year-old son to a racially integrated school, but he also didn't actively support desegregation; in fact, he didn't see why it was such an emotionally charged issue for either side.[8]

Almost as soon as Smith drove his patrol car onto Highway 23, he saw Gary Duncan going the other way. He pulled the Impala over and walked up to the window.

"Hi, Gary," he said. "You have a little trouble up the road?"

"Well, not really trouble," Gary replied. "I tried to break up a fight."

"Would you come up there with me to get it straightened out?"

Gary said he would, and asked if he could ride in the patrol car. That was fine, said Smith, and Gary told his cousin, whose plans of hitching a ride to New Orleans now seemed totally ruined, to find that spare tire and come by the Little Fish to pick him up.[9]

They spoke little as they drove, but Gary did say that he had dropped his nephew and cousin by their homes. Back up the road, Smith saw the four white boys waiting at the convenience store. He knew three of them: Wayne Scarabin, Wayne's cousin Randolph "Ruggie" Scarabin, and Herman Landry, who went by "Bunny." The Landrys he knew very well;

Herman's grandfather was a justice of the peace in Venice. The fourth boy he didn't know, but that wasn't so unusual; families were always moving into and out of Venice on oil-field contracts. The unknown boy said his name was Westley McKinney, which was also a name that Smith did not recognize.

Smith asked Landry to say exactly what happened and show him. The boy launched into an explanation: they were walking down the highway and asked these two black boys their names. They couldn't hear the black boys' response, so Landry explained that he and his friends crossed over to their side of the road, where the bigger of the two black boys asked if he wanted to fight. Landry recounted a disjointed conversation that Smith could barely follow, but in the end, as the boys were working themselves up either to fight or walk away, the car with two black adults had come up. Gary Duncan, Landry said, had threatened him and called him a name he wouldn't repeat in public and then took a swing at him.[10]

"Where did he hit you?" asked Smith.

"Right here," said Landry, motioning to his elbow.

Smith looked and felt around the spot. There was no bruise or redness.[11]

Gary protested that he had just been making a gesture and touched the boy, but Smith went over to Seaway Academy to talk to Latham, who was in the office. Latham told his version of the story, and Smith returned to ask the other boys what they had seen. Ruggie Scarabin grunted that Gary had hit Landry just like he said. Wayne nodded silently. The boy who had introduced himself as Westley McKinney, though, spoke up.

"He didn't hit nobody."[12]

Gary came up to Smith to protest again that he didn't do it.

"I know you never hit him," Smith agreed. "I'd be able to tell."

"Yeah." Gary nodded.

"Okay. Go on about your business."

Whatever had happened, this seemed to Smith like something that would sort itself out. The Landry boy seemed a little disappointed as Gary walked off, but this incident seemed so far from an arrestable offense—if anything had happened at all—that Smith paid the boy no mind.[13]

Smith loaded the four white boys into the patrol car to take them home. No one was at the Landry house, so he waited a bit to see if he could talk to one of the parents about it. After a while, though, no one came, and he left Landry there to take the others home. He dictated the paperwork to someone back in the office, in case the Landrys wanted to press charges. This annoyance out of the way, Smith settled in to finish his accident report.[14]

———

Gloria Landry was at the beauty parlor when F. J. Smith dropped her son off at home in October. She returned to find him wound up and bursting to tell his story. After listening, she told him that they would wait until his father got home to decide what to do, but she was feeling protective and offended. She worried that this was an inevitable consequence of the racial tensions that, in her mind, had been created by the meddling of federal agents in the public schools. She wanted to put Herman in an academy, but those schools had not yet opened, and she hadn't wanted to keep her children out of school. Now she regretted that decision.[15]

Herman Landry Sr., when he returned from work and heard his son's story, was apoplectic. He wanted to file charges that very evening, which meant a trip to a justice of the peace. The justice of the peace in Venice was Herman Sr.'s stepfather, so they decided to drive up to the office in Port Sulphur to avoid the appearance of impropriety. There, they explained what had happened to their son, and the justice of the peace laid out their options.[16]

There were several potential crimes that could fit the incident, he said, and he listed them. Herman Sr. was intent on pushing for the most serious charge possible, so he was captivated by the heavy sound of "Cruelty to Juveniles." That the crime, in its most extreme incarnation, could carry a prison sentence of ten years made it even more attractive.[17]

It was on this complaint that Gary Duncan was arrested. A week later, the juvenile probation officer, Arthur Cope, went to take statements from

Bud Latham and the four white boys. He did not seek out Bert Grant, Bernard St. Ann, or Gary himself. Cope spoke for almost an hour with each of the witnesses, beginning with the Scarabin cousins. One boy was missing, however: Westley McKinney.* His neighbors said they thought the family had moved to Texas.[18]

The Scarabins had their stories mostly straight, and they mostly conformed to what Herman Landry had told F. J. Smith on the day of the incident, though they added some details, explaining that Gary had threatened to "beat all our asses" and called Landry a "bastard." Latham described the scene from his point of view, saying how "the colored driver swung at one of the boys."[19]

Officer Cope finished up with Herman Landry. Landry gave a statement replete with striking details, especially about the end of the interaction:

I had my hand in my pocket and he told me, "If you pull something out of your pocket, I'll make you eat it.["]

He called me a smart motherfucker. After he called me a name, he asked me if I wanted to fight; I told him no but if one of the other Negro boys wanted to fight, I would fight them. He told me, "No, you've got to fight me if you're going to fight anybody." He told us that if we didn't leave those Negro boys, he would beat all our asses.

Landry said he didn't respond to that provocation, but rather turned to Wayne Scarabin to say that Gary "must think he's tough." Then Gary hit him hard on the arm.[20]

Herman Sr. and Gloria Landry seemed satisfied. Justice, they were confident, would be done.[21]

———

* No one ever tracked McKinney down, and no one knows why his family left Plaquemines Parish.

46

The next day, in New Orleans with his wife and newborn daughter, Gary got a call from his mother. "Gary," she said, "baby, they got a warrant for your arrest."

Something his mother had always told him flashed through Gary's mind: "Trouble is easy to get into but hard to get out of."

On the phone, he heard her say, "You come on back."[22]

5—Going to War

THE GLASS IN the door to the law offices of Collins, Douglas & Elie was still broken when Richard Sobol arrived. At night the week before, someone had broken the lower pane and thrown a pipe bomb up the stairwell that led to the modest practice of three young black attorneys.*

Tall and skinny and looking no older than his twenty-eight years, Richard had come down to New Orleans from Washington, DC, where he worked at a prestigious law firm. He planned to spend his vacation days working on civil rights cases before returning home to his job and his family.

By the time he arrived, Richard had little information other than the address of the law firm: 2211 Dryades Street. But it was Sunday, and the office was closed. He found no one, no note, no sign that his arrival had been expected. Everything was unfamiliar to him; even the air felt foreign, pressing thickly on him, made worse by the miasma of hot rain cooking off the pavement. He was drenched with sweat.

The owner of a restaurant around the corner identified Richard instantly as a civil rights worker—well-dressed white people didn't just wander around Dryades Street—and offered him a lift to a nearby motel where activists and lawyers stayed.[1]

The next day, Richard walked up the dark steps to Collins, Douglas & Elie, noticing that he was somehow not especially bothered by the bombing that had taken place in that very stairwell. Richard opened the door at the top of the landing, revealing his home base for the next three weeks. The

---

* The bomb failed to ignite fully, but it broke glass, charred the stairwell, and damaged a car parked nearby. An investigation was opened and almost immediately closed. No one was ever charged or arrested, and the attack barely made the local news.

space was tiny, he thought, and cluttered, though it was clearly a lawyers' workplace: framed diplomas and stacks of extra-long, legal-sized papers announced the profession of its inhabitants. Three miniature offices housed the partners, and an even smaller library with a desk crammed in among the law books was shared by volunteers.

Richard had barely taken in his surroundings before a lanky black man strode up to him and said, by way of introduction, "You need to drive up to Baton Rouge and meet Murphy Bell. He has a school case he wants to bring." This was Nils R. Douglas, one of the partners in the firm, but there was no time for pleasantries. He gave Richard directions and car keys and turned to other business.

Back out on the steaming streets, Richard found a broad, rust-brown Plymouth and drove the unfamiliar roads to Baton Rouge, the state capital. He met with a local lawyer and a group of black people who wanted to desegregate their school district. Less than twenty-four hours later, he had filed his first school-desegregation case in federal court.[2]

It just all moved so quickly. In his job at a corporate law firm, the work was painstaking; Richard's individual contribution to each project was small, his personal impact on any given client negligible. His excitement evaporated when he learned which judge had been assigned his case. E. Gordon West, the others told him, was "a well-known racist," known for diatribes from the bench about how the civil rights movement was part of a Communist plot to destroy America. Richard could not have been assigned a worse judge.[3]

But, within a week, West's objections had been brushed aside by a higher court, and the school-desegregation case was cleared to go ahead. Richard was stunned. He had never seen the legal system move so fast. In his previous work, nothing was measured in days; cases plodded through the courts for years, and the abstruse rulings often provided little in terms of clarity and closure. More important, what had been at stake in those cases was almost always money: corporations bought and sold products and divisions and merged and executed takeovers and continually sniped at one another through their armies of lawyers. Richard had been in the

South for eight days, and he had, more or less single-handedly, won the first round of a school-desegregation fight against the most notorious judge in the South.[*]

After work that day, lawyers and civil rights workers crammed into the office of Robert Collins, as was customary at five or six every evening. Collins, smooth and light-skinned and sharply dressed, was one of the partners. He produced a bottle of Haig & Haig Pinch from his desk drawer, and the gathered men toasted Richard's success. Some friends and acquaintances from the community, knowing of the ritual in Collins's office, came by for a drink or to share a joke.

As the sunlight waned, diffuse in the muggy air, Richard sweated and sipped the liquor and thought that he had never felt so drawn to something in his life. That warm feeling stayed with him for the next three weeks, as he drove all over Louisiana filing lawsuits, and stayed with him as he boarded a flight back to Washington, DC, to his house and his family and his career and the rest of his life.[4]

———

Drinking cheap Scotch in the dusty office of a black lawyer in New Orleans was not what Richard Sobol was supposed to be doing. It had been decided since his birth that Richard would be a lawyer like his father. He never doubted that path, nor did he rebel against it. Richard grew up in a circumscribed world on the Upper West Side of Manhattan. When the family moved, it was from 101st Street to 103rd Street, or from one building on a corner to another building on the same corner. Before college, he rarely left the city.[5]

His parents had grown up in the Bronx, the children of Jewish immigrants

---

[*] As was so often true of school-desegregation cases, *Carter v. West Feliciana Parish School Board* would drag on for years. Sobol and Murphy Bell would shepherd *Carter* to the US Supreme Court in 1970, but even a unanimous decision by the justices could not force West Feliciana into compliance. *Carter* was being litigated in federal court as late as 1983, long after Richard had passed the case on to other lawyers.

from the Russian Empire. Alfred Sobol suddenly became the only man in his household when his father died in 1920. Alfred was fifteen. Still, he supported the family, met and married his wife, moved to Manhattan, and earned a law degree in 1929. After a brief stint working for a railroad after the stock market crash, he opened a law office. In the Depression, this hardly seemed a savvy career move—he may well have made less money in his early years as a lawyer than while working for the railroad—but his wife found work teaching math, and they moved to an apartment building on Central Park West. Their daughter, Marion, was born in 1934. Richard followed in 1937.

Richard went to the Hunter College Model School and the Bronx High School of Science, one of the best schools in the city. Bronx Science crackled with energy, and Richard found himself in an unexpected hub of intellectual life in New York City. Public figures visited the school to give exciting talks. McCarthyism was at its peak, and students debated about the House Committee on Un-American Activities. The academic debate was brought home when a beloved Bronx Science teacher was hauled before the McCarthy committee and, after he refused to testify, was sacked by the city. Amid all the excitement, Richard focused less on schoolwork than his father would have liked, but he graduated and went to Union College in Schenectady, New York, in 1954.[6]

Midway through his sophomore year at Union, Richard received word that his father had died. Like his father before him, Alfred Sobol had not reached his fiftieth birthday. Alfred had long suffered from high blood pressure, and the stresses of his life, especially the intensity with which he worked, had exacerbated this condition. After the funeral, Richard returned to Schenectady.[7]

Richard had never questioned the conveyor belt that his father had built for him, leading from grade school to college to law school to a lucrative legal practice. Alfred Sobol's determination to leave the Bronx and poverty behind had brought comfort and stability to his family, and he was determined that his son would not only follow him, but improve upon his own success. Not just any law school would do: Alfred had gone to

NYU, but Richard was to attend Columbia Law School, where he would be assured a high-paying job and the sorts of connections that could launch his career.[8]

Back at Union, Richard had met Barbara, a student at Emma Willard, an all-girls high school in neighboring Troy. The relationship deepened, and, six days after Richard's graduation, they were married. The couple moved to New York City for the final step of Richard's preordained academic journey: Columbia Law School. Richard thrived at Columbia. He became notes and comments editor of the *Columbia Law Review* and worked closely with Professor Herbert Wechsler on developing the Model Penal Code, an immense undertaking aimed at standardizing criminal law in the United States. Richard loved it all: the intellectual challenge, the structured way of thinking about the world, and the application of complex, intellectual abstractions to the real world. He graduated third in his class in 1961, having exceeded even his father's dreamed-of success.[9]

Right out of law school, Richard was hired as a law clerk to a federal judge and then took a position at the Federal Trade Commission in Washington, DC. The job was sought after, but Richard hated it; he didn't get along with his boss, and he was frustrated by how little work there was to do. It wasn't long before he started looking for something else; a Columbia friend mentioned Arnold, Fortas & Porter.

Arnold, Fortas & Porter was one of the nation's top law firms at the time, at least in part because it had remained a small partnership. When Richard joined, he was just the twenty-eighth lawyer. In part, Richard was drawn to the firm by the fame of Abe Fortas, who had been appointed to represent Clarence Gideon in *Gideon v. Wainwright,* the landmark 1963 Supreme Court case that ordered the government to provide lawyers for poor criminal defendants. *Gideon's Trumpet,* Anthony Lewis's 1964 account of the case, made Fortas a legend and had Richard thinking of all the good work he could do at a firm like Arnold, Fortas & Porter.

The Sobols moved to Capitol Hill, two blocks from the Library of Congress. Richard bought his first car and enjoyed the novelty of driving to work. Within a few blocks lived a bunch of people he knew from law school or work; they were all married, all the same age. The office itself was both opulent and cozy—instead of an office building, the firm was located in a town house—and the structure of the firm was tight-knit and nonhierarchical: there was a standing invitation for all attorneys, partner and associate, to gather in the TV room for drinks from five to six in the evening. Everything about this new life in Washington was agreeable, and Richard luxuriated in the sense of having arrived. In everything, that is, except the work.[10]

Richard knew that the bulk of his caseload at any corporate law firm was likely to be uninspiring. He worked as part of a team of lawyers representing oil companies in places like Oklahoma and doing battle in wars of endless litigation between corporations. He did this work seriously and well, but as he looked around for ways to create meaning in his professional life, he was disappointed by how little the other lawyers seemed to care.

In 1963, Richard listened to Martin Luther King Jr. deliver his "I Have a Dream" speech on the radio. He was vacationing in Maine while the most important civil rights march in American history was taking place just a few blocks from his house in DC. As he heard King's words, a weight gathered and sank in his stomach—he just felt so *guilty*.

What bothered him wasn't so much that Arnold, Fortas & Porter didn't do public-interest law—he knew what he was getting into when he joined a corporate firm—it was that he felt the firm actively discouraged and criticized that sort of work. He tried to get involved in some small way by interviewing a client for the American Civil Liberties Union (ACLU). He scheduled the interview during lunch to avoid interfering with his work, but Paul Porter walked in on the meeting. Later, he told Richard, "We don't have time for that here. That's not part of your job." Deflated, Richard returned to his work.

Fortunately, another young attorney at the firm shared Richard's views and frustrations. Ralph Temple was just five years Richard's senior, but he had already been on the front lines of the social-justice movement.[11]

Temple ignored the firm's stance on extracurricular work; he started taking Richard along after hours to demonstrations, and he brought Richard into his first civil rights case. The incident was small—their client was arrested for "filing a false report" after he reported police officers kicking a defenseless black man on the street—but they won the case by a unanimous decision of the DC Court of Appeals.[12]

This was the first case Richard had ever taken that had been "his," and winning freedom for a man unjustly imprisoned was exhilarating. The decision received little attention in the press, but, to Richard, it felt like a high-profile win. Even better was when Arnold, Fortas & Porter expanded into another town house; from there, he and Temple could work on their cases away from the prying eyes of the partners.

Then Richard was arrested at a protest. As they were being led away in handcuffs, Temple told him not to worry—they had friends in the police department. In lockup, Richard felt sick, not from shame at his arrest but at the thought of how disgusted the partners would be with him. He was relieved when a well-connected friend at the firm arranged for his quiet release without charges. He succeeded in hiding his participation, but, in a way, that just made him feel sicker.[13]

The drudgery of corporate law began to grate more on Richard as he settled back into it. He didn't want to leave the job that had provided this comfortable, pleasant lifestyle, but he started looking around for other ways to do civil rights work on the side. That was when he heard about LCDC.

———

The Lawyers Constitutional Defense Committee (LCDC) was founded initially to defend activists during the summer of 1964. The "Freedom Summer" was the most radical—and most dangerous—phase in the evolving civil rights movement, and it would prove the most difficult to manage.

By 1964, the movement had been gaining momentum for several years, culminating in the March on Washington, which Richard had listened to on the radio. But many activists, especially young ones, were dissatisfied with Martin Luther King's focus on made-for-TV events and his patience with incremental change. They argued that few concrete gains had been made for most black people in the South, especially in rural communities. So they planned to send hundreds of activists into Mississippi to register voters and teach at "Freedom Schools" all over the state. As the summer approached, the volunteers—mostly middle-class white college students from the North—numbered in the thousands.[14]

The Freedom Summer was initially organized by a group of young radicals calling themselves the Student Nonviolent Coordinating Committee (SNCC, pronounced "snick"). Although SNCC was eventually joined in its effort by the other major civil rights organizations, the whole endeavor made many experienced civil rights lawyers queasy. An army of activists going into isolated towns meant thousands of arrests—the Freedom Summer needed an army of lawyers, too.

Carl Rachlin, who was general counsel for the Congress of Racial Equality (CORE), one of the long-standing civil rights organizations that joined SNCC, first conceived of a mass mobilization of lawyers. His idea was to fly a bunch of lawyer volunteers down for a couple of weeks at a time and put them near the places where activists would be working. Then a "dispatcher" would take calls twenty-four hours a day from civil rights workers in need and send lawyers to help them. It would be named the Lawyers Constitutional Defense Committee, and it could all be done for around $15,000.* At least, that was Rachlin's pitch to the ACLU, which agreed to sponsor LCDC.

Reality was more complicated. The organization was not formed until April, just a few months ahead of the Freedom Summer's start. The man hired to run LCDC, Henry Schwarzschild, was an activist, not a lawyer. ("When I came to the LCDC," he told an interviewer later, "I knew law like you know astrophysics—I mean, diddlyshit.")

Chaos reigned at LCDC's tiny home office in New York. Schwarzschild felt in over his head, as the logistics of coordinating transportation and lodging in seven cities for more than a hundred lawyers began to overwhelm him. It didn't help that each volunteer had individual scheduling constraints.

---

* About $120,000 today.

Schwarzschild began taking oversize sheets of thirty-column accounting paper and the stacks of volunteer registration forms over to an ACLU friend's place on 13th Street, where they would spread everything out over the floor, covering the apartment's entire footprint, and painstakingly try to fit each person into the schedule.[15]

The disorder in LCDC mirrored the confusion in the movement as a whole: "Twenty-five hundred kids roaming around Mississippi and Louisiana doing voter registration organizing work, but they're not going to be there in October," remembered Schwarzschild. "Nobody had any grand strategy about this!" But summer came, and they went.[16]

Most of the LCDC volunteers were corporate lawyers with no knowledge of criminal law. Most had never practiced in an actual courtroom— they had jobs like Richard Sobol's, playing out expensive proxy battles for big companies at their desks. Civil rights work was different. "I felt like a soldier or something," remembered one. "I was really scared."[17]

On June 21, 1964, three CORE workers went missing. James Cheney, a black man, and two white men, Andrew Goodman and Michael Schwerner, were murdered by members of the Klan and police officers in Neshoba County, Mississippi. That same day, the first wave of LCDC volunteers arrived. Panicked, an ACLU executive wrote to FBI director J. Edgar Hoover, imploring him to help his volunteers in Mississippi. Hoover replied, "We cannot provide protection for these attorneys."[18]

Those who went with LCDC for the Freedom Summer did not soon forget it. Lawyers flew in for a week or two, passing their cases on when they left. They stayed in cheap motels or homestays or "freedom houses," which were small buildings in black communities that served as schools and community centers by day and bunkhouses by night. Carol Weisbrod, who did much of LCDC's office work that summer, wrote that the atmosphere vacillated between "that of a summer camp to that of an army war room."[19]

LCDC volunteers worked in pairs whenever they could. A call would come to the office: a mass meeting or demonstration was planned, a group of workers had been arrested, a group of workers planned to register black voters or desegregate a restaurant and wanted lawyers present. LCDC rented cars and sent its people wherever they were needed. They drove long hours on highways and back roads to defend arrested activists or file lawsuits.[20]

Volunteers remembered the unremitting heat, the joyous evening meetings in black churches, "singing 'We Shall Overcome': black and white together, holding hands, swaying," as one recalled. "It was one of the most beautiful, exciting, moving, emotional moments of my life." Another volunteer, asked about his experience thirty years later, said,

It was probably the one thing in my whole legal career which made being a lawyer worthwhile. I really saw the effect of what I did. The rest of it is all bullshit. It is all shoveling papers or money or other things around. But for me it was *the* most gratifying—unequivocally—the most gratifying experience of my professional life.[21]

———

Richard Sobol followed the excitement of the Freedom Summer from his desk in Washington, DC. His application to LCDC had been denied.

Ralph Temple and another Arnold, Fortas & Porter associate had gone, and they returned to the office full of stories about mass meetings and panicked calls by arrested activists and impromptu trials in backwater counties without courthouses that convened in real-estate offices or gas stations before judges who were not even lawyers. Richard was entranced and envious.

That winter, Temple arranged for Henry Schwarzschild to be at a dinner party at his house with Richard and Barbara Sobol. At the party, Schwarzschild probably did not expect to be buttonholed by a guest, but Richard was on a mission. When the evening was done, Richard had extracted an assurance that he would go south with LCDC in 1965.

But when Richard got his acceptance letter the next spring, he was disappointed to see that he would be going to New Orleans. He had followed developments in the South, and New Orleans had never really come up. "I wanted to go to Selma or Jackson or one of the places I was reading about be-cause, judging from the newspapers, that's where the civil rights movement was....I thought, gee whiz, I've been relegated to this no-place."

After his last day of work before heading south, Richard ran into Abe Fortas, who had just been appointed to the Supreme Court, in a taxicab. Richard talked excitedly about his plan to volunteer his vacation days and how happy he was to have the opportunity to do civil rights work in the South. Fortas listened and then said, "If you don't want to spend your vaca-tion time for a vacation, you should spend the time working at the firm."

Richard, stunned, realized that he should have kept his mouth shut. Was this the man who had stood up to Joseph McCarthy and represented Clarence Gideon in the Supreme Court? Richard had sought to find a role model in Abe Fortas, but he understood as he stepped out of the cab that he had been wrong. He felt that he could finally see his present situation clearly.

A few weeks later, when Richard was returning to Washington, his disillusionment with Arnold, Fortas & Porter was complete. Civil rights work made him feel alive. It made him feel connected to his clients, to his fellow lawyers, and to events that were shaping American history before his eyes. He went back to the firm after that summer changed in ways that even he was not prepared to recognize or understand.[22]

6—Determination and Unity

THE FALL OF 1966 was one of the busiest times of Leander Perez's life. He was dealing with the continuing impact of the desegregation case, fending off challenges to his control of local voter registration, overseeing the continuing post-Betsy development and reconstruction projects, and trying to move segregationist legislation through Baton Rouge.

These time-consuming responsibilities overwhelmed him to the point that he lost a bit of his attention to detail: Perez, who had always prided himself on immaculately clean and close-mowed levees, was enraged in November when federal inspectors reported that the levees from Port Sulphur to Venice were strewn with debris and rutted from heavy traffic. It was one of several signs that the Judge was spread thin and prioritized maintaining segregation over the other aspects of his work.[1]

Perez took the opportunity to begin the inevitable transfer of power to his sons. At seventy-four, he knew that he would need to shift leadership of the parish before long.

Perez had two sons, Leander Jr. and Chalin. Each had inherited a different admixture of the father's characteristics—his vaulting ambition, attention to detail, sharp legal mind, drive to win, affability with friends, ruthlessness with enemies, and willingness to use underhanded or even illegal tactics—but neither of them exhibited the right combination of these traits to take the old man's place, and neither of them had the most important of their father's many qualities: his unerring focus on the people of Plaquemines Parish.

Leander Jr., who went by Lea, had already settled into his father's long-time position as district attorney, but he was little interested in the minutiae of governance and showed little passion for work. Lea was generally liked in society; he was a regular at lavish parties in uptown New Orleans, and he got along with most of the public officials in Plaquemines. He was, by all accounts, a good-natured and fair boss, and, though he shared his father's racist views, he was less obsessive about them.

Chalin, by contrast, exhibited many of the Judge's less likable characteristics. He had his father's doggedness and intensity, but he was quick to anger and unpredictable; few people wanted to work with him. This fact may explain his limited role in Plaquemines government and social life up through the mid-sixties—he was rarely tapped to perform public duties. But the school-desegregation crisis gave him opportunity: since both Leanders were barred by court order from speaking publicly about the school situation, Chalin was put in charge of public relations.

Meanwhile, through the *Plaquemines Gazette,* Perez pressed constantly on the basest fears of his parishioners. Every week since *United States v. Plaquemines Parish School Board* had been filed, the *Gazette* ran stories from newspapers around the country in which blacks were held responsible for violence and murder, especially when committed against the police. The cumulative effect was to portray a United States that was descending into race war, with Plaquemines Parish as the sole bastion of peace. Crucially, the *Gazette* refused to acknowledge locals, black and white, who opposed the gutting of the public-school system. Blame was always deflected to the federal government and the activist judges who were forcing racial tensions into a naturally harmonious community. "We're just plain sick and tired of these news media trying to make out our people as monsters, bigots and haters," the editors wrote later that year.[2]

At a mass meeting in New Orleans that fall, Perez was presented with a plaque for "courage" and called "one of the greatest heroes of modern times" by the gathered segregationists. In his keynote speech, titled "Why the Whites Have Lost Their Civil Rights," he invoked the Confederacy, declaring that his people in Plaquemines "are unreconstructed rebels!"[3]

Beginning on October 14, the *Gazette* began publishing, in serial form, a lengthy legal treatise by Perez, titled "The Unconstitutionality of the 14th Amendment." The article's language was impenetrable to nonlawyers, and no wonder: it was identical to a brief Leander Perez had tried to submit in federal court in August before a federal judge had shut him down. No law review would accept the piece, so publication of his magnum opus in the *Gazette* must have been a small consolation.[4]

October was a triumphant month for segregationists in Plaquemines Parish. The weekend before the incident with Gary Duncan, Chalin Perez and the Belle Chasse School Association held a party to dedicate the new River Oaks Academy, built in just forty days. Inside the hastily constructed building, which was still missing parts of its ceiling, US Representative F. Edward Hébert thanked Leander Perez over a rendition of "Dixie," announcing that "freedom and independence has not died in Plaquemines Parish, and no one living here ever expected it to do so under the leadership we have." By the terms of the restraining order, Perez could not speak at the event, but he waved and accepted the adulation of his flock.[5]

That very day, Perez achieved his greatest tactical victory yet: the entire faculty body of Belle Chasse High School resigned. The school's doors did not open on Monday. Outside the building, parish attorney Sidney Provensal said that, without a single teacher, it would be unsafe to allow students in. Besides, he averred, Belle Chasse High School cost $500,000* annually to operate, a sum the parish was happy to pay when nearly two thousand students had attended. With barely one hundred students, though, such an expenditure seemed wasteful. Chick Tinsley, the Belle Chasse principal and superintendent of schools, shrugged and declined to comment.[6]

This feat was achieved through a carefully coordinated campaign of enticement and intimidation, and not only at Belle Chasse. Former public-school administrators approached their former teachers and suggested quitting to join the private-school system. Many of these teachers were at first resistant, even indignant. So the ex-administrators first laid out the benefits of private-school employment: a $100–$300† raise, smaller class sizes, and better insurance and retirement benefits. They could use the same

---

* About $4 million today.
† About $800–$2,400 today.

books and lessons they had been using in public schools. If those incentives were insufficient, the teachers were reminded that they still had no contract for the school year and were unlikely to get one.

The administrators also played to racial fears: the courts, they said, were about to order the integration of the faculty; by law, the teachers would need to be "at least 30 percent Negro," and all staff would be required to "share facilities." (All of this was untrue or misleading.) Some especially difficult teachers were told to fill out an employment application "for [their] own protection"—no word on whether that meant job protection or something more sinister—and reminded of their husbands' or family members' comfortable jobs with the parish or in the oil industry. One twenty-year veteran teacher remembered, "That's the first time I was ever frightened down there. [My former principal] gave me the funniest feeling all over. I didn't feel that I was at home anymore."[7]

Civil Rights Division lawyers acted swiftly to force Belle Chasse High School to reopen. On October 20, several administrators and teachers testified in court about the developments of the week. Teachers from as far down the road as Venice described being coached into resigning en masse just before the opening of private schools. In response, Chick Tinsley testified that the allegations were absurd. He had allowed his own daughter to teach at Boothville-Venice High School. Choking back tears, Tinsley said that the stress of working in the integrated school had caused her to miscarry her baby. This melodrama drew guffaws and snickers from some in the courtroom, prompting Perez to leap to his feet to stare them down and request that the judge clear the court. The judge ignored Perez's request, ordered Belle Chasse to reopen, and closed the proceedings.[8]

It was too late. Belle Chasse did not reopen for two weeks, and then only because the archbishop offered to staff the school with volunteer Catholic housewives from New Orleans (Tinsley had turned down the suggestion that nuns could fill in, saying it would violate the separation of church and state). River Oaks Academy opened with twelve hundred students on October 22. It was only half-completed, so the students had to attend classes on a platoon system as elementary classrooms in the morning became high-school classrooms in the afternoon. Promised Land Academy had already opened in September, in a Perez-owned house on the east bank. A three-way dedication for the remaining academies—McBride, Delta Heritage, and Seaway—was held November 6 in Buras and headlined by Representative Hébert and Lieutenant Governor C. C. Aycock, among other top politicians, all introduced by Chalin. As before, Judge Perez did not speak publicly, but he was on hand to thank hundreds of parishioners personally for demonstrating "what a spirit of determination and unity can accomplish."[9]

By January, with the private schools all open and the courts seemingly powerless to change that, Perez could at last redirect himself to the work he loved. The Plaquemines Parish Commission Council meeting that month was a list of Perez specialties: renovations of parish offices, ordinances to remove the irksome debris from the levee, real-estate transactions involving mineral leases and grants, and a photo op with some Girl Scouts, who accepted thousands of dollars from the parish for 1967.[10]

Plaquemines Parish was back to normal.

7—Dire Straits

RICHARD SOBOL WAS run off his feet. In October 1966, fourteen months after he had arrived in Louisiana for a three-week stint, he was the LCDC staff attorney in New Orleans, responsible for more than a hundred cases, and probably the only nongovernment attorney in the state who was working full-time on civil rights.[*]

After returning to DC from his volunteer role in 1965, he felt that he had abandoned his clients in Louisiana—clients who really needed him, unlike the companies that hired Arnold & Porter (which had dropped Abe Fortas's name after his ascension to the Supreme Court). During the Freedom Summer, the civil rights movement had needed an army of lawyers to take one-off cases, mostly defending Freedom Summer activists, and LCDC had filled that role.[1]

In these more normal circumstances, however, the cases were different; there were fewer prosecutions of activists and more complicated lawsuits to be filed, litigated, and followed up on. Where having a rotating cast of lawyers had once been a strength of LCDC, now it was a problem. The volunteer lawyers didn't have enough time to get up-to-date on cases before they had to be training their replacements, and judges became exasperated when a different cast of characters showed up for each hearing. Besides,

---

[*] Civil Rights Division lawyers were in New Orleans at this time, including Hugh Fleischer and Ray Terry, who brought the Plaquemines Parish School Board suit. But people in the civil rights movement tended not to consider government attorneys to be "civil rights lawyers" in the way that Collins, Douglas, and Elie were. Government lawyers could not, for instance, take criminal cases, and their role in affirmative suits was limited by Justice Department policy to desegregating schools and public accommodations and litigating voting rights issues. The archives of civil rights organizations are filled with letters bemoaning the conservatism of "the Division."

Richard thought they spent too much of their time partying on Bourbon Street and going to Antoine's. That might have been fine on a vacation, but it felt contrary to the mission of LCDC.[2]

But Richard felt at home with the black lawyers. Elie, Douglas, and Collins could hardly have been more different—from one another, and from Richard. All three had grown up in households of little means and less education, worked themselves through prestigious all-black private schools, and joined the first integrated classes at their law schools. But they represented different strains of black lawyerdom.

Robert Collins had something of the politician in him; he was well liked and always sharply dressed. Of the three, he had hewed closest to academic institutions. He went straight through from grade school at Gilbert Academy to law school at Louisiana State University, and then to legal practice and a professorship at Southern University. This connection to the establishment showed in his style: Collins was focused on results, and he was careful when making public statements—he would ruffle feathers, but only when he needed to.[3]

Lolis Elie (pronounced "EEL-eye") was Collins's opposite. He was just as gregarious, but unlike the cautious Collins, he relished stirring people up. He was intense and eloquent, given to unprompted disquisitions on race and history. Asked where he was from, Elie always said, "Niggertown," as the impoverished neighborhood of his youth was informally known. Of the three partners, he was the most worldly; he had served in the merchant marine, jumped ship in New York, served in an otherwise all-white army unit in California, attended Howard University in Washington, DC, and returned to New Orleans to join the first black class at Loyola Law School. The parties at his house were a pillar of intellectual life in New Orleans for his many friends—they would discuss art and politics while Elie treated them to his encyclopedic collection of jazz records.[4]

The voice of moderation in the office was Nils Douglas. He held back while the others spoke, he was most likely to gently say "no," and he tried to see problems from as many sides as possible. Introverted and bookish, he liked to work in the law library in the state supreme-court building, where he could do research in peace, surrounded by all the reference books he could want. Every once in a while, an old white lawyer or judge would come through the library on some business and start in surprise at the lanky black man hunched over a stack of law books in these rarefied surroundings.[5]

Richard got along with all of them, but especially with Elie and Douglas. Elie was like family; he made the Sobols feel like part of the cultural scene of New Orleans, and his fearless advocacy impressed and inspired Richard. Douglas felt more like a sibling. His love of research, his deliberate manner, and his sharp focus on complex legal issues all brought him close to Richard. Richard even took to joining Douglas in the supreme-court law library. Douglas was also an avid runner, and he and Richard later developed the habit of running together—the two stick-like men, black and white, striding together all over New Orleans.[6]

The affinity was mutual. In the spring of 1966, Collins, Douglas, and Elie had asked Richard to become a partner in their firm. Flattered, he declined nonetheless. He wanted to go back to New Orleans, but he wasn't prepared to move there permanently. He looked at all the work that the three black attorneys had to do to eke out a middle-class living: divorces, car accidents, bankruptcies, and small claims. All of which left very little time and energy for civil rights work, which was why the firm had needed LCDC volunteers in the first place.[7]

Instead, Richard suggested that LCDC transition to a different model: just a few volunteer lawyers and a paid staff attorney, who could better handle cases. He offered to take the full-time job himself, and, starting in the summer of 1966, he was the LCDC staff attorney in New Orleans.[8]

This time, Richard came down with his family. Barbara was enthusiastic about the prospect, although she was expecting a second child in late spring, and their daughter, Joanna, was not yet two. Arnold & Porter executives were less excited by the Sobols' quixotic plans, but the partners eventually agreed to allow Richard to take an unpaid leave of absence for a year. The LCDC job came with a hefty pay cut—from $24,000 annually to $9,500[*]—

* From $186,000 to $73,000 today.

but the leave of absence afforded him the peace of mind he needed. He looked forward to returning to New Orleans, but only with a set end date and a secure job waiting for him on his return to Washington.[9]

On July 22, 1966, Richard and Barbara Sobol moved with Joanna and infant Zachary to a pleasant house on South Carrollton Avenue in uptown New Orleans. In front of the house, the St. Charles Streetcar clanked and whirred, and Richard could catch it to work in the mornings.[10]

The first morning saw Richard in the familiarly dilapidated office of Collins, Douglas & Elie, where he met Jeremiah Gutman, who had run the LCDC office for a few months. Gutman was fifteen years Richard's senior and famous in civil rights circles as a founder of the New York Civil Liberties Union. On a desk lay a stack of index cards, each of which included a bare-bones summary of a current LCDC case. As Gutman went through them, Richard lost count; there could have been sixty or eighty or even more than a hundred. As Gutman left, it hit Richard that those cards represented a crushing caseload that was now his sole responsibility.[11]

The office finances were also his responsibility, and their disarray may have come as a shock. LCDC, Richard learned, had been close to financial ruin from the moment of its founding. In the first month of his tenure as staff attorney, he received regular letters from Henry Schwarzschild. These mostly warned of the dangers of spending too freely and implored staff to keep the New York office updated on developments and expenditures. "LCDC is in very dire financial straits," Schwarzschild wrote at the end of August. "We are running up a very sizable and very acute deficit in 10-grand multiples." This was not a surprise: the 1966 budget for LCDC was $234,491. Fundraising, however, was never projected to exceed $178,000.* Even optimistic cash-flow projections had the organization running negative balances in its bank accounts for several months in a row after summer operations wrapped up.[12] By mid-September, Richard was forced to write a terse letter to Schwarzschild:

---

* The budget would be about $1.8 million today. Expected fundraising would be about $1.3 million.

Dear Henry:

We have $15.00 in the bank.

Best regards,
Richard B. Sobol[13]

Richard watched the dates of board meetings come and go with trepidation. He always half-expected to open a letter one day saying that the organization had been dissolved and his dream of living for a year as a civil rights lawyer had been dashed.[14]

The work was there, though, and Richard pushed all other thoughts away as much as he could. August was primary-election season, and he traveled all over the state, reporting on violations of federal law. By September, he was so busy that he had to cancel meetings with visiting LCDC leadership, and, frustrated by mundane office tasks, he hired Barbara two days a week to do clerical work and answer phones. Hiring Barbara had other benefits, too: She felt isolated at home with the children and left out of the excitement of Richard's work. Her salary covered the cost of childcare, so she could begin to take part in this otherwise unseen part of her husband's life.[15]

Richard was at the office working on October 21, 1966, when Mazie Duncan called. She said she had called the FBI or someone, and she had been given this number. Whether or not she was surprised to hear a voice that clearly belonged neither to a black man nor to a Southerner, she said she wanted to talk about a matter involving her son and that she needed a lawyer. Richard gave her the address and told her to come on up.[16]

———

Gary Duncan was shocked that he had been charged at all, but it was the specific offense that stung most: Cruelty to Juveniles. He had reached for the Landry boy in a gesture of equal parts paternal admonition and conciliation. The charge was a juvenile matter, to be settled through an

68

informal hearing rather than a trial, but the wrongness of it bothered him. It also bothered him what the boy had said after recoiling from his touch: "My people can put you in jail for that."[17]

When Gary returned home from New Orleans, his mother met him and had just one question: Had he hit that boy? When Gary assured her that he hadn't, his mother said, "That's all I wanted to know. Because I will walk that highway buck naked before I see you spend one day in jail."[18]

Gary turned himself in, and F. J. Smith escorted him to Pointe à la Hache for booking. Shortly thereafter, Herb Collette, his employer, showed up with the bail money. This was not unusual; boat owners in Plaquemines Parish would sometimes post bond for their crew in minor matters. But as Collette signed the bond agreement, Gary remembered something his father had told him when he had started working for a white man: "All you're supposed to do is your job. Don't borrow no money, and don't get nothing because he'll feel that you'll be obligated to do certain things for him and go out of the way to do things for him." Still, Gary didn't see the inside of the jail that day. A few days later, he went up with one of his brothers to New Orleans.[19]

The office was unimpressive. No longer confined to a closet-like room at Collins, Douglas & Elie, LCDC was still cramped in a portion of the CORE office downstairs, where hastily erected plywood partitions barely afforded privacy or sound protection. The decor called to mind a home renovation more than a law office, and the skinny white man seated at the cluttered desk looked, Gary thought, like a hippie.[20]

The man introduced himself as Richard Sobol, a lawyer from Washington, DC, who was working with Collins, Douglas & Elie on various civil rights matters in Louisiana. He led them upstairs to a wood-paneled room that looked more like Gary had imagined a lawyer's office to look. Sitting at the desk was a black man in a suit, who said he was Robert Collins, and they just had some questions for him.[21]

Gary recounted the story: how he had stopped the fight and touched the boy lightly on the arm, how the boy had threatened to put him in jail. Collins and Sobol listened, taking notes. They asked a few questions about the incident and the context. They asked about Gary's relationship to Bert and Bernard and had him reenact the gesture. They reminded him that, as this was a juvenile case, he was not entitled to a public defender, and that his parents had told them that he couldn't afford to pay. Gary confirmed that he couldn't afford to pay a lawyer's fee. They asked whether he thought he could get a fair lawyer down in Plaquemines, which sounded like a rhetorical question, and Gary assured them that "all the lawyers are in politics." In the end, they agreed to take Gary's case and asked him to call them when he was brought back in for arraignment.[22]

As he left New Orleans, Gary felt optimistic. He was back at work, and he had been impressed by the sharpness and intelligence of Collins and Sobol. Sobol, who said he would be doing most of the work on the case, had particularly helped to put Gary at ease. Innocence, he felt, was the best defense, especially with a lawyer like Richard Sobol. Even in Perez's domain, Gary thought to himself, that surely counted for something.[23]

8—Cruelty

R OBERT COLLINS DID not want to take a case in Plaquemines Parish.
Richard had brought Gary's case to him because he was the most conservative of the three partners and the most likely to have reservations. Sure
enough, Collins's initial instinct had been to leave Gary alone. He had only
been to Plaquemines once before, and even though nothing sinister had
happened, he knew the place by reputation. The two of them mentioned the
case to Lolis Elie, who had never been to Plaquemines. Elie, despite his reputation for fearlessness, shared his partner's concerns; he mentioned that
CORE had for years debated whether or not to get involved down there,
ultimately deciding against it.[1]

They all recalled that Perez had built a prison camp for "racial agitators"
on the grounds of Fort St. Philip, a relic from the War of 1812. The stronghold was in the middle of a snake-infested tract of marshland twenty miles
from the nearest road. It had no beds, chairs, or tables, but it boasted cattle
pens, an electrified barbed-wire fence, and machine-gun emplacements.
Perez invited Martin Luther King Jr. and his Communist overlords to come
for a long visit, adding with a wink that it was the only racially integrated
facility in all of Plaquemines.[2]

Fort St. Philip was obviously a publicity stunt, but for Gary's lawyers, the
threat felt very real. Richard registered his colleagues' concerns, but he also
felt strongly that Gary was genuinely the victim of racist harassment and
that he would not find suitable representation in Plaquemines. On that, the
lawyers all agreed. Somewhere in the back of his mind, also, Richard relished
the thought of going up against the most notorious racist in the state.[3]

Nils Douglas worried aloud that Gary might actually face a much harsher
penalty upon conviction if he showed up in court with a civil rights lawyer.

Lea Perez, the old man's son, was the district attorney, and a case like this one was inherently political. Furthermore, Douglas continued, he was increasingly concerned that the Louisiana Bar Association might take some action that would jeopardize the trio's law licenses. So far, he and his partners had been threatened and harassed all over the state, but their standing as attorneys had never been challenged. Douglas knew the political power of Judge Perez, and he knew of Perez's paranoia about "outside agitators" and civil rights lawyers. What scenario could possibly play more directly into Perez's deepest fears than a black and a Jewish lawyer showing up in court in the midst of school desegregation? He felt strongly that the firm was risking reprisal by taking Gary as a client.[4]

The four men debated for a long time. The black attorneys had all faced intimidation before. Police had teargassed a church where LCDC lawyers and Elie were taking statements; later, the lawyers had been detained to "check their bar cards" while the sheriff grimly lined up the department's cattle prods against the wall in front of them. In 1963, Elie, Collins, and Douglas had helped smuggle CORE leader James Farmer out of the city of Plaquemine, in Iberville Parish, where police and a lynch mob had set up roadblocks all over town.[*] There was, of course, the bombing of the office in 1965 and a steady stream of catcalls, threatening comments, late-night phone calls, and other indignities. The three black lawyers were so used to these things that, by 1966, they didn't even bother keeping track of them.[5]

Plaquemines Parish was likely to be different. Not worse, perhaps, but sneakier. Perez was too wily and too sophisticated to use something like a cattle prod. Other lawyers had warned Collins and Elie that they were more likely to have narcotics planted on them than to be threatened with violence in Pointe à la Hache. And then there was the Chicken Shack.[6]

Most civil rights attorneys had heard the Chicken Shack story: two pioneering black lawyers, Earl Amedee and A. P. Tureaud, had gone down

---

[*] They remembered racing back to Elie's house, where they "got drunk—or tried to—within ten minutes."

to Plaquemines to defend a group of more than a hundred black men arrested in 1961 at a party at the Chicken Shack. Amedee and Tureaud knew Perez from Baton Rouge, and, racist speeches or no, they trusted him to keep up at least a facade of respectability. Amedee had handled cases in Plaquemines before with no problem—he had traveled the road alone at midnight without any fear. But on arrival at the courthouse in 1961, he and Tureaud were confronted by Perez and a gang of whites, demanding to know what they were doing there. Amedee was shocked; it was as if Perez had never met him before. "You mean to tell me the NAACP...is meddling in a matter like that?" yelled Perez. "With all these rotten cock-suckers, these motherfuckers? I'll tell you one thing: them niggers have all pled guilty and paid their fines." Amedee, stunned, asked Perez whether he was telling him to leave the parish. "Hell no," replied Perez, "I am not going to give the NAACP an excuse to say that I ran you out of the parish. You say you're a damn lawyer. Well, use your damn head!" Amedee and Tureaud left Plaquemines and never returned.[7]

A lot of younger civil rights lawyers didn't fully believe Amedee's story about the Chicken Shack case, but Robert Collins, who had worked as Amedee's research assistant when he was in law school, took heed. If he and Richard were going to take on Gary's case, they would need to do so carefully. Despite Douglas's vocal opposition, Richard was adamant. A person in his position, he felt, simply had to respond to the injustice of Gary's arrest—he had not left his corporate job to refuse cases that might be tough.

When they agreed to represent Gary, the four men decided that, officially, it would be Collins's case. Richard would do almost all the work, but as an LCDC lawyer without a Louisiana license, he needed one of the three black men to sign on as the attorney of record in every case in state court. No judge had ever refused this arrangement, and all the black lawyers needed to do was make an appearance at the first court date to introduce Richard as out-of-state counsel.[8]

The first thing they discovered about Gary's charge seemed auspicious: there was no way that Gary could be guilty of Cruelty to Juveniles. That law, which barred mistreatment of a child that resulted in "undue pain or suffering," applied only to adults with some sort of authority over the alleged victim, usually parents. It was clear that Gary could have no custodial or supervisory authority over Landry, and it was hard to imagine even a Perez lackey finding otherwise. This discovery made the case seem simple, actually, and the lawyers felt some relief.[9]

Even better, Douglas and Elie recognized the name of the judge, Eugene Leon; he had been a law-school classmate of theirs. Leon had even given Douglas rides to class a few times. He had been appointed just three months prior, and his relative youth and the fact that he was acquainted with the firm all boded well. Richard wrote up a motion to quash, which, they all agreed, should result in the dismissal of Gary's case.[10]

On November 21, Collins and Richard drove down to the hearing. They went through the damp tunnel under the intracoastal canal and entered Belle Chasse, arriving at last in Perez's territory. The west bank of Plaquemines looked essentially like the other stretches of rural Louisiana that Richard had spent days driving through, save for the lack of intersections. The occasional passing ship loomed over the levee as a reminder of the river's presence. If anything, Belle Chasse looked more prosperous, cleaner, and less ragtag than the parishes where Richard spent most of his time. From the ferry landing at West Pointe à la Hache, the red brick and yellow trim of the courthouse's Italianate clock tower poked out above the levee. On the east bank, they parked by the levee and went in to find Gary. Collins noted with a twinge that the bathrooms and water fountains were still labeled "white" and "colored."[11]

The clerk called Gary's case and asked the men to step into the judge's chambers. From there, he motioned them into a small room lined with books. Juvenile matters were not handled in open court, so this space would be their courtroom. Moments later, the judge swept in.[12]

Judge Eugene Leon (LAY-on) had childish features and a round face that was cordial but serious, which was a welcome change for many in the courthouse. He was tapped to fill the seat left vacant by the death of Rudy McBride, a one-legged, cantankerous judge known for always showing up late and often also drunk. At the time of his appointment, Leon was only forty years old, but he had been an assistant district attorney for five years and had been favored by Lea Perez with the title of "first assistant" before ascending to the bench, a sign that his political future was promising. Now that he was judge, he was privy to all sorts of important conversations with the Perez clan, which was a good place for an ambitious young lawyer to be.[13]

Leon's replacement in the district attorney's office was Darryl Bubrig. Bubrig was a big, athletic man and even younger than Richard: twenty-six years old and just eighteen months out of law school. He took the oath of office seriously and felt pride in his work, taking no part in the conspiracy theories of his bosses. At the same time, his perspective on racial politics was blinkered in the way of most white people's; he was no segregationist crusader, but he was worried about school integration and anything else that threatened to upset the established order.[14]

It was a group of young men who gathered to hear Gary's case—Leon, at forty, was the oldest of them—and none of the three white men in the room had been at his job for longer than four months. There were no nonwhite attorneys in Plaquemines Parish, but if either Bubrig or Leon was surprised by the presence of a black man in a suit, they didn't show it. Collins said that he wanted to introduce Richard Sobol, a lawyer from Washington, DC, which also seemed to have little effect on the others.[15]

The reaction came when Collins handed over the motion to quash and explained that the Cruelty to Juveniles charge was invalid on its face. The room fell silent. Leon read the motion a few times—it was only a paragraph long—and looked over at Bubrig. The young prosecutor looked mystified by his own failure to notice the obvious problem. He took a copy of the motion and passed his eyes over it.

"I'm prepared to go to trial now," Bubrig said, flustered. "But I wasn't expecting preliminary proceedings like this. Could I have some time to consider them?"[16]

After a moment, Leon said that he would set a date to consider the motions, and they agreed on January 4. The judge confirmed that Gary's bond was still good, and the hearing was over. As he left the room, Leon turned to Collins and said, "Say hello to Lolis and Nils for me, won't you?"[17]

Gary was surprised and elated. The proceeding had been over in just a few minutes, and he was impressed with how quickly his lawyers had dispatched with the charges. Before he left, Richard cautioned him that the case was not over with, but that he was free to go. He didn't even need to be present for the January 4 hearing, Richard assured him, since that would consist only of the lawyers discussing the motion to quash and, hopefully, getting the case dismissed entirely. Gary was overwhelmed with gratitude to Collins and Richard, and to his mother for having found them.[18]

The midafternoon sun shone low across the Mississippi and through the windows as Gary strode out into the courtroom, feeling like a free man. Collins and Richard followed him out, past a group of seated whites, who gaped at them.[19]

———

Gloria Landry felt the blood roaring in her head as she watched the big black man walk out of the courtroom, smiling. She had sat silently, watching the group of men gather in a closed room, and now it seemed that the court was closed for the day. She had come to see the trial of the man who had hit her child, and she was frustrated by the delay, but it was the sight of Gary Duncan leaving with his smug lawyers that made her mad.[20]

Herman had at first been grateful for the day off from school, but now he was bored. The others in the courtroom were equally restless: Randolph and Wayne Scarabin had come up, and Bud Latham sat in the back. They all expected to see a trial, to be able to testify, to watch a verdict be rendered in the case.

At first, Gloria Landry thought that the case may simply have been delayed until the next day, but she was determined to find out. A few minutes later, Darryl Bubrig scurried out of the judge's chambers. She asked him what had happened, and he said something about how they had filed the wrong charges against Gary, and now it looked like the matter might be dismissed on a technicality. Bud Latham, overhearing Bubrig's comments, declared as he stalked out that he had been there for four hours and he had better things to do with his time than run back and forth to Pointe à la Hache.[21]

When Bubrig left the courtroom, Gloria Landry caught Leon's eye, and he motioned her over to near where the Scarabin boys sat. She asked again what had happened.

"If you want to press charges," he told her, "you're going to have to change the charge."* Cruelty to Juveniles wouldn't hold up, he told her. The proper charge would have been Simple Battery. Gloria Landry took Herman straight to the municipal building at Port Sulphur, walked into the justice of the peace's office, and said she wanted to file a battery complaint.[22]

Four days later, on November 25, Gary Duncan drove home from work, coming up the road from Venice Marina. In front of his house sat Wilbur Buras and F. J. Smith.

"Gary," one of them said, "we got another warrant for your arrest. They filed new charges on you."[23]

---

* There is some dispute over who told Gloria Landry what the "right" charge should have been (it was either Bubrig or Leon, both of whom denied it, and it was a question of some legal importance). Both Gloria and her son, when deposed about the incident in 1970, denied remembering any such conversation. In the same round of depositions, Randolph and Wayne Scarabin remembered it vividly. Bubrig, when I interviewed him in 2015, remembered few details from that day.

9—Klantown, USA

RICHARD WAS IN another part of the state when he learned that Gary Duncan had been arrested again and new charges had been filed. Quite apart from the question of innocence or guilt, the existence of two cases against Gary, based on the exact same facts, seemed patently unconstitutional. Richard researched and wrote a long, detailed memorandum that laid out the illegality of charging Gary with battery while he was still also being charged with Cruelty to Juveniles. He never filed the document, contenting himself instead with berating Darryl Bubrig for his "outrageous behavior."[1]

Gary's arraignment for the new charge was on December 7, so Richard blocked out just enough time to take some depositions in the town of Tallulah, drive late at night back to New Orleans to sleep, and make it to Plaquemines in time for Gary's appearance. But by early evening, Richard was feeling shaky and nauseated and weak.[2]

The stomach bug he caught was only metaphorically related to his treatment by the segregationist lawyers in Tallulah (one of them threatened to "take him outside" during a deposition), but he was in no shape to drive five hours back to New Orleans that evening. Searching for someone to be there for Gary at his arraignment the next morning, Richard tried to reach Collins at the office and at home. When that failed, he called Douglas but got no answer. At last, he called Mazie and Lambert Duncan to see if he could talk to Gary. After apologizing, he walked Gary through the process: he should plead not guilty, and he should make careful note of the trial date and anything else the judge said.[3]

Richard spent the night in Tallulah, violently ill and alone. Staying at a motel in rural Louisiana was unusual for him; he liked to return to the safety of New Orleans each day, regardless of the length of the drive. Gary called back the next day to say that he had pleaded not guilty and been released on a new bond. His first bond—which was still outstanding, as the Cruelty to Juveniles charge had not been dropped—had been $1,000, but this new bond was $1,500.* This sum seemed outrageously high, and the combination of his client's hasty rearrest and this exorbitant bond seemed to be something more than the usual workings of justice.[4]

Gary's case was beginning to appear less straightforward. So far, proceedings had been orderly and collegial, but there were hints that Richard and the other lawyers had been right: this case felt less benign than a simple misunderstanding about how hard Gary Duncan touched Herman Landry on the elbow.

But Gary's case still seemed trivial compared to some of the other work Richard was doing. As he worked on Gary's defense, he was spending most of his time on a series of cases in Tallulah and, especially, Bogalusa, which had become an unlikely hot spot in the civil rights movement. Perez may have made Plaquemines Parish synonymous with white supremacy, but it was in Bogalusa that civil rights lawyers needed armed escorts. Every time Richard drove into town, he was entering into pitched battle.

———

The Ku Klux Klan owned Bogalusa, Louisiana, or thought it did. There were more than eight hundred professed Klan members residing in the town of twenty-one thousand, including the city attorney and members of local and parish legislature, the police, and the housing authority. The local Klan, which had rebranded itself the "Anti-Communist Christian Association" in a name change that fooled no one, began "patrolling" the streets after dark, hurling bricks and bottles at pedestrians and chasing black drivers at ninety miles an hour down North Border Drive, which divided Bogalusa in half.

---

* In today's dollars, the first was about $7,700; the second was about $11,500. Both bonds were much higher than usual.

Black leaders woke to burning crosses on their lawns and at their churches, or to gunshots fired into the houses of suspected civil rights workers. In its February 1, 1965, issue, *The Nation* ran a cover story about Bogalusa called "Klantown, USA."[5]

The Klan needed to be so strong in Bogalusa because black people in town were so organized. The largest employer in town was a paper mill owned by Crown Zellerbach, and it employed both black and white workers in large numbers. In the sixties, the company had a payroll of $18 million[*] in Bogalusa alone. True, the pay rates and job descriptions were not equal between the races, but black workers had their own union, which became a training ground for local activists, and they owned their own homes and cars, which made them unusually independent. Ten years earlier, activists and union members had formed the Bogalusa Voters League to advocate for themselves.[6]

Actually, it was the union that made the first move; in 1963, after years of negotiating about wages and safety, the black union pushed to integrate all aspects of the plant. Crown Zellerbach began to comply—the company was based in San Francisco and was agnostic on race. As soon as the showers and cafeteria were opened to both races, whites in Bogalusa reacted with fury.

What followed was both a metaphorical and a literal arms race. Whites refused to enter the desegregated facilities; blacks pressed their advantage to gain access to some jobs reserved for whites. Whites signed up in droves for the Klan and began threatening black workers with lynching; blacks lawyered up, contacting Collins, Douglas & Elie. Whites started burning crosses on the lawns of black families; the Bogalusa Voters League called in some seasoned CORE workers to train them in tactical resistance. Whites ambushed the CORE workers and laid siege to Voters League meeting places; blacks formed the Bogalusa Deacons for Defense and Justice. The Deacons were a black militia formed to combat the Klan in rural Louisiana. This was not Martin Luther King Jr.'s vision of the civil rights movement. The central message of the Deacons: First, organize. Second, get bigger guns.

---

[*] About $140 million today.

By the time Richard got involved in Bogalusa, the Deacons were well armed indeed. They patrolled the streets in cars, carrying large-caliber rifles and shotguns. There was talk (usually denied with a wink) that they carried military-style weapons in their trunks. They learned to organize the defense of their neighborhoods. "We have groups patrolling each street," a Deacon explained. "And every time a white man comes in, an automatic radio call is dispatched to a car to stop him and ask him his business. When the policeman come around, we right on him, too—we patrol him." They also learned to escort their New Orleans–based lawyers all the way to Lake Pontchartrain to keep them free from harassment.[7]

Richard started working in Bogalusa on a group of cases for Bob Hicks, a shrewd local activist and vice president of the Bogalusa Voters League. Hicks was tireless in putting himself at the center of civil rights cases. When the Voters League staged a demonstration or rally in Bogalusa, whites would break it up, beating people as the police watched or took part. Then Hicks would call Collins, Douglas & Elie, who would inform the federal judge charged with the case. Soon enough, Bogalusa authorities were bogged down under numerous court orders stemming from several lawsuits against them.

Though he seemed to enjoy advancing his activism through the courts, Hicks was no pacifist. It was he who, after spending several tense hours barricaded inside of a café encircled by the Klan, insisted on forming the Bogalusa Deacons for Defense. "It takes violent blacks to combat these violent whites," he said. "It takes nonviolent whites and nonviolent Negroes to sit down and bargain whenever the thing is over…but I ain't about to."[8]

Richard liked working with him. Hicks was a sharp, dedicated activist but warm and amiable as a friend. Like Richard, he was a strategic thinker and, also like Richard, most comfortable working behind the scenes. Richard worked on a slew of "Hicks versus" cases, including lawsuits against the chief of police, the head of the local housing authority, the mayor, and the secretary of housing and urban development. But the biggest and most ambitious by far was the case against the paper mill.[9]

Richard and Hicks alleged an elaborate system of racial discrimination in hiring and promotion practices at the Crown Zellerbach mill. This case was on the cutting edge of the law. Title VII of the Civil Rights Act prohibited employers from discriminating on the basis of "race, color, religion, sex, or national origin." Clearly, the sort of blatant "whites only" segregation that had been the norm in the South was now illegal, but it was unclear whether the law went any further than that.[10]

What Richard argued in *Hicks v. Crown Zellerbach* was that Title VII also banned subtler methods of discrimination, like standardized tests. These tests were just starting to be administered in workplaces, much as they had been used in college admissions for decades. The problem, from Richard's point of view, was twofold: the tests had nothing to do with the actual work, and blacks failed these tests much more often than whites, leaving them unpromoted or unemployed.*

Unlike the targets of most previous civil rights litigation, these tests were not explicitly racist. In fact, the tests may not even have been intended to be covertly racist; they were prepared by people with PhDs at companies like "The Psychological Corporation" in the North and West, and they reflected a midcentury preoccupation with IQ and data-driven analysis rather than Jim Crow–style racism. Still, Richard argued, the tests discriminated on the basis of race whether or not that was their intended purpose, and their use should be barred.[11]

Nothing like *Hicks v. Crown Zellerbach* had ever been tried before under the Civil Rights Act, and the task was daunting. It was just the sort of case that often takes a team of lawyers many years—and many thousands of dollars—to resolve. From his time at a corporate law firm, Richard knew how much work it would be, and he understood how ambitious the case was. He would first need to prove the discrimination, which required processing the test results and employment histories of hundreds of people, and then he would need to make the novel legal argument that

---

* Crown Zellerbach used three tests: Wonderlic, SRA Non-Verbal, and Bennett. The results of all three had large racial disparities. According to Sobol's research in the suit, the passage rates were Wonderlic: whites 36%, blacks 12%; SRA Non-Verbal: whites 24%, blacks 6%; Bennett: whites 66%, blacks 15%.

employment discrimination did not need to be overt or even intentional to be illegal.

He had a lot of moral support at Collins, Douglas & Elie. Lolis Elie, in particular, became obsessed with the potential of *Crown Zellerbach* to utterly overhaul hiring practices, bringing blacks fully into the workforce, at last, as equals. And the partners knew that Richard had the vision, intelligence, and legal instincts to build the case carefully and persuasively. If he succeeded, he would be responsible for redefining workplace discrimination in America.[12]

———

Even if Gary's case was not at the front of Richard's mind as 1966 ended and 1967 began, he was hardly pushing it aside. He saw little of his client, but that was because there was little to discuss. The trial had been set for December, but Richard asked that it be postponed; he was rushing to work out some tricky election issues in Mississippi before January 1. But Gary didn't need to worry about all of that. All he had to do, in the end, was get up on the stand and tell the truth.

Still, Richard had come up with a few defenses apart from the basic claim that Gary was factually innocent. Any good defense attorney will be looking out for potential issues that might help the client: illegal police activities, procedural missteps by the state, violations of the Constitution— what laypeople and prosecutors often dismissively call "technicalities." A technicality (defense attorneys prefer "protection") operates regardless of the defendant's actual innocence or guilt; instead, it calls into question the essential fairness of the proceedings. In Gary's case, Richard's chosen technicality was both unusual and ambitious.

One fact had struck Richard right away about Louisiana's Simple Battery law: a person could serve up to two years in prison for it, yet it was still classified as a misdemeanor. That sounded off. Usually, any crime punishable by two years in prison would be considered a felony. The distinction was meaningful: Felony cases required more elaborate procedures and protections than misdemeanors. Most important, felonies were usually decided by juries, not by a single judge.

Richard dug deeper into Louisiana law, and he found a number of "misdemeanors" punishable by up to ten years in prison, which seemed absurd. For decades, federal courts had provided juries for any crime with a punishment of six months or more. Most states did something similar. But Richard noted in the Louisiana constitution that the state's right to a jury trial wasn't even related to the length of the sentence. All cases not punishable by hard labor or death were to be "tried by the judge without a jury." And even when Louisiana did provide a jury, it was usually not of the *Twelve Angry Men* variety. Crimes punishable by hard labor were tried by a jury, but there were only five people on it—or sometimes twelve, but only nine needed to agree. Death penalty cases were the only ones in Louisiana with the familiar twelve-man, unanimous jury.[13]

An idea arose in Richard's mind as he contemplated Louisiana's bizarre jury system. There was no inalienable right to a jury trial in America. The Bill of Rights promised an "impartial jury" to all criminal defendants, but for almost two hundred years, that had been understood to refer only to federal courts. Every state provided for some sort of jury trial, but there was no law saying that they had to.

But Richard knew that there was a legal movement afoot to apply the Bill of Rights to the states. Slowly at first, the Supreme Court had been advancing clause by clause through the first eight amendments, considering whether each particular segment of the Bill of Rights should be applied to ("incorporated against" in legal jargon) state governments. Incorporation, as it was called, began in earnest in 1925 with freedom of speech and then continued through the rest of the First Amendment before moving on to the others.*

By 1967, most clauses of the Fourth, Fifth, and Sixth Amendments, which

---

* *Gitlow v. New York*, 268 U.S. 652 (1925), was the first case to explicitly argue for the incorporation doctrine. Several cases that incorporated (or rejected) clauses predate *Gitlow*, so a clause-by-clause list of incorporation arguments goes back to 1884, when the court refused to incorporate the grand jury clause in *Hurtado v. California*, 110 U.S. 516 (1884).

protect criminal defendants, had been applied to the states. A couple of the cases were famous: *Gideon v. Wainwright,* which had been argued by Abe Fortas, Richard's old boss, established the right to have a public defender if you couldn't afford an attorney. Not every right was incorporated: Grand juries were explicitly left out, and the protections against excessive bail and fines had not yet been addressed. Nor had the clause about the jury.[*]

It was a long shot, but Richard decided to write up a motion demanding a trial by jury in Gary's case. He knew that nothing would probably come of it, but he was young and feisty and a little bit naïve—and perhaps he also liked the idea of confronting a judge in Perez country with an argument about the US Constitution.

---

[*] The "impartial" part of the jury clause had been addressed in *Parker v. Gladden,* 385 U.S. 363 (1966), which held out some tantalizing dicta about "the Sixth Amendment, made applicable to the States by the Fourteenth." But *Parker* did not do the trick. Interestingly, *Parker* was a case out of Oregon, the only other state to share Louisiana's idiosyncratic system of nonunanimous juries.

10—The Case for the Prosecution

JANUARY 25, 1967, DAWNED COOL and foggy as Richard left New Orleans for Gary's trial. Gary met him on the levee with Mazie, Lynn, and one of his sisters. Together, they walked up the staircase, which curved as it ascended, and into the courtroom. Inside, Bert and Bernard sat to the back on one side, and the Scarabins on the other, by the entire Landry family.

Gary watched Richard unpack his papers—a stack of documents and motions set on a legal pad—and he felt confident. He looked back at his mother, who smiled at him. He was frustrated by needing to miss so much work, and he was upset at the indignity of his arrests, but as he watched his lawyer prepare himself, none of that bothered him. Richard had always been ready for the next move, and Gary was eager to see this case brought at last to a conclusion.[1]

"Be seated," said Judge Leon as he bustled in.

"Your Honor, may it please the court," Richard began, the r-less "cwaht" giving him away as a New Yorker, "I'd like at this time to pass up to you a demand for trial by jury in this case."[2]

He handed up the thin sheaf of papers that contained his quixotic argument about Louisiana's jury system.

Bubrig countered, "Your Honor, the state will certainly oppose a trial by jury. This is a misdemeanor. The Louisiana law is very clear that the defendant does not have a right to trial by jury unless the case is a felony."

"The court is familiar with this statute fixing the juries," Leon nodded, and he rattled off the Louisiana jury law: "Misdemeanors are not tried by a jury with or without hard labor. It's a five-man jury with hard labor or a twelve-man jury with nine men concurring. Capital must be a twelve-man

86

jury, twelve men concurring. These are the requirements under Louisiana law. The court is going to deny your request."

There was nothing unexpected about this denial; Leon was right about Louisiana law. Richard offered a pro forma objection and directed his attention back to the case: "The defendant is ready for trial, Your Honor." And with that, the trial was formally under way.

Bubrig spoke first, a little hesitantly; he was still developing a smooth courtroom persona. "The state will prove...that on the 18th day of October, 1966, Gary Duncan, at about four thirty p.m., did strike Herman M. Landry Jr. with his hand, without his consent—the consent of Herman M. Landry Jr.—that the striking was within the Parish of Plaquemines and, in particular, Boothville, Louisiana. The state would like to call—"

"Now, wait just a second," Judge Leon cut in, and then turned to Richard. "Do you have an opening statement to make, Mr. Collins?"

"Mr. Sobol," Richard corrected him.

"Mr. Sobol. I'm sorry."

No, Richard said, he didn't need to make an opening statement.

Wayne Scarabin walked forward past the bar and between the counsel tables. He sat to the judge's left at the burnished-oak witness stand and raised his right hand high in the air as the bailiff swore him in. Scarabin spoke confidently as he told his story.

"We was talking to the two colored boys on the side of the road," he began, "and Gary Duncan and this other boy passing us in the car. They stopped and backed up to us. They asked us what we was doing. We told them we was talking to the two boys and asked them their name and all. And the two boys said we was lying."

In Scarabin's telling, Gary suddenly turned belligerent, threatening to beat up the white boys and calling Landry a "smart little punk." Then Gary slapped Landry on the arm before retreating to his car.

"What was the discussion between you and the two colored boys about?" Bubrig probed.

"Well, we was talking to them," explained Scarabin. "They had an incident at school. They had a little trouble, and we was asking them about it."

Bubrig had inadvertently made a misstep by allowing the boy to bring up the "incident" at school. Talking about racial tensions in Plaquemines was key to Richard's argument.

"Did Herman Landry ever strike Gary Duncan?" asked Bubrig, moving on.

"No, sir."

"Did he ever threaten him?"

"Well," said the boy, "after Gary Duncan slapped him, he said he was going to call the police."

"But only after he was slapped?"

"Yes, sir."

Richard knew as he started the cross-examination that he needed to get Scarabin to admit that there was animosity at school towards the new black students. If he lost this case, Gary's fate would rely on the transcript of these proceedings. The next step would be to appeal, but today was the only shot Richard would get at asking questions of witnesses; cases on appeal get no second trial. At best, lawyers can speak briefly in an "oral argument" on behalf of their side, but appeals courts decide cases based on the record: the trial transcript and the briefs and motions filed by the lawyers.

He started by asking if Scarabin and the black boys were in the same grade or knew one another in any way. Scarabin replied curtly that he didn't know them at all and had no idea when they had even started attending the school.

Richard moved carefully to the issue of race: "But you took some note of the fact they were there, didn't you?"

"Yes, sir."

"How about in the boys' bathroom in the school," offered Richard. "Had you ever seen them in there?"

"I seen them in there, yes."

Richard phrased the next question as neutrally as he could: "Were you in a group that spoke to them?"

"No, sir," said Scarabin. The boy knew what was coming, so Richard prepared to ask the question outright.

"You were not in the group that—"

But Bubrig leapt to his feet with an objection. The more Richard was able to harp on the racial tensions, the worse for the prosecution. Just as Richard's case relied on making Gary's arrest about school desegregation and racial tensions, Bubrig's case relied on limiting discussion of the incident as much as possible; if Gary touched Landry without Landry's consent, then he was guilty of battery.

Quite apart from strategy, Bubrig was personally skeptical that this incident was related to the desegregation of the schools, except maybe in the most tangential way. Batteries happened all the time, especially after the roughnecks came home from the offshore rigs on payday, and in his few months as a prosecutor, he had already won convictions for crimes much more serious than Gary's that had no motivation other than jealousy, money, or intoxication.

The schools, Bubrig thought, had desegregated relatively quietly, despite Judge Perez's provocations. Boothville-Venice, in particular, had barely missed a step. And, while Bubrig's son was too young for his family to need to decide between public and private schools, he knew folks with children in each system who seemed perfectly happy. Bubrig was a little annoyed, truth be told, at the implication that he was part of some sinister Perez conspiracy. Neither the old man nor Lea Perez had been involved in the case in any way, though both were affiliated with him through the district attorney's office. As far as he knew, neither had ever heard of Gary Duncan.[3]

For another ten minutes, Richard tried to find a hole in Wayne Scarabin's story. He asked about whether Scarabin actually already knew the black boys' names, whether he and his friends had moved to block the black boys' way, whether he in fact threatened the black boys as he crossed the street to talk to them, whether anything in their conduct might perhaps have been perceived as threatening. Had the white boys blocked Grant and St. Ann's path? Had they prevented the black boys from leaving?

"They could have left if they wanted," was the reply.

Richard even asked Scarabin to reenact the slap, approaching the witness stand and asking Scarabin to hit him on the arm as Gary had hit Herman Landry. Scarabin leaned out and touched Richard on the elbow.

As Scarabin stepped down from the witness stand and walked back into the audience, Gary felt vindicated. Scarabin had admitted that the touch was "not too hard," and the way the boy had touched Richard's arm in demonstration had seemed more timid than threatening. Richard seemed in charge of the proceedings, and Judge Leon seemed to be listening carefully and without prejudice.[4]

Randolph Scarabin took the stand next. The stories of the two Scarabin boys fed on each other. They were essentially the same, but Randolph's version was punchier. In his telling, Gary's language was rougher, the black boys were more pugnacious, and Bert Grant had openly challenged the white boys to a fight from across the street. Richard pounced on this.

"It was *Bert* who said, 'You want to fight?'" asked Richard, incredulous.

"Yes."

"And Bert is with one person and you're with three, and he challenges this group to a fight?"[5]

Bubrig again leapt to his feet. "If Your Honor please, the state asks that the last remark—it's a self-serving declaration by the attorney—that it be stricken from the record."

But Richard bore down, asking why Scarabin or any of his friends would cross the road after being challenged to fight. Had they perhaps already crossed before the challenge? Had they perhaps provoked their black classmates before Grant's "threat"?

Bubrig was livid. "If Your Honor please, the state asks that counsel for the defendant control his remarks to the testimony of the witness and not insert any information, Your Honor, into the record. This is a self-serving declaration."

"Your Honor," replied Richard, "I was trying to get clear what he was—"

"No," countered Bubrig, "you're trying to get into the record before the court your own personal remarks."

"I am not."

Judge Leon leaned down at Richard. "You have done this on two or three occasions.... You're changing the declarations of this man completely. Whether you're trying to put something into the record, I have no idea. But

I wish you would confine questions of this gentleman to his answers and not add your own words to his answer."

Richard was not done: "If there's an exception to that remark—"

Then Richard was cut off by another, unfamiliar voice. It came from behind him, at the prosecution's table.

He had not noticed when Lea Perez entered the courtroom, had not noticed as the district attorney picked up the file from Bubrig's desk and leafed through it. He hadn't seen Lea Perez before, so he may not even have recognized the man, though Judge Perez's notoriety made his sons recognizable figures.[6] The younger Perez, tall and thin, boyish even at forty-six, had none of his father's craggy features and swagger. His voice was softer and he was always polite, but he carried himself with the confidence of one accustomed to getting his way.

Richard may not have known who Lea Perez was, but Gary did. Blacks from the parish rarely sought interactions with any Perez; the Perezes were not a topic of daily conversation among black people down in Boothville before school desegregation, but everyone was conscious of the ruling family. When Gary looked over to the prosecution table and saw Lea Perez, dread knotted in his stomach.[7]

Despite his position as district attorney, Lea Perez was not a constant presence at the courthouse. He almost never showed up in the district attorney's office in Plaquemines, leaving all day-to-day operations to Bubrig and Joyce Armstrong, his secretary. He appeared in court even less frequently, and only for high-profile cases. In fact, in his six months on the job, Bubrig had never seen his boss in the courtroom before. But there was Perez, at the prosecution table, and he spoke up, perhaps finding Bubrig insufficiently firm in his objections.[8]

"And further," Perez said, cutting off Bubrig from behind the prosecution table, "if Your Honor please, the state has not objected to the lengthy questioning of certain witnesses, but the state will…prove that the defendant came upon this scene when there were five or six people and that the crime was committed by the defendant, not by these boys. And anything that these boys might have said or done has nothing to do with the particular charge at all."

Judge Leon turned back to Richard and said, "As far as this court is concerned, this…is highly immaterial. I mean, [Mr. Sobol] stated that he wants to show the events leading up to it, but the events leading up to it have no bearing on the crime as far as I've seen."

Richard was left to continue his cross-examination. But just as he was getting back in stride and asking about the fight at school, Perez jumped in to stop him.

"If Your Honor please, the state will obj—"

But Judge Leon was already speaking: "I see no relevancy of this line of questioning, Mr. Sobol."

"Well, Your Honor—" Richard began, but Perez shouted him down.

"If Your Honor please, at this time, I would like to make this remark: I think this line of questioning is more damaging to the defendant, because the state has seen by evidence elicited by counsel for the defense that these two colored boys had been proven to be the aggressors. And I can't understand any further questioning along these lines, which seems to me to prove the *guilt* of the defendant."

When Richard again tried to go back to questioning Scarabin, it was Judge Leon who cut him off: "Now you're trying to go into the fight on the school grounds. This may be a serious—"

"Your Honor, I'm trying to show—"

"The court realizes what you're trying to show, Mr. Sobol," Judge Leon thundered.

Richard tried to explain his argument: that if the boys were threatened at school, then Gary had reason to suspect that they were at risk when he saw them on the side of the road, outnumbered by white classmates.

Judge Leon stopped him short. "The facts of this case are what went on on the side of this road in front of this restaurant, not what went on at school. The court is interested in what went on on the side of the road."

Bubrig chimed in, "Your Honor, I think everything that happened prior to Gary Duncan coming upon the scene would prove nothing. Mr. Duncan didn't arrive at the scene until he drove in front of the store, and all these other questions are irrelevant."

Before Richard could offer a rejoinder, Perez explained that this case was really about the random slapping of a boy by an adult "for no reason at all." Was Richard contending that Gary knew about the fight at school? Was he saying that the black boys had specifically called on Gary to be their "deputy" to hunt down Landry and his friends? Surely, Perez finished, "it's damaging to the defendant to exhibit this type of testimony."

Richard was aghast as Perez explained his objection. Not only was the district attorney speaking out of turn, he was trying to lecture Richard on trial strategy. Richard looked from Judge Leon to Bubrig to Perez.

"I don't know where we are, exactly," he said.

Judge Leon peered down at him. "Well, there was an objection to your line of questioning. I would say—a statement by Mr. Perez. You're damaging your client in your line of questioning."

"I have never heard of that as a basis for an objection before, Your Honor."

Judge Leon probably knew that Richard was right—there is no rule against damaging your own case, if that's what Richard was actually doing— but he was done with the conversation.

"I can't see the relevancy of these questions," he said. "Truthfully, I can't. What has this to do with the crime before me today?"

As soon as Richard prepared to continue his cross-examination, Judge Leon leaned over the bench to admonish him: "The court finds it highly irregular. And I'll state for the record to Mr. Sobol: I think you are injuring your client in this line of questioning. However, if you wish to proceed, the court is not going to stop you, sir."

Finally, and providentially, Judge Leon added, "This is not before a jury."

What the judge meant was that he was tired of the procedural debate, and since the rules are a little looser in trials without a jury, he'd allow Richard to continue. American law considers judges better at ignoring irrelevant or misleading evidence and testimony than jurors, so some things will pass in a bench trial that a jury would be instructed to ignore or disregard. Despite the fact that it carried no legal weight at all, Judge Leon's pronouncement seemed to strike a nerve with Richard, who had asked for a jury trial an hour before.[9]

"Thank you, sir," was all Richard could manage before he let Scarabin step down.

Bubrig called up Herman Landry, whose story was clear and polished. He described how the black boys had shouted threats across the road, and Grant's challenge to fight. He told how he had asked Bert and Bernard their names, and how they had refused to answer.

"So we went to cross over," he said flatly. "And they told us their names."

"Then," he went on and pointed at Gary Duncan, "the boy right over there stopped in his car." Landry described the conversation, saying that Gary had called him a curse word and threatened to beat them all up. Bubrig asked if he had invited Gary to hit him or consented to the attack in any way.

Richard took over and asked where Gary had hit him.

Landry pointed to his elbow. "He hit me right here."

"He hit you hard?"

"It stung a little bit."

"Stung a little bit?" Richard asked. Landry nodded.

As Richard tried to pin Landry down on where everyone was standing and whether anyone had mentioned the fight at school, Gary felt vindicated. The boy looked flustered as Richard bore down on him, and there was no way, Gary thought, that anyone could believe that this kid had been struck, let alone hurt.[10]

The final witness for the prosecution was Bud Latham. His recollection of the moment was dramatic: he recounted how he saw Gary punch at Landry, whose arm flew into the air, and then speed away down the road. When Richard pressed him on cross-examination, Latham's responses were willfully obtuse until Richard finally asked, "Did he wind up and hit him? Do you have any idea? That's what I'm really getting at." Latham replied that Gary had been aiming at Landry's chest and that only the boy's timely dodge had made the blow land on his arm and avert serious injury. Satisfied, Bubrig rested his case.

After Latham stepped down, Judge Leon called a recess for lunch and walked over to Lea Perez. As the men talked, Richard gathered his papers together, and Gary sat with his hands on the table, unsure what to do next. Richard reassured him about the afternoon, when he and his cousins would testify.

In truth, Richard was troubled by Lea Perez's entrance to the courtroom. At worst, the district attorney's presence itself may have determined the outcome of the case. He still hoped to win an acquittal, but every development in this ostensibly routine misdemeanor prosecution indicated that there was, as Gary's parents and Richard's partners had feared, more to this case than a disagreement over what exactly happened on the side of the road. The best Richard could do in that case was to make a compelling record for an appeals court to review. As he tried to ease Gary's concerns, his mind raced ahead to the next steps.

The Louisiana Supreme Court was unlikely to overturn a conviction. Appeals courts are loath to overturn the verdict of a lower court, and stronger cases than Gary Duncan's had been dismissed, even without a racial element. Once a verdict is given, higher courts are required to presume that it is correct.

But a ruling from the Louisiana Supreme Court was probably out of the question anyway. By asking for a jury, Richard had specifically referred to the US Constitution, and state courts are forbidden to reinterpret federal constitutional law. They can only look at the laws of their own states. Even if the Louisiana Supreme Court had been sympathetic to claims of bias against black defendants—which they were not—they could not have ruled in Gary's favor. No state law had been violated. When he spoke in the Plaquemines Parish courthouse that afternoon as the last of the fog burned off and sunlight started to stream in through the high windows, Richard Sobol knew who his likely audience was: the Supreme Court of the United States.

11—The Case for the Defense

I can see what the law is like. It's like a single-bed
blanket on a double bed and three folks in the bed
and a cold night.
    —Robert Penn Warren, *All the King's Men*

G ARY KEPT REPEATING to himself his mother's assurance that, since he
had not hit the Landry boy, he would be found not guilty. Richard
had mentioned that it was unusual for defendants to testify in their own defense, but Gary wanted to explain what had really happened on the side of
the highway.[1]

"All rise," came the introduction, and Judge Leon strode to the bench.
When the judge told everyone to be seated, Gary settled back into his chair
at the defense table, and Richard moved forward to call Bert Grant.

Grant kept his composure during the grilling from Perez and Bubrig. Bernard St. Ann looked terrified as he walked into the witness stand, but he spoke
up loudly to tell his version of the story. Gary felt his confidence grow.

When he took the stand, Gary kept his gaze on Richard; seeing his lawyer
radiating confidence and intensity calmed his nerves. From the beginning,
Richard built up Gary's narrative: he was a working man, a father, and he
had no criminal history. Nothing in his past would indicate a penchant for
violence. Gary filled the room with his baritone voice as he recounted the
incident from his perspective, describing the touch as "an expression…just
to tell him to go ahead on home. That's about all I could do. I told him to
go ahead on home."

"Did you touch him hard enough to hurt him, do you think?"

"No."

"I have no further questions," said Richard, returning to his seat.

Bubrig went after Gary's character. He asked about his driving record, which, like that of most young men who owned a car in Plaquemines Parish, was not perfect. Bubrig reminded him that he had been fined a hundred dollars and given a suspended jail sentence for reckless driving in 1965. Then, suddenly:

"Did you threaten the four white boys?"

"No."

"You didn't tell them anything?"

"No."

"In other words," Bubrig said, gesturing to the jury room where the white boys were sequestered, "those three boys—all three of them—were lying when they took the stand?"

"They were lying when they said I threatened them, and that I was meaning to hurt the boy when I touched him on the arm." Gary stiffened. "If I wanted to hurt him, I could have hurt him, and I ain't ever had no intention to hurt him."

Suddenly, Lea Perez stood up, holding Gary's file in front of him.

"Duncan," he said, "you had stated in response to the questions asked by your attorney that you had never been in trouble before, and then Mr. Bubrig asked you, and he recalled to you that you were charged on three different occasions, is that correct?" Going on, he pressed Gary on his previous statements. Was he in fact a fisherman, as he had stated at one time? Or was he a deckhand, as he had stated another time? Or a captain, as he had just said?

Gary was a little frustrated by this line of questioning. Whether he was a deckhand or a captain depended on which boat he was working on and how the owner worked out staffing for the shift. And when he wasn't working a towboat, he was trawling.

He tried to explain, but Perez pushed on, asking him if he remembered being picked up—and here Perez read the details from Gary's file—on April

26, 1965, after running someone off the road at ninety miles an hour on a curve on Highway 23? Gary protested that he was arrested for driving without a license, but he hadn't tried to run anyone off the road. Perez turned the page and repeated the interrogation with the next driving ticket.

Richard had tried to object to the form of some of Perez's questions, but it became clear that neither the district attorney nor the judge knew or cared as much as he did about the rules of procedure, so there was nothing he could do to stop the questioning. Gary, he thought, had held up very well under the pressure put on him by both prosecutors. His composure was all the more remarkable for the fact that the toughest cross-examination had been done by a man with the last name of Perez.[2]

Gary stepped down and collected himself. He glanced back at his family, who gave him silent looks of encouragement. Sitting at the defense table, Gary listened to the closing argument. In it, Richard talked about the context of the incident—school desegregation, the fights at school, the boycotts, the media attention paid to a place that rarely received consideration by outsiders—and how those influences explained the facts of the case, making clear why Grant and St. Ann had felt threatened, why Gary had felt it necessary to protect them, why Bud Latham had been so ready to call the police, why Herman Landry's parents had filed charges in such a minor matter. It was, Gary thought, masterful. He felt ready to dance out of the courtroom, especially when the judge nodded in agreement towards the end.[3]

"Mr. Sobol," said Judge Leon when the statement was through, "you brought out an interesting point in your closing argument. A very interesting point. The court will take into consideration in deciding this matter [that] your client, in passing up six kids—I call them kids. They are under the age…They're all kids in the eyes of the court. At the time that this incident happened, things were of such a nature in that end of the parish— we should take that into consideration."

Gary thought he would burst with gratitude, especially to his parents. He did not know how they had found Mr. Sobol, but as he listened to the judge affirm the statement about racial tensions and desegregation, the tension that had built up inside him, taut and wound tighter by each new injustice from when he touched the Landry boy until this moment, began to slacken.

"The fact that six boys were standing on the side of the road would mean nothing to anyone who would be driving by," continued the judge. "I have witnessed this myself, and I am sure you have on many occasions. I'm sure the defendant has, where there are conversations on the side of the road between white boys and colored boys.

"However," Judge Leon said, nodding at Bubrig and Perez, "you described the civil-law definition of battery. The court is well aware of it: a mere touching…every touching or holding, however trifling, of another person or his clothes, [in] an angry, resentual [sic], rude, or insolent, or hostile manner shall be battery, as defined in the code.

"Mr. Latham testified that he was 150 to 200 feet away, yet he saw the blow. And he saw the boy's arm go up in the air from the blow. He stated that, if the boy would not have backed up, it would have been even more serious. The court is taking into consideration Mr. Latham's testimony, a man who was not even in the discussion—or whatever we may call it—between six boys on the side of the road. And the testimony of the victim himself, Mr. Landry, that the blow was sufficient to sting him. I think the state, for those reasons, has proved to me beyond a reasonable doubt that the defendant is guilty of Simple Battery. Will you stand up, Gary Duncan?"

Gary felt himself fall through the floor even as he mechanically stood tall to comply with Leon's request. He was short of breath, as if his body were constricted by thick lines or pressed under weights. His family was behind him, and he turned slightly to look back at his mother. She was weeping, and the sight of her face fractured something behind his ribs. "I know what this is," he thought. Gary saw how people could just take and do things to you, and he understood that his family had known that truth for a long time and protected him. He felt naïve, and he felt foolish. "I know what this is," he repeated to himself as he turned back to the judge.

Leon looked him in the eye. "The court is going to find you—"

"Your Honor, we'd like to have a delay," Richard cut in quickly.

Leon looked annoyed. "I will give you a delay between the verdict and the sentencing. I'm going to render my verdict now."

"I see," said Richard, a little sheepishly. After hearing the word "guilty," he had thought Leon was going straight to sentencing.

"The court at the time finds you guilty of the crime of Simple Battery. The court will at your request—you do not wish to be sentenced this afternoon. You want a delay?"

"Yes," replied Richard, and he confirmed that Gary's bond was still in effect. Sentencing was set for a week later, and court was adjourned.

Richard sat and turned to Gary, who was staring through the top of the table. "Don't worry," Richard said. "It's not over. Let us fight this. Go live your life."[4]

12—Investigation

THE WHOLE SITUATION irked Lea Perez. Despite his victory in the case—which had never really been in doubt—he was troubled that such a big deal had been made of what was, after all, a minor issue, best dealt with expediently by local authorities. Now, it seemed, even a battery prosecution was magically about civil rights when it was in the "notorious" Plaquemines Parish and had the name Perez attached to it in some way.

Lea did not share his father's unflinching belief in the vast Marxist-Zionist conspiracy, but he had to say that the sudden appearance of a Jewish lawyer from Washington made him wonder whether the old man had been right. Forced race mixing had upset the carefully constructed balance in Plaquemines, as it had everywhere else it had been tried, and everyone suffered. It was bad enough that gangs of black and white boys were fighting, breaking the fragile peace that had once been maintained. But some fighting among schoolboys was normal and expected, he thought, and maybe even a good way for hotheads to blow off steam. It was that Duncan, an adult, had taken sides in a harmless brawl between children—that had been the transgression. It confirmed a narrative that seemed to be playing out in front of him: school desegregation was the gateway first to sporadic violence and then to a war between the races.

Lea Perez was irritated that the mainstream press, run by smug elites with deep pockets on Wall Street and in the Capitol, could not see what had been so obvious to his father and everyone else he knew: putting black and white children together bred more, not less, racial animosity. It was well known in Plaquemines that if you picked a fight with a black man, you picked a fight with his whole family—and what had begun with a slap or a punch would spread like a brushfire until, in short order, an entire community was caught up in the conflagration. Just look at Los Angeles, still scarred by its rioting a year and a half previously. Or Chicago, Cleveland, San Francisco, New York City, Philadelphia. The *Plaquemines Gazette* had dutifully reported the devastation caused by rampaging blacks in each of these places as a solemn warning of the storm to come. Every one of those cities, he might point out, was part of the supercilious crescent of Northern and Western do-gooders that arced from California to the capital. And yet the liberal media were too busy caricaturing the Deep South—where, it might be noted, no such degeneracy had yet erupted—to turn their poison pens on their own hometowns.[1]

And, to be honest, it was also personal. Sobol's condescension in court still bothered Perez. The boyish lawyer had shown no deference to him, had dared to lecture him on the law of his own state. That Sobol could steamroll Bubrig was understandable: Bubrig was even younger than the newcomer and even newer to the job. But the man's impudence, especially in light of how inconsequential his client's case was, made Perez angry. Had Duncan been beaten? His life threatened? Paraded before a mob like the savages in the Klan insisted on doing? Everyone had been happy before this business with the schools, and for Sobol to implicitly equate the eminent respectability of Plaquemines Parish or the Perez family with the boorish horror show of Selma or Birmingham felt unfair, particularly when it was Sobol himself and his fellow travelers who were edging the community towards violence. To be accused of racism by the very people who were stirring up racial resentment was simply too unjust for words.[2]

An idea grew in the mind of the younger Leander Perez. Lolis Elie had taken some cases from the Orleans Parish district attorney, moonlighting as a prosecutor to make ends meet. Nothing wrong with that. But on the first of the year, not even a month previously, a law had come into effect that barred active prosecutors from also practicing criminal defense. As a partner in the firm defending Gary Duncan, Elie's work as a prosecutor cast doubt on the firm's ability to take any clients in criminal cases. If Collins, Douglas & Elie were disqualified from Duncan's case, Sobol would be disqualified, too. So Lea Perez reported Elie to the district attorney in New Orleans. He also notified the Louisiana Bar Association. It was a long shot, since it didn't implicate Sobol directly, but he thought it might work. But when someone mentioned that Sobol was not a member of the Louisiana Bar, Perez saw a much easier path open before him.[3]

If Sobol was not licensed to practice law in Louisiana, then what was he doing in a Louisiana courtroom? It is a bedrock principle of American law that each court system gets to determine which lawyers are allowed to practice before it. Being a member of "the bar" allows one to pass, literally and metaphorically, beyond the railing that traditionally divides officers of the court and their clients from the public seating area behind. Just having a law degree does not qualify a would-be lawyer to practice law—each state has its own system of tests that, in theory, admits only those who understand not only the general legal principles taught in law school, but also the idiosyncrasies of local law.

Perez rushed to his office to make a phone call before Sobol came down for Duncan's sentencing. If Sobol was not licensed in Louisiana, he had been even more brazen than Perez had thought. Perez fumed at the thought of this outsider lecturing him, a native, on Louisiana law without even having taken the state's bar exam. He recalled a favorite quote of his father's: Huey Long had once said, quite rightly, that "there were more carpenters licensed to practice law in Louisiana than there were lawyers."

Still hot, Perez dialed Thomas Collins, the secretary of the Louisiana Bar Association. A secretary answered, saying that Collins was out of town. Perez asked if she could check her records to see if there was a Richard B. Sobol admitted to the Louisiana Bar. After searching for a few minutes, she returned to the phone to say that there was no one of that name—nor anybody named "Sobol" or "Sobel"—authorized to practice law in the state. Perez, exultant, asked if she could have Mr. Collins write a letter to that effect, on letterhead, and send it to him. She said of course she could, and Perez went upstairs to tell Judge Leon.[4]

The sentencing hearing came and went—Duncan got sixty days and a $150 fine—and neither Perez nor Leon revealed their discovery to Sobol.

But on the way back to New Orleans, when Sobol was stopped and cited for driving without an inspection sticker, the deputy called back to Pointe à la Hache with the car's registered address.[5] Sobol was released, but Perez had what he needed to get started with an investigation.

The district attorney checked records of the address for Sobol's car. He was a little surprised to find that 2211 Dryades was not a house, but on a commercial block in a black neighborhood. The Pontiac had actually been a rental car originally, he found, but had been purchased by the Congress of Racial Equality, and then by the Lawyers Constitutional Defense Committee. Perez knew all he wanted to know about CORE—it was one of his father's favorite punching bags—and, though he had never heard of a committee for constitutional defense, it sounded Communist enough.[6]

For decades, the elder Leander had hosted powerful lawyers and other political allies on frequent fishing trips, and Lea rarely passed up a chance to socialize with the state's elite. Deep-sea fishing was certainly done on these trips, but they were mostly opportunities to let loose in private with other politicians and power brokers. On February 10, an entourage set out on the parish yacht, the *Manta,* traveling to Judge Perez's lavish camp at remote Port Eads. As they motored down the river, Lea went to greet Woodrow Irwin, district attorney of Washington Parish. Irwin complained to his counterpart about all the agitators in Bogalusa, which was in his jurisdiction, and the trouble he was having with the federal courts and the media. He wished that he had a Perez to keep Communists out of his parish and federal judges out of his local affairs. With particular bitterness, he talked about the trouble he was having with a dogged and obnoxious lawyer named Sobol.[7]

At that moment, Lea Perez realized that he had been thinking too small. He had assumed that Sobol was some troublemaker sent down to be a thorn in the side of the Perezes, and that the threat of uncovering Sobol's lack of a Louisiana law license was simply a nifty way of abating the nuisance of the Duncan case. It was possible that Sobol had worked in federal court, which would allow a lawyer from any state to practice—

he knew that activist lawyers were causing trouble in federal courthouses all over the South. But it had never occurred to him that Sobol was actively practicing law in local courtrooms all over Louisiana. That must be against the law.[8]

The investigation of Sobol grew both in pace and scope after the fishing trip ended on February 13. Perez began calling other district attorneys all over the state to see if they had heard of Sobol, and he recorded that Sobol had been spotted in local courtrooms all around southeastern Louisiana and as far upriver as Madison Parish, near the Arkansas border.

Meanwhile, no letter had arrived from the Louisiana Bar Association. Impatient, Perez called on February 13 and learned that the letter had gone to the wrong address. He fumed at the hapless secretary before carefully dictating the address of the Perez law firm in New Orleans, where he and his brother conducted their private practice. On February 14, the letter arrived, certifying that Sobol was not a Louisiana lawyer and had no business in Louisiana courtrooms. Perez had certified copies of it made, and he sent them to DA offices all over the state.[9]

From information learned after Sobol's traffic stop (the charges were filed on February 6, and Sobol went to Pointe à la Hache to plead guilty and pay his fine), Perez found his home address on South Carrollton Avenue in New Orleans, where a car was parked with Washington, DC, plates. From Washington, DC, Perez tracked Sobol to the firm formerly known as Arnold, Fortas & Porter. That Abe Fortas had recently become one of Judge Perez's favorite targets of abuse on the Supreme Court felt like one more piece of the puzzle that fit perfectly.[10]

Perez found that Sobol had a family: a wife and two young children. And he decided that a man like Sobol—who had a phone number, a driver's license, a place of work, a utility bill, a New Orleans Shoppers credit card, a car, a house, and a family living in that house—could not possibly claim to be in Louisiana on a temporary basis.

It is not clear exactly when Lea Perez told his father about his investigation and its results. The Judge always maintained that he had no idea who Sobol was until late February. Sobol himself suspected that the elder Perez had been orchestrating Duncan's prosecution from the beginning, "taking out his frustration" at having been muzzled by the federal court. But Lea's investigation seemed more representative of the father's bulldog approach than the son's dabbling. In any case, by February 20, both Leander Perezes had their evidence.[11]

13—Trouble

VIVIAN DUNCAN TOOK Gary's arrest the hardest. She was not only the eldest Duncan child but also the most like her father: proud, upright, and burdened with an overdeveloped sense of fairness. God, she trusted, had sent them Richard Sobol, and she believed that it was good. She liked and trusted the fastidious lawyer. But where her brother's prosecution fit into the Almighty's plan, she could not say. Vivian knew better than her siblings how far Perez's power extended, and how hard their parents had worked to protect the family from the sort of persecution that Gary now seemed to be suffering from.

Mazie and Lambert were frank about the risks of being black in America, especially in the South, but they insulated their children as much as they could from the harsh realities of racism. The boys were warned many times to avoid any interactions with white women, and Gary recalled being told by Mazie to cut off a friendship with a black woman who, rumor had it, "could have been fooling around with a white man." Nobody needed that sort of trouble.

But trouble had begun to bleed into the family's relationships. Some members of the extended Duncan clan had always been quietly envious of Lambert's financial independence and success. This envy had bred resentment among a few, which was compounded by Richard's representation of Gary. A white lawyer—a Yankee, no less—must have cost a small fortune to retain, they grumbled. Where had the Northern attorneys been when they or their sons had been arrested for various crimes, trumped-up or valid? That no money had changed hands was not always believed.[1]

Some troubles were of Gary's own making. He had been the recipient of many talking-tos by his father, but none as dire as the one about his son. Gregory was born on February 17. This was less than five months after Geralyn's birth, and Lynn, needless to say, was not his mother. Less than a year earlier, Lambert had given Gary a lecture about the responsibilities of being a husband and a father, so he thundered his disappointment at his youngest son while his daughters comforted Lynn.[2]

It was the nature of the Duncan family to enclose within its bounds as many members as possible, even those whose ties might be considered tenuous. "Cousin" was a stand-in for nearly all relatives outside the nuclear family; no distinction was made among degrees of parentage or so-called legitimacy. So after Gary had weathered his comeuppance, it was understood by all that Adrian Taylor and her son Gregory were family.[3]

Still, Gregory's was another mouth to feed, so Gary threw himself even more into his work. He was rarely home; he worked for days at a stretch on crew boats and tugs for the offshore oil industry and then returned home only long enough to catch a few hours of sleep before leaving in the morning to trawl for shrimp with his brothers.

His relationship with Lynn survived the infidelity and his long absences, helped along by her family's delight with the Duncans generally and Gary in particular. City folks, they treated the Duncan property like a getaway, and they were heartily welcomed in. Lynn's father went out fishing with Gary, and her brothers, Stanley and Calvin, brought friends down to enjoy the open space and relaxed pace of life. Soon enough, Stanley and Calvin met and fell in love with sisters Cheryl and Paula Franklin, which gave them even more reason to be in Plaquemines.[4]

There was a lot to like. On summer Sundays, the Duncans might have a picnic on one of the boats or gather to watch the men play community baseball. The Boothville Drifters played across the road from the Duncan property. On home-game days, cars would be parked on the shoulder of Highway 23 for a mile, and fans would cram onto the makeshift bleachers to watch the game, drinking beer and sweating in the sun. Gary played catcher or center field, as needed.

Then they would migrate to the Good Rockin' Club in Sunrise, a dozen miles up the road, to drink more and play pickup ball. The other teams came from black communities up the river as far as Baton Rouge, and families would carpool to games after church or ride in the back of a truck still sticky from hauling watermelons.[5]

After a long Sunday, the Duncans would return home. There, they talked and argued, picked at leftovers for supper, or drove with friends to bars in Port Sulphur or, if they were feeling ambitious, as far as New Orleans. The best prospects for a good time, though, lay across the river, on the east bank, where the women were. Bars and informal clubs hosted all-night parties, and Gary and his friends and brothers would take the ferry after dark.

If exhaustion or the exigencies of romance took hold before the ferry reopened in the morning, individuals and couples would make a pallet on the floor and sleep until dawn. Or they might head towards the closest bridge, in New Orleans, driving through the Ninth Ward, stopping at black bars and clubs along the way. Once over the bridge, they would begin the ninety-minute drive back to Boothville. More often than not, by the time they got back, the ferry was running again anyway. Then they would deposit their cars carefully at home, stealing final kisses with a wink, getting their stories straight if they had told daddy that they were staying local. An hour or two later, it was back to the boats, back to picking shrimp and hauling mud.[6]

And, even though he was working overtime, Gary found some time to relax. He trusted his family to move on from the trouble in his marriage, and he trusted Richard to stand in the way of Perez. In the end, he felt, his blessings far outnumbered his troubles.

Lambert worried, though. He worried about Gary's work. He worried about the bail bond in his son's case because Richard worried about it. He knew better than to let his guard down. Growing up, the Duncan children were unaware of Lambert's involvement in the New Orleans NAACP, which continued even after 1956, when the organization was forced to go underground by a Louisiana law (championed by Perez, of course).* Adults

---

* The statute used to drive the NAACP out of Louisiana was a zombie law. It required that advocacy organizations file annual membership lists with the state, and it had been initially passed in the twenties as a way to combat the Klan. Perez advocated for the law's resurrection and led the subsequent raid on the New Orleans NAACP office himself.

often gathered in the Duncan home after dark and spoke in whispers, their guns propped by the door.

Lambert told his children that he was a Freemason, but he did not explain that black Masonic lodges in Louisiana were full of radical activists who smuggled civil rights workers past police and vigilantes into the most hostile corners of the Jim Crow South. It was understood that the Plaquemines sheriff kept track of NAACP and Masonic-lodge meetings in New Orleans, and the first few miles of Highway 23 in the parish would be crawling with cops looking to stop black drivers for any reason or no reason.[7]

Lambert also worried about the family's good standing with the many white gatekeepers throughout lower Plaquemines Parish. He had always been respected by respectable white people down the road, and despite the burning of his boat and the intermittent vague threats he had endured all his adult life, he was generally positive—if cautious—about white natives of Boothville and Venice. After a long day on his boat, Lambert used to grab a beer at Fitzgerald's Bar in Venice, which served white fishermen. When some out-of-town whites had protested against Lambert's entry one day, Fitzgerald himself had come out and declared, "If Lambert Duncan can't walk in the front door and get a beer, I'm gonna shut this place down!" There were a lot of good people.[8]

Lambert and Mazie Duncan continued to shelter their youngest son from the dangers he faced. His good nature and his faith in justice gave them hope, even though they knew the ugliness that skulked in the dark corners of Plaquemines Parish—and in its courthouse.

14—No Error of Law

RICHARD BRACED HIMSELF as Al Bronstein's hurricane-force person-ality whipped in through the front door. Bronstein ran the Jackson LCDC office and oversaw all of the other field offices, so he was nominally Richard's superior. In practice, he and Bronstein worked as coequals, bound by mutual respect—although they didn't necessarily much like each other.

Except for being Jewish and from New York, Bronstein appeared to be Richard's opposite in every way. Where Richard was physically imposing but restrained in his speech, Bronstein was short, fiery, and possessed of a thundering bass voice that he wielded like a club. He boiled with energy at all times, speaking in incantatory paragraphs that explored ideas from several angles or attacked contrary positions viciously before pivoting to an alternative suggestion. "After being cross-examined by Al," recalled a lawyer who later worked closely with him, "you knew you'd been through something."[1]

Born in Brooklyn in 1928, Bronstein was nine years Richard's senior. After working his way through an accelerated law-school program, he delighted his parents by becoming a partner at his uncle's small law firm and then disappointed them by neglecting his work to hang out with activists. He married a woman, Kate, whom he met at a CORE event, and a few years later the couple and their three daughters moved to the Adirondacks to found an alternative school. Shortly, it became clear that neither the school nor the marriage was working out (Kate later left him for the school's third founder), so Bronstein was happy to see a notice in

111

the ACLU magazine that called for lawyers to volunteer in the South. A summer of shouting down segregationists in sweaty courtrooms suited his mood perfectly.[2]

Bronstein spent the summer of 1964 working for LCDC out of a closet-sized room in the back of a black dentist's office in St. Augustine, Florida. When the Freedom Summer ended, he left the South and closed up shop—the lawyers' work was done. This did not sit right with Bronstein, so he went straight to New York City, charged into the LCDC central office, and announced to Henry Schwarzschild, "There is no way you can morally close down this operation." Schwarzschild commiserated but said that LCDC had only a few weeks to live. So Bronstein showed up unannounced at the LCDC board meeting that had been called to dissolve the organization. He offered to work for a comically inadequate salary if they would agree to keep LCDC running.

A few months later, in January 1965, Schwarzschild called him to say that the board had agreed to guarantee his pay—for three months. That was good enough for Bronstein. He left for Jackson, Mississippi, in February to start LCDC's first full-time field office, and he had been there ever since. Among the first items of mail he received at the new address was a divorce complaint from Kate, but even those who worked most closely with him remember no public reaction to the end of his marriage. Every iota of his being was directed steadfastly at his work.[3]

Bronstein's intensity was legendary. "There were no limits to his guts," recalled a co-worker from Jackson. "None. He was the toughest, bravest guy I've ever run into. He just took no shit from anybody." Another said that Bronstein "strode around like he owned the earth—and he really did. He had earned it."[4]

He earned this trust with his dedication to living in and frequenting the communities he served, and also by unflinchingly ignoring the danger he was in. He was followed late at night by cars. A sign appeared on his office door one day that read, "The eyes of the Klan are on you." He was often threatened with beating by police officers and the white supremacists they represented. He was in fact beaten by a police officer and a jailer at a courthouse in Magnolia, Mississippi, where he had arrived for a bail hearing, seeking the release of forty-two blacks arrested for demanding their right to vote.[5]

For all their differences in style, Richard and Bronstein shared this earned respect, as well as a view of the limited role of a white civil rights lawyer. The lawyer, they felt, always supported the actions of civil rights workers—the lawyer never dictated or participated in those actions. Richard and Bronstein zealously enforced the line between representation and activism—volunteer lawyers who worked under both of them recalled being sharply corrected if they marched in a demonstration or tried to participate in a sit-in. "You go, you get arrested, you become a client," Bronstein told one. "We need more lawyers, not more clients."[6]

February 13 was the due date for Gary's appeal; as the day neared, Bronstein consulted with the other lawyers at LCDC and the ACLU on strategy, and Richard readied his memos and motions, sending drafts not only to Bronstein but also to his former colleagues in Washington. When the day arrived, Richard was prepared with an application for a writ of certiorari to the US Supreme Court, a petition for a stay of enforcement, and several bond applications—one to Judge Leon, one to the Louisiana Supreme Court, and one to the US Supreme Court. He figured that one of these courts would surely grant Gary a bond that would keep him from serving his sixty-day sentence while the justices made their decision. Richard sent copies to Daniel Rezneck, the Arnold & Porter attorney who had gotten him out of jail three years earlier, and waited.[7]

But February 13 came and went. Richard was relieved to hear that Gary was not arrested, but he was also ready for the next step and a little impatient. Richard had plans to spend some time in the North, which would provide a welcome respite. On February 22, he was to fly to Washington. If the appeal had moved to the US Supreme Court by then, he could stop in at Arnold & Porter, where he was still on a leave of absence, to be sure that everything was in order. If not, he still looked forward to a few days away from New Orleans.[8]

When he arrived at the LCDC office on February 21, 1967, Richard had a letter from the Louisiana Supreme Court, which tersely announced its dismissal of Gary's case: "The application is denied. No error of law in the ruling complained of." Richard, on cue, had Daniel Rezneck fill in the blanks and file his application with the US Supreme Court. As soon as the Plaquemines Parish courthouse opened at ten o'clock, he called Judge Leon to make sure he could get his papers signed and Gary Duncan could get bail.[9]

The secretary at the courthouse told Richard to wait as she conferred with Leon. When she returned, she asked if he could schedule a meeting with the judge for Thursday morning, February 23. Richard said that no, he needed to see the judge today. Thursday would be far too late for Gary, he thought, and besides, he himself was flying away on Wednesday. The secretary left the phone again, and Richard waited with the hiss of the receiver in his ear. At last, she returned.

"The judge said, 'If he will be here by noon, I can see him this morning,'" she reported.

Richard hung up and dashed upstairs to see if Robert Collins could go with him, but Collins's office was empty. In fact, the entire upstairs office was deserted. Downstairs, Barbara Sobol, at the secretary's desk, was the only person present in the LCDC office.

Richard called Gary, hastily dated the papers he needed, stuffed the case file into his briefcase, and got in the car alone to drive down to Plaquemines Parish. It was ten thirty. If everything went perfectly, and he timed the ferry crossing just right, he could be at the courthouse in an hour and twenty minutes. That left him only a few minutes of buffer to make it to Pointe à la Hache in time.

He eased the LCDC Pontiac across suburban Jefferson Parish and into Plaquemines through the clammy tunnel, which had been one of Leander Perez's signature infrastructure achievements. He sped along the gentle curves of Highway 23 and down the narrow funnel of farmland and borrow pits until he arrived at the ferry landing. He was in luck: the ferry was waiting for him.

Richard arrived at Leon's chambers at ten minutes before noon. The secretary told him to wait, so he sat nearby and worried. Gary had not been waiting for him at the courthouse as he had hoped. He had briefly considered waiting for him, but there was no point. The ferry ran frequently, but even so, the next crossing would not be until after noon, and Richard had not wanted to be late. He had hurried up the courthouse steps to present himself a few minutes early for the judge, and there he sat. The clock showed noon and then five and ten after. He felt certain that Lea Perez or Darryl Bubrig would request a warrant for Gary's arrest at any moment—indeed, it could be happening right then—and there would be very little he could do about it unless he could beat them to Leon and get the judge to sign the papers he was carrying. If not, Gary would be arrested. He could cancel his flight to Washington, which left in less than twenty-four hours, and come back on Thursday, but Gary would still spend two days in jail.

The door to the judge's chambers swung open, and Leon strode past him and down the hall. Richard remained sitting, not knowing what else to do. A few minutes went by, and then, just as suddenly, Leon returned and bustled into his office, at last turning to Richard and inviting him in.[10]

Leon settled down to eat the rest of his lunch as Richard handed him the papers. Leon perused them, chatting briefly about how interesting Richard's argument about trial by jury was—really very unusual. He signed the papers, and, at Richard's insistence, he signed an order for a new $1,500 bond to cover Gary through the Supreme Court's process—Richard wanted everything in order before he departed for Washington.[11]

"You planning on being in the building for a while?" asked Leon as Richard gathered his things.

"I'm going to make a telephone call," Richard replied, a little confused.

Richard did not see Gary in the courtroom as he walked out. There was no sign of his client downstairs, nor had the telltale Impala been on the levee by the ferry landing, where his own car was parked. He walked to the courthouse's phone booth to call Gary. No one answered. He tried again. Still no reply. Perhaps that was a good sign.[12]

He heard a knock on the glass of the phone booth and spun around.

Directly before him stood two men. The first was in the uniform of a Plaquemines Parish deputy sheriff. The second, scowling and powerful and clutching a fragrant cigar, was unmistakably Leander Perez.

"You Sobol?"

"Yes," said the young lawyer mechanically.

"You're under arrest."[13]

15—The Chief Engineer

H IS PARISHIONERS DOWN the road had disappointed Judge Perez. The anemic boycotts of Port Sulphur, Buras, and especially Boothville-Venice had not forcefully sent the message that racial integration was unacceptable to the people of Plaquemines. The east bank had responded to dog whistles, Belle Chasse had needed a brief campaign of intimidation to bring it in line, but the downriver communities had survived threats, disruption, and even the horrifying reality of mongrel classrooms. The truth that many of Perez's subjects did not see race mixing as an existential threat—or that, in real life, an integrated classroom was not the rape factory of his imagination—was unacceptable to Perez, so he found other ways to explain the situation. He blamed his political opponents down the road, the craven oil industry that had even started allowing blacks to secure service contracts, and the vast Zionist-Communist conspiracy that, it seemed, had somehow managed to infiltrate even the most isolated parts of his domain.

On the east bank, by contrast, the process had gone perfectly. Woodlawn School had not opened on an integrated basis for a single day. Whites had moved to Promised Land Academy with only a two-week delay, and the black students who had tried to transfer to the defunct Woodlawn were back at Phoenix School, where they belonged. Belle Chasse High School, while not subjected to an airtight boycott like its counterpart across the river, still struggled to attract one hundred students on any day. Judge Christenberry had ordered it to remain open, but Perez figured that the boycott would outlast the court order, sending the last few straggling whites to River Oaks Academy and the troublesome blacks back to Scottville School. In his upriver homeland, his parishioners' solidarity gratified him, and he did what he could to encourage its continued strength.

As ordered, the Plaquemines Parish School Board wrote a report in January 1967. It claimed that the schools had peacefully integrated. The description emphasized how onerous the court's demands had been and how hard it was to maintain discipline with unruly black boys present.[1]

The report masked a reality that had gone from dire to absurd. Between the time of the initial orders in *United States v. Plaquemines Parish School Board* to late February, the local government actively sought to fulfill Perez's prophecies when reality did not match up with his expectations. The Judge had said that an integrated school system would descend into chaos, so he made sure that chaos came.

The Plaquemines Parish Commission Council created artificial staff shortages and financial crises in the schools. The repairs from Hurricane Betsy were halted, leaving some classrooms and athletic facilities in dangerous disrepair. Meanwhile, the council slashed public-schoolteacher wages while broadly advertising the comfortable salaries available at the private schools.[2]

The public schools didn't even advertise job openings until ordered to by a judge. Next to an eye-catching advertisement for private-school teachers, the board took out the smallest available classified-ad space in the *Plaquemines Gazette:*

TEACHERS WANTED

Apply Plaquemines Parish School Board office,

Pointe-a-la-Hache, La.

Plaquemines Parish School Board[3]

The school board eliminated all courses that had not been offered at all-black schools the previous year. This included driver's education, industrial arts, and kindergarten. After Judge Christenberry ordered cafeteria service restored, the board increased the cost of meals 150 percent (from ten to twenty-five cents) and eliminated the free-and-reduced lunch program. This policy applied both to formerly all-white and formerly all-black schools, and hundreds of children, mostly black, did not eat lunch at all.

Buras High School's brand-new cafeteria, construction for which had been started before the desegregation suit was filed, sat half-finished and never opened.[4]

Getting to school in the first place could be a challenge. The school board dutifully ran buses after Christenberry required it to, but service was comically bad. In towns covered by several buses, the newer ones were reserved for private-school use; the older ones were retained for the public schools, and their maintenance was often neglected.* In hamlets with only a single route, the public-school bus sometimes just did not come. All over the parish, public-school routes were meandering and indirect—an impressive feat given the straight-line geography of Plaquemines—and seemed designed for maximum redundancy. To accommodate an earlier start time and the longer rides without interrupting (free, timely) bus service for the private schools, pickups were often scheduled long before dawn. This disrupted the routines of parents and children, which, no doubt, was the intended effect.[5]

Throughout the school year, equipment disappeared from the public schools and resurfaced at the academies. On a Monday in October 1966, the new principal of Boothville-Venice High School discovered that all of the football and basketball equipment was missing. He tracked the items to River Oaks Academy, where he was told by a man named Duver that "I was instructed to remove the equipment. That's all I know." From Port Sulphur High School, Duver removed the weight-lifting equipment and everything from the sports supply closet.[6]

At Belle Chasse High School, the new assistant principal suggested offering informal intramural sports to make up for the lack of uniforms and equipment. The next day, he was approached by Chick Tinsley, the superintendent, who told him that his students could no longer use the track, the playing fields, or the auditorium. Later, he saw teens running around the track. He was about to reprimand them when he realized that they were not his students at all, but from the private school.[7]

---

* A veteran white teacher at Boothville-Venice High School stated that the public-school buses were "so old that the tires are giving out and the engines just stop."

Classroom materials, too, began to disappear. Textbooks were the first to go. Students sometimes had books in only one or two subjects, which they would share when they could. Orders of new books sometimes ended up mysteriously being delivered to the private schools. Some frustrated teachers of history and geography abandoned the textbooks altogether and used a subscription service called the Weekly Reader. But since the school board had cut its teacher supply fund entirely, the teachers had to make their students pay for the readers or reach into their own pockets. There were no music classes or band practices, as there were no instruments.

As teachers left for the private schools, they were encouraged to raid their classrooms and bring whatever supplies they could with them. Later, they were sent back to get loads of smaller and smaller items. At Boothville-Venice High School, one classroom was progressively denuded, losing first its books, then its record player, and then its charts, prints, and maps. Even the classroom aquarium went missing, along with its fish.[8]

As all of this went on, Perez kept up a relentless propaganda campaign in the pages of the *Plaquemines Gazette* and in public appearances big and small. His associates showed up at the houses of teachers, administrators, and parents. Everything was done to make real the truth he so desperately believed. The desegregation of Plaquemines Parish was a worse disaster than Hurricane Betsy. And if it wasn't, he'd make it that way.

His efforts were effective. Charles Simmons, the principal of Boothville-Venice High School, testified in early 1967 that "there has been an amazing belief that has been sort of widespread—not only in nearby communities but elsewhere in the state—that we don't have public schools in Plaquemines Parish anymore. And I have had several instances where people have expressed surprise that we do have public schools still operating in the parish."[9]

It was a victory, however Pyrrhic, for Leander Perez, but it came during a time of gathering troubles. Increased federal scrutiny following the Voting Rights Act and school desegregation meant that Perez heard reports of FBI agents all over the parish. Some of these were true and some not, but the proliferation of sightings fed his paranoia.

Compounding his woes, Agnes Perez, the Judge's beloved wife, died on February 10, 1967, three months short of their fiftieth wedding anniversary.[10]

Perez took little time to mourn, or, more truthfully, he mourned in the only way he knew how: he worked. The next morning, he drove to inspect a new section of state highway on the east bank. He stopped the work crew when he objected to the construction of a curb. It was "dangerous," he hollered at the parish highway director. "I want it out. Better than that, I'll knock it out myself—today!"

At three o'clock that afternoon, Perez showed up at the offending stretch of road with a bulldozer. He declared to all present that he was "the chief engineer" of the parish and he'd make sure the job was done right, and then he bellowed at the driver of the bulldozer, "Move it!"

The six-inch hump of asphalt cracked and buckled under the force of the machine.

16—Bailing Out

O N FEBRUARY 21, GARY took his eldest brother, Robert, and his father up to the courthouse with him to meet Richard. Trouble seemed to have followed in the wake of Gary's arrest. Members of the family kept getting pulled over, only to later be released, for minor traffic violations almost every time they would go up or down the road above Port Sulphur. Lambert himself had been stopped for speeding that week, and he had been astounded to hear on February 20 that, in lieu of a speeding ticket, he had been charged with operating a vehicle in a reckless manner.[1]

They parked by Richard's car and hurried into the courthouse. Inside, though, Richard was nowhere to be found. Back in the entryway, they tried to decide what to do. Gary looked across the road at Richard's brown Pontiac, sitting empty on the levee, and, for the first time since his arrest, he began to feel genuinely frightened.

A court employee came up to them, shaking his head.

"Man, things are getting bad around here," the man said. "They're putting lawyers in jail!"

Gary's pulse hammered his skull from within. "What lawyer? What does he look like?"

The man described a tall, skinny white Yankee.

"That sounds like my lawyer."[2]

———

That morning, when Richard called Judge Leon to see about Gary's bail, he set off the chain of events that led to his arrest. After Richard was done talking to his secretary, Leon told Bubrig that Richard was trying to come down that day around noon. The young assistant district attorney called Lea Perez, who was in the St. Bernard Parish office.

"I think he'll be here today," Bubrig said. Over the phone, Perez carefully described how to draw up the papers charging Richard Sobol with practicing law without a license, while Bubrig wrote as fast as he could.

In a hastily convened hearing in open court, rushing so it would be over before Richard arrived, Bubrig handed the charging papers to Leon, who signed them.*

Richard came at the appointed time, talked with Leon as the judge ate his lunch, secured Gary's bond, and left. When Richard closed the door to Leon's chambers, Bubrig rushed in to collect a bench warrant instanter, which is just what it sounds like. Deputy T. K. Devitt was waiting below to execute the warrant, and so was Judge Perez.[3]

An hour later, Lea Perez called Judge Leon.

"Has Sobol been arrested?" he asked.

"Yes," confirmed the judge.

Downstairs, Richard Sobol had gone along with the arrest procedure in stunned silence until the sheriff requested his briefcase; Richard protested that it was full of privileged information—it contained his entire Duncan file, among other things. A deputy removed it anyway. Richard was fingerprinted, and his mugshot was taken as Devitt asked questions to fill out the arrest report. Richard gave Collins, Douglas & Elie as his address, and refused to answer when asked who his employer was. After processing, he was asked for his belt and his tie, apparently to keep him from hanging himself.[4]

Richard used his phone call to dial the LCDC office. Barbara picked up. In as even a voice as he could manage, he told her what was happening to him—and what he needed her to do.

Lolis Elie joined Barbara on the phone. He asked if bail had been set.

---

* Bubrig denied this account, which is drawn from multiple sources, when he testified about it in 1968. When I interviewed him in 2015 and 2016, he had no recollection of this specific incident.

Richard didn't know. He asked the sheriff, who shrugged. Perez was gone; Richard hadn't even seen Bubrig. He said he'd try to call back.[5]

When he hung up, a different deputy insisted on fingerprinting Richard for a second time. His hands were still stained with ink, but he submitted. As the pads of his fingers were being pressed onto the paper, word came down from the courthouse that Judge Leon had set a bond: $1,500, the same as Gary's. Richard called the office back to tell them. Barbara said they would figure something out; she had already called Al Bronstein in Jackson to inform him.

"Barbara," he said urgently, "it's got to be *today*." He did not want to spend a night in Perez's jail.[6]

Richard hung up, and a third deputy, as if it were simply the routine, requested that he be fingerprinted yet again.[7]

Richard was marched back upstairs towards Leon's chambers and the courtroom and then ushered across a narrow, screened-in walkway to the jail. The deputies put Richard in a cell with a few other white men—like every other public accommodation in Plaquemines Parish, the jail was segregated—and locked the barred door.[8]

Richard and his cellmates sized one another up. The cell slept six on folding bunks, the bottom ones doubling as benches, as in a train compartment. He guessed it was ten by fourteen feet.

"What you in for?" asked one of the other men—the inevitable first question in lockup.

"Practicing law without a license," said Richard.

His answer was not what his cellmates had expected. They fell to discussing it among themselves—a lawyer arrested. What could have gone wrong?

As they spoke, Richard felt apprehension rising in him. He was a man of action, a restless and compulsive worker. The shock of the arrest had propelled him through booking, leaving him little time to fear for his safety. Now that he was confined to this tiny room, not knowing for how long or with what result, he began to fend off the worries that now closed in on him.

"I heard about a lawyer in Alabama got arrested for representing niggers," one of the other men said.

Richard's breath shortened a bit; the man seemed just to be making small talk, but Richard knew the lawyer he was talking about. Don Jelinek was a legendary firebrand, working at various times for the ACLU, LCDC, and SNCC. Jelinek was the kind of lawyer that made Richard and Bronstein nervous: foulmouthed and freewheeling, he blurred the line between activist and attorney, which brought him close to leaders of the militant wing of the civil rights movement. He had been arrested several times and shot at to boot, but the incident in question happened in Greene County, Alabama, in 1966, and the facts of it hewed more closely to Richard's experience than any of them knew. Accused of practicing law without an Alabama license, Jelinek had been held for a day or two in jail, but his prosecution had not been pursued after his release.[9]

"Can you imagine?" the man asked Richard. "He's representing these niggers, and they got his ass!"

Richard feigned surprise and went right along with it. "Oh, really?" he said, as the man continued. "Really? Is that right?"

After that, he tried to say as little as possible.[10]

———

Robert Duncan had called the LCDC office after learning of Richard's arrest. Gary's fear had been overwhelming, and it took some stubborn prodding by his father and brother to persuade him to stay at Pointe à la Hache and to wait for someone to come down. In part, the decision to stay was practical—Gary needed a new bond, or he risked arrest—and in part it was born of a sense of loyalty to Richard, who surely would not have wound up in the Plaquemines Parish jail were it not for taking Gary's case.

For four hours they waited at the courthouse before a big white man who sounded like he was from Cajun country pulled himself out of a car and introduced himself as Don Juneau, a brand-new LCDC attorney.

Juneau had no sooner shaken hands than he was raising hell. A torrent of foul language surged from him as he asked about Richard's situation. Lambert, Gary, and Robert followed Juneau into the courthouse as he offered a vulgar narration of what he was seeing. The "whites only" and "colored only" signs over the restrooms drew his particular ire. As he stalked around the courthouse, he fulminated about how this backwater parish was going to feel a pain like no other it had experienced, and how these must be just about the stupidest white folks he'd ever met. The Duncans were enchanted.[11]

In the courthouse's records room, he found Leon talking to a deputy clerk. Leon cringed when he saw Juneau advancing and then directed the huge lawyer to the sheriff's office to secure bail. A bondsman from New Orleans had come to Pointe à la Hache with Juneau—actually, Juneau had caught a ride with the bondsman, since the LCDC car was still parked on the levee by the courthouse—and Richard's release was secured in short order.[12]

Gary watched as his lawyer claimed his belt and necktie. Richard had an intense expression on his face, and he was speaking quickly to Juneau. He caught Gary's eye and walked over to him.

"Don't worry about me," he said. "About your bond: The judge has allowed it, but it's a new bond. It is in the same amount: $1,500. You should have it set the same way as the others."

Gary nodded, but the bulb of dread that had planted itself in his chest refused to wither.[13]

Richard strode with Juneau to the Pontiac. The bondsman had returned to New Orleans, so the lawyers would ride back together. Before getting into the car, and without thinking, Richard dropped to his hands and knees to check beneath the car for a bomb. The action felt instinctual, even almost automatic, but as he was looking, he wasn't sure why he did it. It was not an irrational fear—civil rights workers regularly found bombs affixed to their vehicles after returning from court or mass meetings. But, he realized as he scoured the undercarriage, he didn't even know what a bomb would look like.[14]

After Richard and Juneau left, Gary and his family went into the courthouse to see about the new bond. Lambert had come with deeds and papers to put his property up as collateral; they didn't have the cash, and, although Herb Collette had kindly posted Gary's previous bonds, Lambert still disliked relying on a white man for anything.[15]

126

Inside, the sheriff said he didn't know about any bond, and he refused the surety papers the Duncans offered up. This didn't seem right, and they needed to hurry: the courthouse was closing. Gary got in touch with Herb Collette, who called to see if he could post a cash bond later that day or in the morning. Once again, the clerk said he couldn't accept it—there was no bail order.[16]

Gary and his puzzled family members returned to Boothville. Gary was headed out for several days on a crew boat, so he hoped that the Collettes or Richard would figure out the bond problem. Gary was actually relieved to be out on a boat again for a few days—the Gulf felt safe to him, isolated from sheriff deputies and surety bonds and Perez and Leon, but still "his," still home.

The next morning, February 22, Richard went with Al Bronstein to the federal court in New Orleans, where he brought a lawsuit against Judge Leon, Lea Perez, and Leander Perez Sr.

17—Where Is Your Law?

I see the blade,
Blood-stained, continue cutting weeds and shade.
—Jean Toomer, *Cane*

GARY DUNCAN WAS working on a crew boat on the evening of February 23 when a call came over the radio: the boat was to return to shore at once to drop Gary off. The caller had given no reason, nor even a name.[1]

Gary had parked at Shell Oil Company's dock, so that was where he came ashore. In the semidarkness, he could see that his car was there, as before, and the dock was otherwise deserted. The short stretch of Highway 23 between the dock and home rose pale in his headlights as he drove up the road. He parked in front of his parents' house and went inside. The place was deserted, and he felt fear prickle the length of his spine. He checked Calvin's house next and found his entire family huddled in there.

"Where's Calvin?" one of them asked when Gary appeared in the door. He looked around and realized that Calvin and his parents were missing from the group.

"I didn't see Calvin."

"The police came. They want to take you to jail."

Wilbur Buras and F. J. Smith had come earlier to tell the family that they had a warrant for Gary's arrest. Calvin volunteered to go meet Gary at Venice Marina with them; he sensed that his brother would take this action hard, and he hoped to act as an intermediary. Lambert and Mazie were up in New Orleans, and they didn't know yet. On their way to the city, actually, they had been pulled over and Lambert arrested on the speeding charge from a few days before. Lambert had been released after paying a fine, but the coincidence of these events made everyone in the Duncan family uneasy.[2]

As his siblings filled Gary in, the admixture of dread and grievance boiled up in him, slowly precipitating an angry despair.

A car pulled into the drive, and he was instantly on alert. It was Herb Collette, his boss, demanding to know why he wasn't on the boat. Gary and his family explained that the sheriff had called for him, which did not please Collette.

About fifteen minutes later, two more cars pulled up: Calvin's and the sheriff deputies'. Calvin said they had waited for a long time at the marina before returning. He told Gary that he had seen the warrant, that this was real, and that there wasn't any use in fighting. As he spoke, Gary protested.

"I'm not going to nobody's jail," he said. "I'm tired of going to jail." He raised his voice, knowing that the deputies were just outside. "I'm tired of y'all picking me up and taking me to jail!"

"Y'all not coming in here," he heard Calvin declare out the front door. A conversation followed, but he couldn't make out the words. He felt simultaneously small and dangerous.

"He's not coming out," he heard Calvin say.

Gary looked above the lintel to where his brother's shotgun rested. He shocked himself as he imagined taking it and barricading himself inside. Turning away, he decided to leave it where it was—but he would die before he'd let them take him to that jail again.

For a long time, Gary stayed inside, and the deputies stood on the lawn in the cold. Calvin went back and forth between them, negotiating. The rest of the family stayed put, hushed into silence for once as midnight came and went.

At last, Gary agreed to come to the door. Standing tall, he looked down at Smith and Buras.

"Don't put no handcuffs on me," he said. "Ain't nobody gonna put no handcuffs on me."[3]

He sat in silence in the back of the police cruiser as they rolled up the road. There was a small jail in Port Sulphur, and the ferry had stopped running for the night, so he prepared himself as they entered the town's limits. Outside the jail, he saw a clutch of eight or ten men and several cars. With a pang, Gary recognized Dutch Asevedo, Judge Perez's bodyguard and investigator, among them.

The two deputies seemed as confused as Gary felt. "I don't know what's going on," Smith said as they pulled up and the gathered men squinted into the headlights, "but I'm going to make sure you get to lockup."

The car came to a halt, and Smith said urgently, "Don't look around."

Gary's perception narrowed to the dirt at his feet, which looked ghostly in the headlights. Smith and Buras were talking to the men around him, but he didn't take in what they were saying.

Then there was a hand on his shoulder, and Buras was leading him forward. "Get in that other car," said the deputy, and Gary did as he was told. He felt the engine turn over and the vehicle heave, and then they were on the road again.

"I don't know what you did," mused Buras, "but I've never seen anything like this before." He said that they had taken worse men than Gary—people who had killed people—to jail without this level of security. "You might as well be prepared for anything," he advised.

Across the river from Pointe à la Hache, Smith and Buras pulled over the levee and onto the ferry landing. There, the boat bobbed gently, its engine idling, its deck lit, and Gary knew it was waiting for him. The full moon gave a pallid cast to the riffles on the water. Across the Mississippi, the courthouse feebly glowed.

Atop the levee on the east bank stood Ralph Ferranto, the jailer.

"Where's that nigger at?" Ferranto asked when they pulled up to him. "Give me that nigger here."

No one spoke for a moment, but then Smith shook his head, "No, I'm going to lock him up myself."

"I said, give me that nigger here," repeated the jailer. "He got him a NAACP lawyer."

"I have orders to lock him up," Smith said. "So I'm going to lock him up. What you do with him after that, I don't know."

Gary Duncan had never felt so *black*. His vulnerability lurched into an overwhelming urge to fight. He looked at Ferranto. This man, he told himself, will have to shoot me or bust me in my head before he takes me.

But the car burst forward and away from Ferranto, towards the courthouse. Buras and Smith flanked Gary as they went into the darkened building. Smith stood by as Ferranto booked him and Buras sleepily filled out an arrest report, struggling to form legible words. Both deputies went with him as far as the cell, and they did not leave until Ferranto had closed and locked the cell door behind him.

Alone in the dark with Ferranto, Gary struggled to maintain his composure. "Look at this nigger, got his self a NAACP lawyer," Ferranto said to no one, spitting the letters of the acronym like bile. Gary glared at him from the bunk.

The cell contained some meager bedding, which Ferranto removed. As he passed by Gary with the blanket and pillow, he stopped and chuckled. "Nigger, what's that?" He motioned at some marine paint that had dried on Gary's skin. "You trying to paint yourself white?"[4]

Sometime after two a.m., Ferranto left Gary alone in the cold with his thoughts about his family, imagining the look on his mother's face when she would find out about his arrest. He conjured his brothers and sisters and Lynn and Geralyn and infant Gregory, and he wept.[5]

———

Back at home, Vivian lay awake, her pain vivid and sharp. As the eldest and most responsible—and sixteen years Gary's senior—she had been tasked in part with raising her baby brother.

"That was my blood," she recollected almost fifty years later. "That was my brother. The same blood. Same mama, same daddy. How would you feel? How would you feel?"

Ordinarily, she had an uncommon ability to control her thoughts, to wrench her mind from thoughts she deemed unchristian. Today, though, she struggled. "I felt hatred," she recalled, putting a hand to her heart and wincing again from the remembered ache. "It hurted me here, and there was hatred there. I had this feeling—I wondered: Where is your law?"[6]

18—Absent and Unrepresented

O N THE MORNING of February 23, the day of Gary Duncan's late-night arrest, Lea Perez had been in the Plaquemines Parish courthouse, typing. His letter was addressed to every district attorney in Louisiana; it reported Richard's arrest and encouraged Perez's colleagues to investigate Richard and LCDC themselves.

As his secretary made copies, Perez walked into the courtroom, where Judge Leon was waiting for him.

"If Your Honor pleases, in the matter of the state of Louisiana versus Gary Duncan," Perez began, "it has come to the state's attention that the defendant has not yet posted this bond, so the state requests a bench warrant instanter, that the defendant be incarcerated in the parish prison until such time as bond can be posted."

In an exchange that lasted barely a minute, Leon signed the warrant that would lead to Gary's arrest, and Lea Perez went back up to New Orleans.

In the official transcript of this brief proceeding, Perez is listed as the only lawyer appearing. "Defendant," the cover sheet reads, "absent and unrepresented."[1]

———

The Duncans were waiting outside the courthouse when Don Juneau arrived at nine a.m. on February 24.

Juneau had woken just after dawn to a call from Richard, who had himself been awakened by a call about Gary's arrest. Richard had been quietly furious, but Juneau was apoplectic. He asked the Duncans what they knew, and then he stormed into the courthouse.

"Where's Leon?" he demanded of assistants in the offices of the clerk and sheriff. The judge wasn't in, he was told. The judge was out of town and unreachable. The judge doesn't usually come in on Fridays, anyway. The judge will be back on Monday.

Juneau demanded to see the bail order for Gary Duncan, but he was told that there was no such bail order. They had a Gary Duncan in custody, yes, and he had been arrested on a bench warrant. Trailed by Robert and Lambert Duncan, Juneau stalked from one office to another in the courthouse, looking for anyone who knew how to get his client out of jail.

At last, he found Tony Mattice, who was not happy to be found. Mattice worked for the parish jail and, after some prodding, said he thought Gary was on a $1,500 bond. Juneau explained who he was and that Gary's father was here to put up his property to make the bond.

Mattice pulled out a slip of paper and painstakingly wrote out Juneau's name in block letters—they would later learn that he was only semiliterate—and then looked Lambert over and asked if he had certificates of non-incumbrance, showing that his property was owned outright, without mortgages or liabilities. He said he did.

After a moment, Mattice told Juneau that it was actually policy that someone looking to post bail with property needed to put up twice the cash bond amount, so he asked to see $3,000* worth of property. Lambert, Robert, and Juneau exchanged glances. Lambert said that, between Robert and him, they might be able to come up with $3,000; were two or more people allowed to pool resources to make the bond? Mattice said that was fine; they would just need the approval of a judge. But Judge Leon, unfortunately, was away that day. Juneau felt anger growing inside him as Mattice frowningly suggested that they either return on Monday or come back with $1,500 cash.

Juneau gathered the family on the levee to strategize. He explained

---

* About $23,000 today.

the situation and asked whether they knew anyone who owned $3,000 of property outright. They did not. The answer, offered one of Gary's sisters, was quite simple: they had to find some way to come up with the cash before the courthouse closed. Juneau cautioned them against putting up a cash bond. Knowing how these courts operated, he said, they were unlikely to get that money back for years. The family members listened to him, but every one of them agreed that the most important thing was to get Gary out that day—every hour spent in prison was a humiliation, an injustice, and a danger.

Lambert said that the family might have $1,500 if they all pooled their various savings accounts. To avoid using Delta Bank—a Perez-affiliated operation that blacks gave a wide berth—the Duncans kept their money in banks in New Orleans. Lambert and Robert said that, if they left right then, they might have time to scrape together the money by the afternoon. Juneau offered to give them a ride. A few family members said they would stay at the courthouse to keep an eye on things, and the rest piled into a car to return to Boothville.

As Juneau drove up the road, Lambert and Robert told him about how Perez rose to power, about the land grabs and the huge oil contracts and the stockade for "racial agitators" at Fort St. Philip. Juneau had heard of Perez, but he had never understood just how far-reaching the man's power was until he heard it explained to him. As they described Perez's absolute power, Juneau marveled. A Louisiana native, he might have been shocked by the shady dealings of his home state, but he was rarely surprised by them anymore. He dropped the Duncans off on Baronne Street, in the downtown of a black neighborhood, and then continued uptown to check in with Richard.

At noon, Juneau picked up Lambert and Robert and went back down the road. On the way, they showed Juneau a shorter route from New Orleans to Belle Chasse, turning off the Westbank Expressway early and threading through Jefferson Parish on Belle Chasse Road. The two men had cobbled together enough money—barely—from all of the various savings accounts. If they felt any trepidation about putting their entire family's savings into the care of the Plaquemines Parish government, they did not tell Juneau about it or betray it on their faces as they sped back into Perez country.

Back at the courthouse, Juneau asked again to see Leon, just in case. He was told again that the judge was away, so he went with Lambert and Robert back to the jail office. There, he found not Mattice but a red-haired woman who introduced herself as Mrs. Ralph Ferranto. It was not clear what her position was at the courthouse, but Juneau talked her through the events of that morning. She stopped him when he told her that a property bond needed to be twice the cash amount. That, she told him, was just wrong. They have been mistaken, she said. Just then, Ralph Ferranto appeared behind his wife.

What followed was as illegal as it was frustrating. Ferranto invented numerous barriers to the posting of Gary's bond, citing obscure tenets of the Napoleonic Code and informing them of certificates that would need the signatures of multiple absent parties as well as a judge's approval, all delivered in a laconic drawl that made Juneau want to leap across the desk and throttle the jailer.

Juneau eventually argued Ferranto out of his position, and the jailer was forced to hand over bond papers. At last, the Duncans signed the last of the forms—in black ink, Ferranto insisted; blue ink was not accepted—and posted Gary's bond.[2]

When Gary at last emerged, he embraced his family members tightly. The midafternoon sun grounded him; in his two cells, he had lost track of time. In the first, there had been no light at all. In the second, the light had burned constantly. Both had been windowless. He would later learn that the dark room was the solitary-confinement space, and the light one, with padded walls, was for the incapacitation of those termed "criminally insane." And as Gary held his father, he promised that he would never set foot inside that jail again.

19—The Fruits of Benevolence

"LIKE A VOICE crying in the wilderness," wrote the *Plaquemines Gazette,* in prose overwrought even by its own purple standards, "Judge L.H. Perez and other far sighted patriots, too few in number, have been cautioning people over the years that their rights would be eroded by the Communist infiltration of our Government's ideology." If any had doubts of the boss's foresight, the paper reminded readers,

> Turning back the pages of the *Gazette* brings to light pictures taken during the dedication of the $2 million tax-free Belle-Chasse High School May 21, 1959 and the warning issued then by Judge Perez.
>
> During the dedication ceremony, Judge Perez said that… "We must ever be mindful of the threat that is hanging over our people… Our Constitution is not an automatic instrument. It is only a means to preserve the liberty and freedom of people."[1]

Ironically, this was precisely the same argument about the Constitution made by the civil rights lawyers who opposed them.

The *Gazette's* histrionics were not without cause; by late winter of the first desegregated school year, the resistance scheme in Plaquemines Parish was under fresh threat from within and without.

The trouble started on February 23—coincidentally, the day of Gary's arrest—when the Louisiana Financial Assistance Commission, which administered financial aid to white students attending academies, announced that it would have to delay private-school-voucher payments because of a $1.5 million shortfall.* The deficit was largely due to the thousands of applications from Plaquemines Parish. Perez soft-pedaled that news to his constituents, but it was devastating; without those vouchers, most people in Plaquemines could not afford tuition at the academies, and, despite the efforts of Perez lackeys, the nonprofit scholarship fund was not nearly enough to make up the gap. Perez may have been upset, but he could not have been surprised: the Louisiana Financial Assistance Commission had warned that it would collapse if every white student in Plaquemines Parish applied for aid.[2]

Meanwhile, the entire system of tuition vouchers, called grant-in-aid, was under attack. Perez had masterminded not only the Louisiana Financial Assistance Commission, but also the statutes that funded and protected it. In typical Perez fashion, no important measure was allowed to exist without a fail-safe. Eventually, every fail-safe had a fail-safe. By 1967, grant-in-aid laws resembled a Russian nesting doll: the cracking open of each one revealed another beneath.[3]

The progression was partly to slow down the litigation that would dismantle it—the legislative equivalent of dropping tacks in a car chase—and partly because Perez's approach became more refined over the years. The scheme had begun with Act 258 of 1958, which called for tuition vouchers to be offered to students in districts where there was "no racially separate public school." At the time, not one public school in Louisiana was integrated. Then, after New Orleans schools desegregated, Perez drafted Act 3 of 1960, which created the Education Expense Grant Fund and removed the obvious language about racial separation. In 1961, another act transferred millions of dollars to the fund, which was to disburse that money to private schools. When the Education Expense Grant Fund came under attack in court, the legislature passed Act 147 of 1962, which gutted the fund (though, for maximum misdirection, did not dissolve it) and replaced it with the Louisiana Financial Assistance Commission, which gave grants directly to parents, rather than to schools. When the commission itself

---

* Almost $12 million today.

came under attack, Perez set about building a new fail-safe. Act 99 of 1967 was a sleeper; it was designed to spring into action only if Act 147 were dismantled. This final act, which took pains to avoid racially charged language, set up yet another fund to replace the Louisiana Financial Assistance Commission. In all, by 1967, more than $15 million[*] of state money was given to support the segregated private schools.[4]

The assault on Act 147 came in March, when the trial began in *Poindexter v. Louisiana Financial Assistance Commission.* It was actually the second lawsuit with that name; the first had been brought by A. P. Tureaud in 1964 and decided two years later by Judge John Minor Wisdom and two others. When that opinion failed to dismantle the voucher program, Tureaud sued again, this time joined by the NAACP Legal Defense Fund and the Justice Department. With both the US government and the nation's foremost civil rights law firm on board, *Poindexter II* promised to finally dismantle grant-in-aid and ban the use of public money to prop up segregated school systems. "The free lunches and textbooks Louisiana provides for all its school children are the fruits of racially neutral benevolence," Wisdom would write in his opinion. "Tuition grants are not the products of such a policy. They are the fruits of the State's traditionally racially biased policy of providing segregated schools for white children."[5]

The *Plaquemines Gazette* covered this newest assault on traditional values with breathless horror. Meanwhile, the paper devoted much of the space in its spring issues to its typical fare: development, modernization, and fearmongering reprints from newspapers in cities with racial unrest. And, as usual, alongside stories about $150-million marine lifts and elevated reservoirs (all tax-free, of course), the *Gazette* reported on the dances, sports, field trips, and honor rolls of the local schools—the private schools.[6]

In early April, when the academies were retroactively accredited by the Louisiana Department of Education, the paper reprinted the full text of

---

[*]   More than $110 million today.

the reviled HEW (the Department of Health, Education, and Welfare) guidelines for school desegregation, putting in bold the parts about faculty being integrated. A week later, eight thousand books arrived at the office of private-school chief Frank Patti. They had been donated by supporters all over the country after an appeal in *The Councilor,* the magazine of the White Citizens' Councils. These books, which were to form the basis of a new scholastic library system for the white students of the parish, were each marked, "Best Wishes to the Brave People of Plaquemines Parish."[7]

That there were far-ranging hearings in *United States v. Plaquemines Parish School Board* in the spring went mostly unreported in the *Gazette.* The Justice Department brought shocking stories to court in April, including several days of testimony from public-school parents, students, and teachers about the privation, intimidation, and discrimination they had endured. Most explosively, a former school-board member testified about Perez's complete erasure of every check and balance in Plaquemines. "We could have saved quite a bit of money by having a $1.75 rubber stamp," he said.[8]

Back in Plaquemines, the story was carefully controlled: the only mention of the public-school system that spring was after a tuberculosis scare. After a black girl at Port Sulphur High School was diagnosed with the disease, all public-school students were tested. It was the first mention of the Port Sulphur school since McBride Academy's dedication. The *Gazette* noted the "fear" and "apprehension" of the "tiny tots" as they lined up to be tested, and lauded their "courage" in such adversity.[9]

Leander Perez was still under a court order barring him from directly influencing the progress of desegregation in his parish. He continued to work behind the scenes to orchestrate his resistance scheme, and he became a bit bolder about speaking out. As the school year drew to a close, he announced the launch of "Save Our Children," a self-styled grassroots campaign, the "only all-white organization dedicated to the preservation of the purity of the races." Perez had become frustrated with the White Citizens' Councils, which had for a long time served as the white supremacist organizations of choice for respectable citizens and the urban elite.* Perez felt that the Citizens' Councils had produced more talk than action when finally put to the test. In an April letter to members of the Citizens' Council of Greater New Orleans, Perez was blunt: "The lack of interest among white people in this city has brought disgrace upon us."[10]

Part of the problem with the councils was that their mission had been so broad. Save Our Children, however, was tightly focused on winning elections through using white voter drives to counter black voter drives. As more and more blacks registered to vote in the South, the possibility of actually losing elections because of demographic shifts in the electorate had preoccupied politically savvy segregationists. It was assumed that all blacks would vote unthinkingly for whichever candidate they were instructed to vote for—the "Negro bloc vote" was a favorite Perez bogeyman. In May, when Perez kicked off the Save Our Children "Crusade" in New Orleans, his apocalyptic language indicated the urgency of his appeal. "You have the power in your hands, my friends, but only once every four years," he said at the meeting. "If you keep one thought uppermost in your mind—and that is the welfare of the children—you can win, you can protect them, you can save them from bondage, in which so many of them have been sold for filthy federal bribes."[11]

Against all odds, the private schools of Plaquemines Parish graduated their first students on time. By having classes on Saturdays and extending the school day, the academies had made up for their delayed start, an accomplishment that, to hear Perez tell it, overshadowed even the headline-making recovery from Hurricane Betsy. Chalin Perez, in his new role as his father's political surrogate, spoke at each of the academies' ceremonies, lauding the seniors for embodying "the true spirit of freedom." Chalin, however, had not inherited his father's oratorical skills, and the rest of the speech was a convoluted metaphor about "rounds" and "squares" and fitting round shapes into square

---

* "White" was never part of the official title of the Citizens' Councils, although everybody knew who counted as a citizen and who did not. In addition to providing a home for segregationists who were too refined for the Klan, the Citizens' Councils were sometimes the only civic organizations available to white supremacist Catholics and Jews.

holes and how the real "squares" were the "rounds," or something like that. The speaker's incoherence seemed to matter little to the beaming graduates and their parents, who sang, in unison, songs picked for the occasion: "Born Free" for the fifty-four seniors at River Oaks, "The Impossible Dream" for the twenty-three at Delta Heritage, and so on.[12]

Chalin's performance must have been good enough for his father, because a month after the graduations, it was announced that Judge Perez had named his younger son to replace him in his position on the Plaquemines Parish Commission Council. If voters had any doubts about his record—really, other than acting as a stand-in for his father in the private-school system, he had not done anything—the *Gazette* tried to put them at ease by claiming that Chalin had been "burning midnight oil over the years handling the highly legal and technically involved work of Parish interests in relation to the oil and gas industries." It is probable that the only true part of this statement was the last few words: Chalin had become a millionaire through his father's dealings. He would now become the Judge's successor.[13]

20—Losing Everything

JUDGE?" AL BRONSTEIN said as he entered Judge John Minor Wisdom's chambers. "Judge, have you seen the morning papers?"

Wisdom had a copy of the *Times-Picayune* on his desk, the front page blazoned with a reference to another school-desegregation opinion that Wisdom had written. The judge looked quizzically at Bronstein and then leafed through until he saw a story about Richard Sobol's arrest.[1]

"What the hell is goddamn Perez up to?" grumbled Wisdom.

Bronstein nodded and said he had just filed a lawsuit, but he was worried. If Perez won, he said, it would totally upend their entire operation, which relied on out-of-state lawyers to do what local lawyers could or would not.

Bronstein said that he hoped to get a three-judge panel, which was customary in civil rights cases. But, he added, "I'm concerned about who the other judges would be, if…"

"You're in luck!" Wisdom interrupted, understanding the request. "Come on with me. Elbert happens to be here in town."

Elbert Tuttle was the chief judge of the Fifth Circuit and so determined which judges would sit on the panels. Where Wisdom exuded an informality born of privilege and comfort around money and power, Tuttle was upright and strict; he had served in combat in both world wars before retiring from the army as a general. Bronstein had expected Wisdom to have his sleeves rolled up, but he was surprised to find Tuttle with neither tie nor jacket.

"Elbert, you know Al Bronstein from the Lawyers Constitutional Defense Committee?"

"Oh, yes," said Tuttle. "Sit down, sit down."

"Al, you know, is practicing in Mississippi."

"Oh? How is Judge Cox these days?" William Harold Cox was a

notorious racist, known for referring to blacks as "baboons" from the bench and for dismissing all indictments against the murderers of Michael Schwerner, James Chaney, and Andrew Goodman in 1965.[2]

Bronstein said he got mostly unfavorable rulings from Cox.

Tuttle probed a bit more and then shook his head. "Why doesn't Judge Cox—who is an intelligent man—ever learn?"

Wisdom bobbed his head in agreement, and Tuttle continued quizzing Bronstein about the behavior of federal judges in Mississippi, who were all under his charge.

After twenty minutes or so, Wisdom segued: "Say, Elbert, you know what happened?"

"What?"

"That goddamn Leander Perez has gone and arrested one of Al's staff attorneys yesterday—charged him with practicing law without a license. Al's just filed a case on it, asking for a three-judge court."

"Hm," grunted Tuttle, noncommittal.

The two judges went back to chatting, and Bronstein listened. As he stood there, he realized what was happening: Wisdom was bringing Tuttle in, gently, so that the chief would have an understanding of the nature and implications of the case when he sat down to assign judges for the panel. Wisdom's approach seemed to work: when it came time to assign judges, Tuttle picked Robert Ainsworth, a liberal New Orleanian who knew Bronstein well, and Frederick Heebe, who was close with Richard. Heebe had come on the bench just before Richard began working full-time for LCDC, and Bronstein knew they had a "father-son relationship." He remembered, "Heebe thought Sobol was the brightest. And he was."[3]

Bronstein also added a second lawyer to the case on Richard's side: Anthony Amsterdam. Amsterdam, who went by "Tony," was already a legend at age thirty-two. He was tall and unremittingly intense, his body always in motion, leaning back and gesticulating or inclining forward to stare at his interlocutor or to place his forehead on his fingertips in an exaggerated posture of deep thought. Words spilled from him in paragraphs of discursive thought, his high, thin voice gathering speed as it moved along the contours of an idea before striking at the heart of it and moving on. "The general consensus," remembered Owen Fiss, a Yale Law professor who knew him, "was that he was the genius of our generation."[4]

Amsterdam's physical presence was part of his mythology. He was good-looking and, as one judge noted, "suave," a fact accentuated by the slim cigarettes he smoked when he was not masticating cheap cigars ("Cuesta Rey or some such los stinkos," he remembered). Sleep appeared to have no hold on him, and he worked eighteen- and twenty-hour days, giving rise to the theory that he had cloned himself and that the clones worked in shifts. Somehow, he seemed to subsist entirely on Diet Rite Cola; few can remember ever actually seeing him eat.

Though only two years Richard's senior, he was already among the most recognizable figures in the legal profession, especially among those who practiced civil rights law or criminal defense. His near-perfect memory was fabled, and almost everyone who worked with him over the years tells some version of a story from his early years as a lawyer. In an off-the-cuff response to a judge's question, Amsterdam cited an old Supreme Court case by name, volume, and page. Irked by Amsterdam's quickness, the judge told a law clerk to fetch a copy of the case cited, and he found there that Amsterdam had erred in his citation. The judge stopped Amsterdam and revealed the mistake. Amsterdam responded, "Your Honor must have a misbound copy," and continued with his argument without pausing. On further inspection, the judge's copy was, indeed, bound to the wrong cover.[5]

Raised in Philadelphia, Amsterdam was born into a prosperous family of nonobservant Jews, and his far-ranging interests would not have hinted at the singular focus on the law he developed in adulthood. His childhood was marred by polio, which isolated him in his early teenage years, but he had recovered enough by his late teens to attend Haverford College and the University of Pennsylvania Law School. He worked as editor in chief of the law review, but he recalled spending most of his time painting, reading French poetry, and auditing art-history courses at Bryn Mawr College. Two months before graduation, he realized that he had not completed his mandatory article for the law review. He quickly penned "The Void-for-Vagueness

Doctrine in the Supreme Court," which ended up having outside influence on the law. "It was incredible—encyclopedic," said a prominent lawyer of his generation. "You couldn't believe that one person could have written it." After graduation, he clerked for Felix Frankfurter on the Supreme Court, worked briefly in the US Attorney's office in Washington, DC, and returned to Penn Law in 1962 as a professor. He was twenty-seven.[6]

From his office in West Philadelphia, he masterminded many of the legal innovations that allowed civil rights lawyers to keep up with the segregationists they opposed. He was a proponent of moving civil rights cases to federal court for almost any reason, but his real innovation was to force courts to respond quickly to civil rights claims, even when they didn't want to. He came up with a variety of novel strategies intended to out-maneuver segregationist or sluggish judges in the South, and he distributed boilerplate motions to overworked civil rights lawyers, who could simply fill in the details of their cases. In the meantime, he worked with the NAACP Legal Defense Fund to study racial bias, wrote briefs in support of important criminal-justice cases like *Miranda v. Arizona,* and began to represent clients on death row, which was the genesis of his lifelong struggle to end the death penalty in America.[7]

Amsterdam had helped establish LCDC; he was on the board, and he had been involved from afar with developing a strategy for the organization. His connection to LCDC stemmed in part from the fact that it was full of people like him: young, dedicated, radical, and disdainful of the cautious approach of older, established organizations. That fondness also perhaps came from the lively correspondence he kept up with Henry Schwarzschild, whose joy at cramming erudite and multitiered witticisms into even short letters matched Amsterdam's own. Armed with the sharpest legal mind of their ascendant generation, Richard and Bronstein could feel ready to handle whatever Perez or the state of Louisiana might bring against them.[8]

On March 25, 1967, the *Sobol v. Perez* team met in person for the first time. Richard, Bronstein, Amsterdam, and Schwarzschild gathered in New York City to strategize. The case had already gained some notoriety, and not only among civil rights lawyers in the South. On March 12, the *New York*

Times ran a story about the arrests of Richard and Don Jelinek. The article portrayed their plight as representing the newest battleground in the civil rights movement. Just that month, the piece noted, the state of Mississippi had called up an Unauthorized Practice of Law Committee to investigate lawyers practicing illegally. Louisiana had a similar body, and, although the mission statements of both committees were politically neutral, there was little doubt that they were aimed directly at LCDC.[9]

A few weeks before the meeting, Richard had received a settlement offer from Sidney Provensal, in which Lea Perez agreed to call off the prosecution in exchange for Richard dropping the suit. The offer was tempting. Several of Richard's advisers, including his friends from Arnold & Porter, urged him to take it. Amsterdam and Bronstein urged him to hold out, though, since the settlement would also have left the issue of Richard's eligibility to practice law in Louisiana unresolved. That matter had become pressing when Richard received letters from three district attorneys that threatened to "challenge" Richard's right to practice in state court if he appeared in their jurisdictions.[10]

To avoid forcing the issue, Richard had stopped appearing in state court after his arrest. Don Juneau was a member of the Louisiana Bar, so he would go instead, but Richard felt bitterly disappointed that he could not continue the state cases he had worked so hard to develop. He was frustrated at having to stay in the office when he was most effective out and practicing.[11]

But even his presence in the office was a source of tension. Collins, Douglas & Elie had received a letter from the Louisiana Bar Association's Commission on the Unauthorized Practice of Law, threatening all three of them with disbarment for allowing Richard to continue his criminal-defense work.[12]

Provensal's settlement was attractive, but capitulating to Perez would send the wrong message; Richard worried that settling would set a dangerous precedent and look weak. He felt that the case had gained momentum over the month of March, and he hoped that Perez might lose the trial simply by being himself. Amsterdam felt strongly that Perez's unfiltered bigotry gave the case "sex appeal."

When all three men decided to reject the settlement and go to trial, they were not only trying to prevent Richard's prosecution, but also to protect every civil rights lawyer from similar harassment. "It was going to be a hell of a fight," Amsterdam recalled. "There were all sorts of substantive problems. All sorts of procedural problems. We were trying to prove some incredible propositions."

"Winning Dick's case is vital," Amsterdam wrote to Bronstein a couple of weeks after their meeting. "If we win, we will have shown the other side that we <u>can</u> win; and the scope of the victory will doubtless remain sufficiently unclear to put <u>us</u> in a threatening position." Thinking in grandly tactical terms, he added, "Renewed attacks by Perez or his counterparts elsewhere will tend to look like counterattacks not merely on us but on the courts which have protected us, and the ordinary process by which courts are urged into the frame of mind of going further and further."

He thought Richard was the perfect person to lead that charge, moreover, and to begin to shift the courts' position further to the left. "Dick is an attractive fellow," Amsterdam mused, "and no federal judge in Louisiana could have qualms about degrading the local bar if Dick is let in." As long as the case avoided looking like a coup for "the carpetbagging bar," Amsterdam thought, they had a shot. Against Richard stood the embodiment of segregationist dogma—massive resistance in the flesh. "We have been damned lucky to get Perez as a defendant," he wrote to Bronstein in closing.

"To put the matter another way, the <u>Duncan</u> ground is our best assurance against losing the first round; and, of course, we could not lose the first round without losing everything."[13]

21—Having a Field Day

THE AIR ON the morning of August 11, 1967, already felt heavy, like damp wool, and radiated a warmth that clung to passersby, eddying behind them as they ducked into air-conditioned lobbies. Richard and Bronstein made their way to the once-grand Maritime Building, where, on the fourth floor, a court reporter was waiting for them. It was the day scheduled for Leander Perez's deposition.

Bronstein had never seen Judge Perez before, but the man's authority impressed as soon as he entered the room, flanked by Lea Perez, Judge Leon, and Sidney Provensal. The older Perez grumbled that he'd like a cigar, and Bronstein absurdly felt himself patting his pockets to see if he had one to offer. Bronstein was rarely intimidated and even more rarely overmatched in confidence, but he was disarmed by Perez's aura; it was as palpable as the swampy air that occasionally snuck in around the room's window air conditioner. As Bronstein discussed the terms of the deposition with Provensal—he wanted to be sure that everything said in there was on the record—he felt Judge Perez's eyes boring unblinkingly into him. He had the distinct feeling that the man was looking through his skull and into the workings of his brain.[1]

"I'm Mr. Bronstein, Mr. Perez," he began, "the attorney for the plaintiffs. This is Mr. Sobol, one of the plaintiffs."[2]

Perez cut him off: "Would you write that on a piece of paper? I'd like to see the names written out because Soboloff and Bronstein—it sounds like Russians to me."

Bronstein found himself writing the names out and passing the paper to Perez, who grimaced.

"Now, isn't that a quartet," mused the Judge. "Where are you boys from?"

Already, Provensal did not like where the conversation was going. "Let's go on with the deposition," he corrected.

Bronstein could not resist inserting, "I'm from Jackson, Mississippi."

"Let's get on with it," grumbled Provensal.

The tension in the room did not dissipate, even when Bronstein asked straightforward questions about Perez's positions on boards and committees or made innocuous inquiries about the parish. The Judge alternately bristled and held forth, at first resisting the young lawyer's queries and then answering them in exhaustive detail only to stop abruptly and comment on the "irrelevancy" of questions that didn't "have a darn thing to do with the case." When Bronstein asked him to answer a question based on his "expertise," Perez interrupted to say, cryptically, "I don't like that word. I've seen it used federally."

At times, Perez quoted laws and constitutional provisions verbatim, complete with citations, and he launched into a complex historical and legal argument about the differences between a police jury and a commission council. In between answers, he nitpicked Bronstein's words, objecting, for instance, to the implication that he was "involved" with the passage of a constitutional amendment. "That's the wrong word," he said, and then continued, as if it made all the difference in the world, "I was one of the principal sponsors and authors."

If the intent of this syncopated rhythm was to throw his opponent off, Perez failed. Bronstein, notwithstanding his intense reaction to Perez's presence, was dogged in his questioning and blunt in his wording. "Out on the playing field," recalled Anthony Amsterdam fondly, "he's a defensive back."[3]

Still, Perez was in his element when the questions were about the workings of local politics. When Bronstein tried to get a simple answer about the powers of the Commission Council president, Perez described the changing responsibilities of various commissioners over time and then interrupted himself to wonder aloud why Bronstein had asked the question in the first place: "There is nothing exceptional or unusual about it. We do have an

Gary Duncan in 1973 *(Courtesy of Gary Duncan)*

Richard Sobol on a civil rights march from Bogalusa to Baton Rouge in 1967 *(Courtesy of Richard Sobol)*

Plaquemines Parish after Hurricane Betsy in 1965 *(Lynn Pelham / The LIFE Images Collection via Getty Images)*

"Judge" Leander Perez Sr., the "third house of the Louisiana legislature," in 1955, shortly after he dedicated the rest of his life to preserving racial segregation. *(Robert W. Kelly / The LIFE Picture Collection via Getty Images)*

The scene that greeted the first racially integrated class at Our Lady of Good Harbor, a Catholic school in Buras, in 1962 *(Plaquemines Gazette)*

The site where, as public schools were forced to desegregate in 1966, Gary Duncan touched Herman Landry on the arm to end a fight. Duncan was arrested for battery, beginning his odyssey to the Supreme Court. The scene, looking down the road along Highway 23 in 2018, is remarkably similar to the way it looked at the time. *(Matthew Van Meter)*

Leander Perez Jr. ("Lea") in 1970. He succeeded his father as Plaquemines district attorney. *(Sendker Publishing)*

Chalin Perez in 1970. He succeeded his father as Plaquemines council president. *(Sendker Publishing)*

Justices of the US Supreme Court in 1967. Standing, from left: Abe Fortas (Richard's former boss), Potter Stewart, Byron R. White, and Thurgood Marshall. Seated, from left: John Marshall Harlan, Hugo LaFayette Black, Chief Justice Earl Warren, William O. Douglas, and William J. Brennan Jr. *(Bettman via Getty Images)*

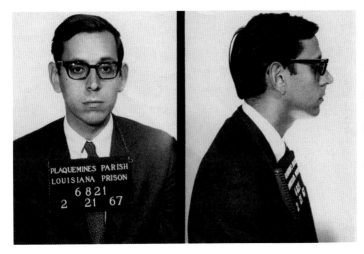

Richard Sobol
after his arrest at
the Plaquemines
Courthouse in 1967
*(Courtesy of Richard
Sobol)*

The partners at "the most
radical law firm" in New
Orleans in the early 2000s,
forty years after its founding.
From left: Nils Douglas, Lolis
Elie, and Robert Collins.
(Courtesy of Richard Sobol)

Gary Duncan and the author in 2018 *(Nancy Buirski)*

Richard and Gary in 2020 *(Matthew Van Meter)*

"This gentleman here."

The confusion might have been funny in a different circumstance. Bronstein, short and scruffy, looked nothing at all like the wiry Richard. Richard simply looked at Perez and said, "Yes," which was the first time he had spoken on the record. Perez, wrong-footed, was silent. Mostly, Richard was awed by the malevolent force seated across from him. He was also sweating profusely. Without the air-conditioning, the small room had grown oppressively stuffy, and the soporific smoke from Perez's cigar drifted in slow whorls over the conference table.[4]

The Judge was more guarded in his subsequent answers, as Bronstein asked him about his opinions of CORE and other organizations.

After ten minutes of these questions, Provensal finally intervened: "I've been sitting here for some time, and we've gone very far afield from the stated cause of action."

Perez again seemed confused. "What is the basis of this suit?" he asked. "I haven't read the petition, even."

"I think you can consult with your attorney after the deposition is over," Bronstein suggested before barreling forward. "Fort St. Philip was to house demonstrators and civil rights workers. Is that an accurate statement?"

"Because civil rights workers, in my books, are simply tools of Communist agitators in this country," Perez opined, and then he turned to the civil unrest that still shook the nation. "And they have succeeded beyond their fondest dreams to extend an armed rebellion and destruction of billions of dollars of property with Molotov bombs and shooting of police and firemen in the back, and all this is agitated and sponsored by the Communists who organize these various, so-called 'civil rights' actions."

Bronstein read from a *Washington Post* story in which Perez offered Martin Luther King Jr. safe passage across the Mississippi to the prison camp for "racial agitators" at Fort St. Philip.

"Part of the way," Perez corrected.

"Is that—?"

"It depended on his conduct," said Perez.

"And you made that statement, is that correct?"

"Possibly." Perez responded with a sly smile. "Hey, are you defending Martin Luther King? Is he one of your idols?"

Bronstein did not take the bait, and the questioning wandered from desegregation to the unwelcome presence of government lawyers in Plaquemines to the lies and slander, according to Perez, that appeared in the *Louisiana Weekly,* New Orleans's black newspaper. When his cigar burned down, he mentioned that he hadn't brought another one. Ronald Hotz, the court reporter, offered one (Perez often joked that he only smoked a given number of cigars—as many as he was given). Perez proclaimed it "pretty good."

When Bronstein's questions turned to the schools, Perez lamented the events of the previous year. "I was responsible for building some $14 million of public-school facilities in my parish," he said, "which gave to our children the best possible educational opportunities." Now, he said, "our public schools have been taken over by the federals.... They have virtually been destroyed," he said, growing emotional at the injustice of it.

"And the same pattern will follow, and ultimately those beautiful schools will be virtually all Negro students. And that carries out the Communist conspiracy to destroy the educational opportunities of our white youth in this country. Not only in this parish, but in this country! And they are succeeding very well."

Having summoned this statement, Perez withdrew briefly, as if spent. For half an hour, he sleepwalked through questions about the attorneys in Plaquemines and whether they would represent black clients ("They never suffered from lack of legal representation," he said).

At last, questions about black lawyers seemed to enliven Perez. Bronstein asked whether he had called Earl Amedee "a very stupid Negro who didn't know how to draw pleadings."

"That's possible," allowed Perez. "He was stupid."

Bronstein pressed. "Haven't you on occasion in the past expressed an opinion that Negroes are inferior morally, as well as having inferior intelligence?"

"I know that Negroes, generally, are immoral. I know that a large number—or a large percentage—of Negroes have illegitimate children; attest to that fact. There's no doubt about that."

Again, Bronstein pushed. "What about intelligence, Mr. Perez? Do you believe that the Negroes have equal intelligence as a rule with white people?"

"Of course not!"

How about black lawyers? asked Bronstein. Or black jurors?

Perez countered that he had nothing against black jurors at all, but there was a problem: "One of the qualifications of jury service is a good moral character."

Bronstein asked whether Perez had ever urged his people to not cooperate with the FBI.

"Yes," replied the Judge. "At one time, secret police were knocking on doors. And I told the people throughout, as president of our police jury, to tell them to go to hell. It was none of their business. Yes, we resent federal interference in our local government, absolutely. It's un-American. It's unlawful. It's dictatorial. It's oppressive."

As tactically adept as Perez was, he was also staring across the table at two Jewish civil rights lawyers—the embodiment of everything he feared and reviled. Here, in this room, he saw the doom predicted by the dozens of apocalyptic tracts that lined his bookshelves at home. Perez seemed unable to coyly frustrate and confound his questioner, who drew him into the political and moral issues that had defined his life for the past thirteen years. Confronted by two men he was convinced were enemies of the American people, Perez began to debate.

This was just what Bronstein wanted, and he pressed his advantage. He asked if Perez thought the Civil Rights Act was a Communist conspiracy.

"Of course it is," came the reply. Then, as if it were the same topic, he said he had read a "secret book report" by Zionists that took credit for *Brown v. Board of Education*. From there, Perez launched into his favorite topic: the unconstitutionality of the Fourteenth Amendment and, therefore, of

Brown. In the stuffy, smoke-choked room, he delved into pseudoscience, history, and pseudohistory. His tour-de-force argument was as detailed as ever, addressing point by point the assertions of the Supreme Court (which, he noted, itself had a "dubious origin") and unveiling the Communist underpinnings of *Brown.*

Bronstein goaded him into elaboration by asking him about the Ku Klux Klan, which Perez readily agreed was "originated by Southern gentlemen of the highest character—professional men, former military men, and so forth—to protect the white womanhood from Negro rapists."

Perez allowed himself to be egged on and held forth on the Voting Rights Act ("It flagrantly violated the Constitution"), the ACLU (which had no "respect for decent womanhood"), and the role of the judiciary in American society ("It should not be accepted as the law of the land").

"Let's get on with it," Provensal intervened at last. "We're going from voting rights to civil rights to just about everything under the sun."

"You're having a field day," shouted Perez. "What has that got to do with this case, Mr. Sobol? What has that got to do with this case?"

"Go ahead and ask your next question," pushed Provensal.

Perez leaned over at Bronstein. "With a mind as pigmented as yours, and as limited, and with the ideologies that undoubtedly you have, I'm impressed that it's not the proper legal principles."

"Let's move on, gentlemen," muttered Provensal. "It's getting hot."

"One minute," said Bronstein, who was shaken or amazed or overheating.

"That's what you said an hour ago!" Provensal protested. "Let's get on with the questioning."

Bronstein had one more line of inquiry: Lawrence Rousselle, an anti-Perez businessman who had been imprisoned after he decided to run for office. Perez dismissed the matter: "Personally, as a man, I would have confronted Rousselle and handled it myself, as a man....Do you know Rousselle?"

"I don't," Bronstein replied.

"It's a matter of self-preservation," said the Judge. "You try it and you'll see what happens."

"I'm not in the habit of threatening people," said Bronstein.

"I guess not."

"Would it be a fair statement, Mr. Perez, to say that you are the wealthiest man in Plaquemines Parish?"

"That's not a fair statement. I wouldn't accept that, and that's none of your business."

"Would it be a fair statement to say that you are *one* of the wealthiest men in Plaquemines Parish?"

"That's none of your business. And I would not say it's a fair statement," repeated Perez. "How much further afield do you want to go, lawyer?"

"Let's go," Provensal said, rising.

"I'm just checking now to see whether we've covered everything." Bronstein looked over his notes. "I have no further questions. Thank you, sir, goodbye."

"Don't thank me," Perez shot back. "I'm not thanking you."

"Your manners, sir, are no concern of mine," said Bronstein.

"What?"

Bronstein repeated himself. Perez flushed and demanded to know if Bronstein was questioning his manners.

"Judge," offered Provensal, "he's not questioning your manners. He knows better than that."

"I guess he does," grumbled Perez. "That's one thing I demand, is respect."

Bronstein retorted, "Respect is given where respect is received, as a general rule."

Before his client could rise to this provocation, Provensal interjected. "Who's your next witness? Call your next witness."

"Well, we're going to break for lunch."

Lea Perez and Judge Leon, who had been waiting, protested that they wanted to give statements and be done with it.

"We have every intention of finishing today," said Bronstein. "It is now one thirty. We have been going since nine thirty. I have suggested a half-an-hour lunch break, both for the reporter's sake and for the sake of everybody else."

"In the first place," said Provensal, "we are *not* going to break for half an hour."

"We are going to go down to get something to eat," Bronstein repeated.

"Why do you have to be gone a half an hour?"

"Well, we never had the privilege to listen to Judge Perez before," said Bronstein. "I've got to clear my mind a minute, Mr. Provensal."

22—Flambeaux

THE PEREZ DEPOSITION had come in the middle of the most intense period of Richard's life. In addition to Gary's case and his own, he was litigating dozens of lawsuits around Louisiana, including *Hicks v. Crown Zellerbach,* the case against the Bogalusa paper mill's promotion and hiring practices.

Crown Zellerbach had gone from a quixotic employment suit to a test case for the Civil Rights Act. Through it, Richard had a good chance to expand the definition of workplace discrimination. If he won, even inadvertently discriminatory practices would be illegal; it would no longer be necessary to prove racist intent.

This case also made him the most interesting equal-opportunity-employment lawyer in the country. Hundreds of academics, government workers, law firms, and employers were watching the daily progress. And job offers started coming in; he was offered professorships at UCLA, Michigan, Columbia, and Yale. (Which he declined.)[1]

He had requested another leave of absence from Arnold & Porter, but he didn't really have any intention of going back. The work he was doing now was too exciting, too vital for him to ever work in corporate law again. What was more, Al Bronstein had accepted a teaching position at Harvard's Kennedy School of Government, and Richard was asked to succeed him as chief legal counsel for the LCDC. He accepted, and, at Henry Schwarzschild's urging, the board raised his salary a bit, which allowed Barbara and him to send Joanna, their daughter, to Carrollton Presbyterian School, a friendly private school across the street from their home.

Against this backdrop, the situation in Bogalusa had become explosive again. A. Z. Young, the charismatic president of the Bogalusa Voters

League, had grown tired of being ignored by John McKeithen, the governor of Louisiana. "He is our governor as well as the whites' governor," Young announced. "And we have to remind him of that."

What Young had in mind was a massive demonstration—a march from Bogalusa to the state capital in Baton Rouge, inspired by Martin Luther King Jr.'s famous 1965 march from Selma to Montgomery, Alabama. The route was almost unthinkably dangerous. At 105 miles, it was almost twice the length of the Selma-to-Montgomery march, and it led through the heart of Klan country.

If anyone could pull off something this ambitious, it was A. Z. Young. Young was striking: six feet four and possessed of a preacher's voice and cadence, he had been a tank commander in World War II and a leader in the Crown Zellerbach black union after the war. His toughness and magnetism had made him an obvious choice to be the public face of the voters league.[2]

The marchers set off from Bogalusa on August 10, 1967. The next morning, Richard needed to be in New Orleans for Perez's deposition. Except for the day of the deposition, Richard drove early in the morning to meet the marchers wherever they were. He was dressed conspicuously like a lawyer; he wanted the police and everybody else to know that they were being observed. Every night, he would drive back to New Orleans to work and catch a few hours of sleep.

Acting as a lawyer for the march was exciting, frightening, and exhausting. Danger could spring from almost anywhere: crowds of whites who eyed them menacingly, apparently empty buildings, the thick woods that lined the road. The first leg of the trip proceeded without major incident, but Richard learned that Young had started receiving credible threats of violence on the road ahead, and he was worried.[3]

Working in the civil rights movement in the summer of 1967 felt like standing in a field of parched grass during a lightning storm. It is hard now to appreciate how close the United States felt to a race war. Newspapers ran riot stories together, and the collection sometimes sprawled to several pages. More than 150 incidents of unrest troubled the summer of 1967, and no region was immune: East, South, West, Midwest, all of America saw racial violence. The National Guard was deployed in a dozen locations, most famously to Detroit, which weathered the largest domestic disturbance in America in more than a hundred years.

Black Americans were becoming more assertive, even performative, about their rights. In May, twenty-four black men and six black women marched into the California State Assembly, bristling with pistols, revolvers, and shotguns, which were legal as long as they were displayed openly (Governor Ronald Reagan swiftly signed a bill that criminalized "carrying a loaded weapon in public"). Police were on edge, which did not improve relations with the black communities they policed. That problematic relationship was, as much as anything, responsible for the frustration and despair that led to widespread unrest in the first place.[4]

The Deacons for Defense and Justice had organized a support team for the march from Bogalusa to Baton Rouge. Cars and trucks would creep alongside the crowd to provide food, water, and means of defense or escape. Since long stretches of the route were without toilets, and some people worried about being arrested for indecent exposure if they relieved themselves outdoors, one deacon rigged up a latrine in the back of his truck. Peter Honigsberg, who was volunteering with the LCDC at the time, recalled seeing a Coca-Cola truck that was seemingly loaded with cold water, but was actually filled with firearms for the deacons, in case it came to that.[5]

Richard hoped it would not come to that, but he wanted to be present to witness whatever might occur. Each morning, he and Don Juneau drove the LCDC car to where the marchers were and idled behind them. The lawyers stuck out in their suits and ties, which was exactly the point.

After three days, the march arrived in Hammond, having covered half the total distance. But that had been the easy section, lying mostly within the relatively peaceful St. Tammany Parish. Between Hammond and Baton Rouge lay fifty miles of US Highway 190, which passed through the most dangerous part of the state: the piney backwoods of Tangipahoa and Livingston Parishes. "Bloody Tangipahoa" and its neighbor had been the site of some of the most grotesque displays of mob violence in all the postbellum South.[6]

The first attack came shortly after the marchers left Hammond. In the town of Albany, a gang of white men with knives came at them. Women and children loaded into the support vehicles for protection, while members of the Deacons for Defense stole straight razors from nearby barbershops and used those to fend off their attackers.[7]

In tiny Holden, the next village on the route, a group of fifteen whites burst through the state-police cordon as darkness fell and began a brief melee before being repulsed. The march organizers decided it was safest to drive back and spend the night in Albany, where members of the small black community had offered to put them up. As they bedded down, the sky glowed orange as a line of crosses burned by the highway.[8]

After each attack, the number of marchers dwindled. Almost one hundred had left Hammond on August 14. By the next day, there were fewer than fifty. Then only twenty-five. As they marched west along the left shoulder of the highway, they saw a crowd of whites, seventy-five or so, marching three abreast and headed east on the other side of the road.[9]

The front ranks of the march and the countermarch closed in on one another and at last drew even, glaring across the highway through the drizzle as cars rolled between them. Then, bizarrely, both groups kept going in opposite directions, and for a moment it seemed as if the tense emotional line that stretched across the twenty feet of asphalt separating them would tauten but not break. But then, with a shout, the whites streamed across the highway and into the line of troopers as the black protesters braced to defend themselves. Hand-to-hand fighting spread over the highway, stopping traffic for miles in each direction.[10]

A. Z. Young thought the white men had made a tactical mistake by hitting policemen. For the first time, the police and the protesters seemed to be on the same team. "Watch out, A. Z.!" shouted one trooper as two whites leapt at him, fists flying. Blood spilled over the highway, and when the brawl was over, it was whites who were arrested for disturbing the peace. Still, only fifteen activists had finished out that day.[11]

Young had no intention of giving up, but the final stretch of highway lay through notorious Denham Springs, the biggest town in Livingston Parish, and rumors of Klan-organized violence there had been reaching the demonstrators for days. The handful of exhausted activists needed some time to regain their strength.[12]

As the marchers rested up on August 17, the lawyers worked overtime. Richard threw himself into negotiations with the police, and he called the Civil Rights Division to see if the federal government could do anything to help, but he heard nothing in reply.[13]

The next day, hundreds of whites lined the shoulder of Highway 190 through Denham Springs. They had strewn roofing nails and glass along the road, and they carried clubs and bottles, cradling Confederate flags and children in their arms. The air was stifling as the sun cooked the pavement. At last, they saw the line of demonstrators approaching on the road. As the column grew nearer, though, it became clear that they were not looking at the black marchers at all. Four mounted policemen led the procession, which was flanked on both sides by a solid wall, four or five deep, of rifle-bearing National Guardsmen, their bayonets glinting in the hot sun.[14]

It is not known who spoke to Governor McKeithen the previous day to persuade him to call up the Louisiana National Guard. McKeithen tried to pass it off as his idea: "Those crazy rednecks out there," he said, "they'll jump on a policeman but they'll never jump on an American soldier. They're so patriotic, they'll just never do it!" Whoever was behind it, the order was not a half measure. Six hundred fifty guardsmen had appeared overnight in Walker, so many that Honigsberg, the LCDC volunteer, actually laughed when he saw them. The number of troops was shocking, not least because it came on top of the 175 state policemen already present, who were armed that day not with billy clubs but with submachine guns.[15]

Richard's intervention, it seemed, had worked. The throng of frustrated whites jeered and heckled the protective force that encased the unseen marchers, begging to be given a shot at roughing up the demonstrators—"just two minutes; that'll be enough"—but they stayed well away from the guardsmen. A few whites began hurling bottles and raw eggs towards the marchers, but they were swiftly arrested. Helicopters circled overhead as a convoy of jeeps and military trucks trundled down the road alongside vehicles from the Bogalusa Voters League and the LCDC car. Guardsmen had gone ahead to post by every bridge on the route to prevent sabotage. It had the feel of a full-scale military operation. From afar, the scene more closely resembled something from the current war in Vietnam than the United States—the summer of 1967 had been full of such comparisons.[16]

Eighty or so marchers had shown up for the event, more than at any time since the first days. They were not just from Bogalusa; others had joined the procession to make it clear, as they marched through the seat of the Louisiana Ku Klux Klan, that they would not be turned away.[17]

As they entered Baton Rouge, the marchers numbered more than a hundred. In driving rain, they walked to Capital Junior High School in Baton Rouge while whites taunted them from the shelter of cars or awnings. Sodden and exhausted as they were, the demonstrators were elated. They were about to finish their historic journey; the state capitol lay just a few miles away. A. Z. Young pulled together a rally in the auditorium of the school, which all of the marchers attended along with Richard and the others from LCDC.[18]

Young spoke about the importance of voter registration and pushing for equal employment. "I'm not here to incite a riot or create a disturbance," he said, "but to get jobs for black folks!" Four hundred people or so attended the meeting, mostly young people, and they cheered and sang civil rights songs, led by the Bogalusa Voters League.[19]

Lincoln Lynch, of CORE, stood up to speak. His message was less conciliatory. "If it takes a Newark or a Plainfield or a Detroit," he said, "then that's how it has to be! White feet on black necks have been there too long. We've prayed. We've marched. Now the time has come to break that hold!"

The crowd applauded as Lynch prophesied, "There is no power on earth that can prevent violence or revolution!" Then he led the assembled in a chant: "Black Power! Black Power! Black Power!"

A few miles away, four hundred whites attended a Ku Klux Klan rally, where they burned a fifteen-foot-tall cross.[20]

On the steps of the state capitol the next day, six hundred black men and women gathered for their long-awaited rally. A triumphant A. Z. Young surveyed the crowd, which was bigger than he could have hoped for. Governor McKeithen still refused to meet—he claimed that he had to be at church—but the size of the crowd and the presence of television and print journalists from all over the country validated his instinct that the march had been necessary. The 105-mile journey had not been in vain. Young wanted to demand the governor's support for the dozens of blacks running for election in November all over Louisiana. He wanted more blacks hired by the state. And he was beginning to think that he might get those things.

But then, without warning, the rally split apart. A pastor from the Bogalusa Voters League opened the meeting with a prayer, only to be shouted down with cries of "No!" when he prayed for wisdom for the governor. A group of 115 blacks broke off from the rally to stage a sit-in, only to be headed off by a leader of the Deacons for Defense, who shooed them back.

A. Z. Young gave his appeal to McKeithen and urged blacks to vote against him and for black candidates in November, but the event's real draw was Lincoln Lynch.

"The revolution is spreading," Lynch proclaimed. "And it has spread right here in Louisiana. It can be a peaceful revolution, or it can be a violent one. If peaceful change is not forthcoming, then we will have violent change!"[21]

Richard was a little lost. He knew the people from Bogalusa—Hicks, Jenkins, Young, and their friends and families. He knew the people from the Crown Zellerbach unions, and he knew the people in the Bogalusa Voters League. He had been to their churches and meeting halls; he had defended them in court. But now it occurred to him that he was surrounded by people he did not know and who did not know him.

All at once, Richard felt exposed and unwelcome—"a 'get the hell out of here' vibe," as he would later describe it—and he was conscious of being one white face in a sea of black faces. He had operated smoothly in the black world for two years, and, although he didn't think he had taken that for granted, he had grown accustomed to it. Just at that moment, he realized that something new was happening, something different, something he was not a part of.

"What are you doing here?" a voice beside him said with concern. "You better get your ass outta here!" So he did, not waiting for the rally to end, and he drove back to New Orleans in a daze. He felt blindsided and betrayed, and, for the first time since his decision to return to the LCDC, he felt a little lost.[22]

———

The basic premise of Black Power, Stokely Carmichael of SNCC wrote, was a struggle "to reclaim our history and our identity from what must be called cultural terrorism." Carmichael would know; he popularized the slogan just a year before the march on Baton Rouge, and he wrote a manifesto, called *Black Power,* that was published a few months after the march.

In the book, he argued that black Americans were a colonized people and that it was time for them to empower themselves on their own terms, not simply by demanding access to white institutions. He dismissed many of the white volunteers who came south ("All too frequently," he wrote, "young, middle-class, white Americans, like some sort of Pepsi generation, have wanted to 'come alive' through the black community"), and he complained that established black leaders "accepted [middle-class] values and institutions without fully realizing their racist nature."[23]

Whatever else it did, the nascent Black Power movement demanded a response from segregationists, politicians, white liberals, white civil rights workers, and from the establishment of the civil rights movement.

The leaders of the movement were confounded. At the same time as the marchers were leaving Bogalusa, Martin Luther King Jr. was at a Southern Christian Leadership Conference (SCLC) meeting in Atlanta, attempting to gain some control over the Black Power message. King's approach, as ever, was highly intellectual. He spoke about needing a positive "sense of negritude" and offered a disquisition on the linguistic violence done to black people by the negative associations with the word "black." The elders

166

of SCLC unanimously passed resolutions calling for "identity workshops" and "unity conferences" in order to "establish a dialogue."[24]

The younger generation of civil rights leaders scoffed at all of this. While King wanted a dialogue, the newly branded Student *National* Coordinating Committee (the new leadership had rid the organization's name of the anachronistic *Nonviolent*) had just expelled all of its white members en masse.

In principle, the white lawyers who did much of the legal work of the civil rights movement in the sixties were supportive of what they saw as the aims of Black Power. In practice, there was little agreement in 1967 about what those aims were, exactly, even among proponents.

White lawyers who had been deeply entrenched in black communities for years—some even more deeply and for longer than Richard—suddenly felt "other," and most felt betrayed by the change. Nearly all of them bristled at the perception of being lumped in with Southern whites and racists, and few accepted their exclusion from the movement's culture gracefully, even if they understood why they were being pushed out.

Some even saw hypocrisy. Al Bronstein grew frustrated with Carmichael, who publicly disowned the liberal whites who came to work in the civil rights movement but then privately told Bronstein that he'd still call LCDC if he ever got arrested.[25]

Carmichael's statement revealed the complexity of the Black Power shift: while the movement was changing to become more radical and ambitious, hundreds of lawsuits still needed to be filed, and arrested workers still needed defending. Despite the moral force of Black Power, the fact was that there were not yet enough black lawyers to do all of the work, so hard-line rhetoric came up against the realities of the struggle for equality.

Black Power produced no such division on the right. Segregationists, Klan leaders, conservative intellectuals, and the moderate Republicans of the Northern suburbs were united in their horror of the language of racial exclusion and armed rebellion. The perceived violence and incivility of Black Power rhetoric drove moderates, who may have been quietly against segregation and agnostic about programs intended to aid black Americans, into the open arms of the far right. Republican leaders were on hand to help this trend along, including a political has-been from California, Richard Nixon, who would weaponize the growing fear and resentment.

That was all still to come, but its seeds were planted. A few days after the March for Jobs and Justice ended, Governor McKeithen called for the hiring of more black police officers, but he put little energy into actually recruiting or training them. After A. Z. Young threatened to repeat the march, McKeithen put employment for blacks on the agenda for the Louisiana Commission on Human Relations, where it was debated and forgotten.[26]

23—Suppression

Novemver 4, 1967, had none of the markers of an explosive election day. Pundits and politicians were already buzzing about the much-anticipated general election of the following year. George Wallace was expected to mount an internal coup attempt against Lyndon Johnson from the Deep South. Republicans had not come up with a satisfying candidate, but Johnson was showing weakness: his approval rating had tumbled from its 79 percent high in 1964 to a troubling low of 37 percent after the turmoil of the summer of 1967. With so many polarizing issues on the table, from the space race to hippies to Vietnam to Black Power, the run-up to the 1968 election offered endless opportunities for discussion, debate, and histrionics.[1]

So it is perhaps unsurprising that the election of 1967 was seen as a proxy for the forces that would play out nationally a year later. This was especially true in Louisiana, which elects its governors and other important state officials in off years.

Twenty-six black candidates were running for seats in the state legislature, where no black person had served since the end of Reconstruction. Many more were running for local offices. Some of them came from districts that were majority black and that, despite fervent efforts by segregationists to suppress the vote, had seen large rises in black registration after the Voting Rights Act passed.

Watching these races closely for signs of foul play were Richard Sobol, Robert Collins, Nils Douglas, and Lolis Elie, who were already involved in voting-rights cases all over eastern Louisiana. The black attorneys, especially Douglas and Elie, had come to the conclusion that nothing would truly change in Louisiana without a massive shift in racial representation.

Douglas himself had run an unsuccessful campaign for state representative in the Ninth Ward. Newly empowered and forcefully represented in court, a group of brave, ambitious black leaders was beginning to test the limits of segregationist stonewalling.[2]

At the same time, Leander Perez was trying his best to use the events of 1967 to turn his state against the ruling moderate faction. His pick for governor was John Rarick. They had worked together in 1966 to unseat a moderate congressman by attacking him as a slave to the "black-power voting bloc." In thanks for Perez's help with his campaign, Rarick introduced a bill in the US House of Representatives "to declare the Fourteenth Amendment illegal," the language of which bore a striking resemblance to the Judge's beloved treatise on the topic.[3]

But the segregationists were on the defensive now. It was more important than ever that conservative whites vote together and that blacks and opponents of segregation stay home, split their votes, or fail to qualify in the first place.

For his entire career, Perez had been a leading innovator in voter-suppression techniques. And though he had honed his skills against white political rivals, it was in his war on racial equality that his gamesmanship achieved its fullest expression. As was true of his resistance of school desegregation, his tactics for mass voter disenfranchisement were notable for their ingenuity, their number, and their dogged application.

Arrayed against him were the combined resources of the Department of Justice, LCDC, and a number of invigorated local activist organizations in big cities and small towns. These groups hoped to press their advantage and make it a landmark year for Louisiana; they wanted history to remember 1967 as the year that ended the stranglehold of white supremacists on the electorate.

The techniques of voter suppression authored by Perez ranged from deceptively simple to intricately convoluted.

The most notorious—and complex—of these was his constitutional-interpretation test. While literacy tests had been used all over the South for decades to disqualify blacks, who were disproportionately illiterate, they were blunt instruments that caught up many illiterate whites in their net. They also did not work well in Plaquemines, where blacks were increasingly well educated. Perez's supercharged version of the literacy test was a quiz on portions of the US and Louisiana Constitutions. He personally devised and printed twenty-five "test cards," each containing three constitutional provisions that the hopeful voter needed to "interpret." He also typed up "sample correct answers" for each form, which the registrar could use for reference.[4]

The constitutional-interpretation test might have suffered from the same collateral-damage problem as the literacy tests, except that almost all of the white registrants—86 percent of them—received either Form 2 or Form 8. It happened that those two cards were comically straightforward. Form 2, for instance, asked the reader to "interpret" the following:

Congress shall make no law respecting the establishment of religion, or prohibiting the free exercise thereof (U.S. Const. 1st Amendment)

Every person has the natural right to worship God according to the dictates of his own conscience (Art. 1 No. 4 La. Const.)

Any person may speak, write, and make public his sentiments on all subjects, being responsible for the use of that liberty (Art. 1, Sec. 3, La. Const.)[5]

The acceptable answers were short and obvious: two responses of "freedom of religion" and one of "freedom of speech." Form 8 ("states' rights," "freedom of the press," and "freedom of religion") was similarly elementary.* Of the 2,384 voters who successfully registered between 1955 and 1960, 2,059 filled out one of these two cards. Not one black registrant received Form 2 or 8.[6]

The twenty-three other cards contained few easy answers. Indeed, they

---

* It is worth noting that the only acceptable "interpretation" of the text of the Tenth Amendment was "states' rights," which is the obvious answer only to someone with a particular political mindset.

seemed to delight in rolling out abstruse or legalistic language. Form 9, for instance, asked for an interpretation of three parts of the state constitution:

> The Legislature shall provide by law for change of venue in civil and criminal cases (Art. 7 Sec. 45 La. Const.)
> The exercise of the police power of the State shall never be abridged (Art. 19 Sec. 18 La. Const.)
> Prescription shall not run against the State in any civil matter (Art. 19 Sec 16 La. Const.)[7]

Perez's suggested answers to these prompts were themselves convoluted and ran several lines each.

Simpler but no less effective was the statewide policy of requiring registrants to calculate their age to the day. Not only did this test one's math skills, but it required knowledge of one's exact date of birth, which was less common among blacks than whites. It also presumed that the registrar could independently calculate the proper response, which was not always a given; people still talk about the 1961 Civil Rights Commission hearing in which the Plaquemines registrar, in the middle of walking the commissioners through filling out a registration card to prove how straightforward it was, miscalculated her own age by nearly a full month.[8]

These and other provisions awaited those few black citizens who were actually able to track down the registrar and make it inside the door. Arbitrary rejections abounded: grammatical errors were grounds for dismissal, as were "incorrect" statements of skin color (only "Negro" would suffice, not "black" or variants of "African-American"). One black schoolteacher was disqualified for writing her name as "Norma J. Cosse" and signing it as "Norma Johnson Cosse." Answers to constitutional questions were disqualified for no discernible reason when written by blacks, including, for example, an interpretation of the right to peaceful assembly that read, "That one may assemble or belong to any group, club, or organization he chooses as long as it is within the law."

Meanwhile, harmless errors were universally overlooked when the applicant was white. Whites were also allowed to crib from the sample answers to the constitutional prompt—one applicant actually signed the sample card by mistake. If they didn't simply copy the responses, whites could write almost anything, including "FREE .MAN" or "FRDUM FOOF SPETGH" for the right to free speech, both of which were accepted. A white Venice housewife successfully registered by neatly penning the following interpretation of three constitutional passages: "I agree."

Unsurprisingly, a mere seven black people managed to register in Plaquemines Parish between 1955 and 1960. Of the more than two thousand whites who attempted to register in the same period, only nineteen were disqualified for any reason.[9]

———

Vivian and Robert Duncan, the eldest of Gary's siblings, first tried to register to vote in the 1950s. Along with their mother, they joined a large group of black men and women from lower Plaquemines who carpooled to Pointe à la Hache, arriving before the registrar's office opened at ten o'clock. The doors opened momentarily, then closed, and the crowd of black would-be voters waited. At four o'clock, when the office closed, the Duncans followed their neighbors back across the river.[10]

For a time, this scene repeated itself every Monday, which was the appointed day for voter registration. The crowd sometimes grew as large as three hundred. Sometimes the registrar's doors would open to allow white registrants in and then close again suddenly. Sometimes a secretary would inform the crowd of black citizens that the registrar was working from home that day. Since there is nowhere to hide in Plaquemines Parish, they would decamp to the registrar's home, only to be told by his wife that he was still at the office.[11]

Every once in a while, a black person would be allowed inside. More often than not, he or she would walk out with nothing to show for it. Leander Perez had made sure of that.

Mt. Olive Missionary Baptist Church, the Duncans' congregation, was the epicenter of resistance to Leander Perez's efforts at voter suppression. Beginning in 1947, the church hosted clinics that coached eligible black residents through the registration process. Similar clinics also occurred at other black churches, all started by pastors and deacons who had served in the US military in World War II and were disgusted by the thankless treatment they received at home. Reverend Joe Taylor of Boothville put his feelings simply: "If I was sufficient to serve my country in a time of need, I should be able [to vote]."[12]

Word spread throughout Plaquemines that you could go to Mt. Olive to learn how to register. In meetings in the modest building, members of the Plaquemines Parish Civic and Political Organization would teach tutorials on age calculation, constitutional interpretation, and how to answer all of the questions about previous registration and residence—a single blank field was ground for disqualification, even if the answer was "none" or "not applicable."[13]

As much as they focused on instruction, though, the task of building confidence back into members of the community who had given up on voting was at least as great. And much of the work needed to be done blind; the constitutional-interpretation test cards, for instance, were not publicly available. It was not even publicly known that there were twenty-five of them. So instructors needed either to rely on the memories of the few black people who had actually made it that far in the process, or to memorize interpretations of every clause of the constitutions of the United States and Louisiana, hoping that those answers matched Perez's sample responses closely enough to pass muster.[14]

The deacons of Mt. Olive, including Lambert Duncan, carefully guarded information about the meetings, and they organized security for the lawyers and civil rights workers who would sneak into the parish to lead clinics. Visiting instructors came down in the trunks of cars and stayed with families in the community overnight as men with shotguns kept watch in shifts. They left in the morning to avoid suspicious late-night drives up the road. Sometimes, a clinic would need to be called off when word got out of a roadblock in Belle Chasse, which would send the community into bouts of paranoia about people snitching to Perez, which some probably were.[15]

Still, obsessed with the menace of "outside agitators," Perez had underestimated the capacity of the black community within his parish, and for years he scoffed at the Civic and Political Organization. Even when, in 1960, members of the organization complained to the US Civil Rights Commission, which hauled Perez in for testimony, even when the Civil Rights Division filed a lawsuit against the registrar, and even when Percy Griffin, the organization's president, ran against Perez in the 1963 election for chairmanship of the local Democratic Party, the Judge seemed unable to grasp that the greatest threat to maintaining an all-white electorate came not from Moscow or Washington, but from Boothville.[16]

The work of resistance was not easy, nor was it often successful. When Percy Griffin ran against Perez in December 1963, there were still only eighty-nine black voters in Plaquemines Parish. That year, 6,754 whites voted, all but 102 of them for Perez.[17]

But cracks were starting to appear in the formidable wall Perez had built. At least six of the black voters in the Griffin-Perez race were Duncans. Vivian, Robert, and Mazie all registered on December 8, 1962, passing the constitutional-interpretation test. Lambert, Calvin, and Gaynelle registered soon after. The Duncans still proudly carry their voter-registration cards with them, eager to point out that they were among the few who made it through the gauntlet of early-sixties voter registration in the white-supremacist dictatorship they called home.

What had started as cracks in the wall soon threatened to destroy it. John Minor Wisdom, in a scathing and sometimes insulting opinion aimed squarely at Perez, dismantled the constitutional-interpretation test in 1963. Two years later, Perez watched in horror as President Johnson promised in his State of the Union speech to "eliminate every remaining obstacle to the right and the opportunity to vote."[18]

Despite Perez's efforts to stop it, the Voting Rights Act passed in August 1965. On the same day that President Johnson signed the act, the United

States Attorney General Nicholas Katzenbach announced that all Louisiana parishes would be subject to its strictures.[19]

Having been stripped of his most effective disenfranchisement techniques, Perez announced that he would counter the Voting Rights Act with white registration drives. "Are the white people going to surrender their government to so-called 'civil rights'? Racial strife? Demonstrations? Insurrection?" he asked in a televised statement. "My friends, we cannot surrender! If we fail to register every white man and woman in this crisis, we will only be inviting far more serious trouble in the future." His stated goal was to register at least two new white voters for every new black one.[20]

A month after the Voting Rights Act passed, a kind of karmic justice was served when Hurricane Betsy ravaged Plaquemines. Busy as he was with recovery efforts, Perez still found time in October to gather leading segregationists at the Hotel Washington in New Orleans to "fight the constitutional battle against the Voting Rights Act in every way." By that time, though, the news was even worse for the Judge: it was announced that Plaquemines Parish was one of just four parishes in which black disenfranchisement was so bad that its elections would be conducted under the watchful gaze of federal election observers.[21]

Federal election observers were nonlawyers whose duty under the Voting Rights Act was to go to counties in the South where voter intimidation was most intense. Contrary to the fears of Plaquemines officials, the observers could not themselves register voters. They compared the voter rolls to their own list of eligible voters, watched polling places to be sure that blacks were allowed to vote, and, most importantly, they handed out registration forms and helped in filling them out.[22]

One irony—there were many—of Perez's pitched battle against black voter registration in Plaquemines was that it never much mattered how many blacks in the parish registered. Black people were a minority in Plaquemines; as long as Perez could carry most of the whites, he was safe. That he expended so much time, energy, and ingenuity on his decade-long struggle to stamp out every last black voter in his domain indicates not only the depth of his hate, but also its unsustainability.

On November 4, 1967, election day, six federal election observers showed up early in the morning to their makeshift Plaquemines Parish headquarters in the Belle Chasse Post Office. Three of them crossed the street to the Belle Chasse Fire Department, where they would be helping blacks fill out voter-registration forms and overseeing the casting of ballots.

At 8:20 a.m., a short white man in a three-piece suit burst into the fire department, flanked by two taller men. If the observers didn't know him already, the telltale cigar hanging from the man's mouth gave away his identity. Saying he was "a parish official," the man turned to one observer, who was seated, and growled, "Please stand up and show respect."

"Yes, sir," said the bemused observer, and he stood.

The man wrote down their names and tossed back their documents, muttering that they were "federal spies" who were part of a "second Reconstruction." "I'd rather eat shit," he spat, "than do this sort of spying."

One observer recalled that the man "began talking about things that did not make sense but were directed as insults toward us."

After ten or fifteen minutes, the irate man suddenly left the building. The three officials sat for a moment in stunned silence, and then one went back to the post office to talk the incident over with his boss. Shortly after he entered the office, the door swung open, and there was the man again. Introducing himself as "Tom Hicks," he repeated the scene from across the road. He counted the observers, skipping the one he had seen previously.

"There are three more across the street," he said to them, "and that makes six of you federal bastards here." Again he asked for identification and wrote down the names. Then, snatching the list of federally eligible voters, he held it aloft and said sarcastically, "I suppose I cannot look at this."

When they responded that he was welcome to it, he thumbed through, grunting at a few of the names in disgust.

The man tossed the book down and walked behind the counter. There, he grabbed a briefcase, turned it upside down, and shook it until pens and paper clips and pages of documents fell to the floor and scattered like leaves.

"Where in hell are the machine guns? I know damn well there must be some," the man said to no one in particular.

He repeated the process with the other briefcases and then began rummaging in the filing cabinets, the observers watching silently as he ransacked their office.

"What's the matter, don't you have any arms? Where are your machine guns? What kind of people are you, anyway?" the man asked, too loudly.

Having failed to discover a massive federal armory, the man stalked out, flanked by his companions. And as he flung the door open and thrust himself out, he ran straight into a black man coming up the steps, nearly knocking him over.

Both men were silent for a moment, standing inches from each other.

"What's he doing here?" demanded the white man, turning back to the observers. They made no reply.

"I want to know!" he thundered.

His friends took him by the arm and led him across the parking lot and back to his car. When he was gone, the black man continued up the short stoop, crossed the threshold, and stepped forward to register, for the first time in his life, to vote.[23]

24—The Facts of This Case

Gary Duncan had never been on an airplane before; he had never even left the state of Louisiana. So he surprised himself a little in mid-January 1968 by boarding a jet bound for Washington, DC. Lynn was with him, and she talked him through what it would entail; she had flown before, so her worries were more about going up north in the winter. For Gary, this was one of the first high points in an odyssey of horrors that had begun when he saw his nephew and cousin and the four white boys on the side of Highway 23.[1]

Since his arrest, Gary had been afraid to get in his car. For a time, he refused to drive too far up the road, for fear of what might happen. Memories of the arrest intruded on his thoughts, and family stories echoed inside him: his father's boat set aflame, a cousin institutionalized after a dubious rape conviction, a cousin found dead in a ditch years back, which everyone agreed was "just another black man dead," took it as a warning, and moved on.[2]

He threw himself even more fully into work. Out on the water, he felt protected, insulated from the outside world. Richard had been in touch with him about the case, but not much had happened, it seemed, in the eleven months since he spent the night in jail. More often, he had spoken to Richard about *Sobol v. Perez,* since he was likely to be called as a witness. But that case, too, had moved more slowly than Gary had thought. On September 10, he turned twenty years old, and there still seemed to be no resolution. In October, Richard called him to say that they were going to Washington, DC, to argue his case before the United States Supreme Court.[3]

The court had given Richard the good news on October 9, made better because the clerk had indicated that the justices wanted *Duncan v. Louisiana* through. This meant that Richard had only thirty days to file his brief, far less time than usual, but it would at least keep the case from dragging on.

Richard felt that Gary's case was worthy, but it had been no sure thing that the court would hear it. Only a tiny fraction of cases ever make it to consideration, and most of those are dispensed with summarily. Gary's case was one of just 110 that year that would receive a written opinion. It was the first time an LCDC attorney had argued before the Supreme Court, and Schwarzschild offered to fly Gary and Lynn Duncan up to Washington for the event.[4]

The flight to Washington took only a couple of hours, but the chilly sting of the air when Gary stepped out of the terminal felt both invigorating and alien. On his way into the city, he looked out and saw the Washington Monument and the dome of the Capitol. The city was clean and sophisticated and well maintained, and so were the people, with none of the bedraggled ostentation of New Orleans, the sagging wood-frame shotgun houses, the gaudy fashions, the public drunkenness. LCDC had put the Duncans up at the Albert Pick Motor Inn, a fashionably modern hotel on K Street, and Gary and Lynn walked into the glassy lobby as if through a portal to another world. From their downtown lodging, they could stroll past the White House and onto the National Mall, which lay under a crusty layer of snow.

Richard had warned them of the cold, so they had come with their heaviest clothing, but the snow was a novelty. Both Lynn and Gary had seen snow before; of the ten measurable snowfalls in New Orleans in the previous hundred years, three had been in their lifetimes. The air in Washington felt clean, without a hint of menace. The parish jail and Simple Battery and Leander Perez all seemed hazy, as insubstantial as the fog that flashed before Gary's face with each breath.[5]

Then, on the morning of January 17, the Duncans approached the Supreme Court Building. At first, it seemed no larger than the buildings around it, but as they approached the steps, its facade seemed to grow. The seated figures that flanked the path—the female Contemplation of Justice and the male Authority of Law—loomed over them and looked out at nothing with their blank eyes. Richard was waiting on the steps with Don Juneau and Al Bronstein. He looked alert and energized but not nervous. After a moment, they mounted the final steps and entered.

Gary seated himself in the audience area of the courtroom, which was surprisingly small—not much bigger than the one at Pointe à la Hache, although certainly better appointed. The counsel's table was startlingly close to the empty nine-seated bench. Others similarly filed in, mostly white people in suits and a few journalists. They sat all over, their voices echoing oddly in the lofty room. Richard had told Gary that there was at least one case to be argued before *Duncan v. Louisiana* that morning, but that each case would take only an hour, so he settled in. All at once, a gavel sounded; everyone in the room rose to their feet, and Gary joined them.

"The Honorable, the Chief Justice, and the Associate Justices of the Supreme Court of the United States," announced a singsong voice. "Oyez! Oyez! Oyez!"

As the voice droned on, Gary looked around at the elaborate trappings of justice. He glanced at Richard, whose face bore a statuesque look of determination.

"The Court is now sitting. God save the United States and this Honorable Court."

Gary felt expansive. He had made it.

———

"Mr. Chief Justice, and may it please the court," began Richard, "this case is here on appeal from the Supreme Court of Louisiana..."

The argument seemed to Gary as if it was over before it began. Richard had told him that it would last only half an hour and that there would be little in the specifics of the language that would make sense to a nonlawyer, and he was right. In fact, it was not so much a rehearsed argument as a conversation with the justices, especially with one (Abe Fortas, though Gary did not know that), who interrupted Richard often to clarify or interrogate or ask for an example. Gary saw most of the justices nodding along, and their questions, though incomprehensible, sounded encouraging. Richard, too, seemed confident and poised as he answered the questions.

Although Gary could not understand most of what was said, what he knew, he knew well: he had been entitled to a jury trial in his case, and that jury would need to be of his peers, not some assemblage of timorous whites and Perez cronies. On this point, he could follow Richard perfectly.[6]

"There's a five-man [jury] in certain cases?" asked a justice.

"Right," said Richard.

"And here there's no jury with the crime at all?" wondered the justice. He continued to ask if Louisiana would perhaps require twelve-member juries? Or six?

Most tellingly, several of the justices asked Richard to suggest a ruling. Barely ten minutes in, one of the justices had plainly said, "I think it would be easier for me if you tell me what you think we ought to decide. What rule should this court adopt?" By the time the chief justice asked Richard to sit down, it was clear that the argument had gone well.

Arguing for the state of Louisiana was Dorothy Wolbrette, who was a notable attorney in her own right. Graduating first in her class from Tulane Law School in 1945, she had been the editor in chief of the *Tulane Law Review,* recipient of the school's two highest honors, and among the first two dozen female attorneys licensed in New Orleans. She was a straight-forward litigator, smart but without much trial experience, conservative but not given to outbursts about states' rights. She looked tense, and her argument ran into trouble from the beginning.[7]

"The facts of this case are exceedingly simple," began Wolbrette (pro-nounced "wall-BRET-ee"). She said that Gary had admitted to making "in-tentional bodily contact" with Herman Landry. He had been given a fair trial, she said, and a fair sentence. And even if Richard was right, even if the Sixth Amendment applied to the states, Gary's sixty-day sentence did not come close to the six months of imprisonment that triggered a federal jury trial.

Justice Hugo Black, a Southerner and former Klan member who none-theless defied easy categorization, immediately tore into her argument. He asked if she really intended to argue that you would only know whether you deserved a jury trial after the sentence was imposed. Wolbrette kept saying "Yes" to Black's queries, but she was clearly wrong-footed.

"Wouldn't that be a very silly ruling in court?" asked Black, but Wolbrette redoubled her efforts to argue the matter. Precious minutes passed as Black made Wolbrette explain her position again and again. No sooner had Black finished than Chief Justice Earl Warren asked her whether her position might violate the protection against double jeopardy.

She admitted, "Well, frankly, Your Honor, I haven't researched that point."

Wolbrette kept her composure well, despite the missteps, at least for a while. She even managed to sneak in a winking reference to the crime of "wearing a hood in the streets except on Mardi Gras," which drew real laughter, despite being an actual statute, punishable by up to three years in prison.* But after twenty minutes of badgering, Wolbrette sounded defeated. She kept trying to go back to her central point: that the important thing about a criminal trial was not the presence or lack of a jury, but the fairness of the proceeding. But the justices were incredulous, asking where her idea of "fairness" came from and whether the Constitution would allow a judge to give the verdict in a death-penalty trial, for instance.

"What's your *principle* for which you're arguing?" asked Justice Fortas at last. "That's what I fail to get."

Wolbrette vacillated for a moment before replying, "Your Honor, Louisiana provides for the trial of a capital case *with* a jury."

"Yes, ma'am," affirmed Fortas, expecting her to answer his question. After a beat, he continued, "Is that your total answer, ma'am? I'm trying to find out what your view of the principle—"

She snapped back, "Well, I tried to answer, but you said that that wasn't the answer."

"—but if that's your answer to it, then that's alright." Fortas shrugged.

---

* It is still a crime in Louisiana to wear "a hood or mask." Exceptions are made in a few circumstances, including on Halloween and for people participating in "promiscuous masking on Mardi Gras."

Wolbrette continued arguing, without much more success. Fortas repeatedly brought her back to the issue of a death-penalty trial without a jury, asking again if she was "still prepared" to say that it was constitutional for a judge alone to convict and sentence a man to die. She tried to dodge the question and soldiered through her lengthy historical arguments until, mercifully, in the middle of some point she was trying to make about the Magna Carta and the colonial constitutions of Massachusetts and New Hampshire, a red light switched on, indicating that her time was up.[8]

Long before the light cut Wolbrette off, Gary knew that he had won. He had learned better than to trust the justice system, but he had trusted God, and he had trusted Richard. Watching Wolbrette struggle, though, he felt sure. He even felt a pang of vindication. "They laughed her right on out of there," he recalled with a grin fifty years later.[9]

That evening, Richard Sobol took the Duncans out to dinner at his hotel, luxuriating in the success of the day. For Gary, the day had had a significance beyond the apparent victory at the court; one moment outside of the courtroom had been almost more important than the oral argument. At lunch, he and Richard had gone down to the Supreme Court cafeteria, a windowless room in the basement. Being in the courtroom for the oral argument had not made Gary nervous—he had sat in courtrooms before—but the prospect of eating a meal with all the high-powered lawyers made him self-conscious; what would they think of him, this rough boatman from the bayou? He worried as they descended to the cafeteria that he would make some mistake, that they would discover his lack of sophistication and ridicule him.

But the cafeteria was just a cafeteria, and the lawyers talked with their mouths full and ate burgers with their hands. He wasn't so out of place after all, he reflected, as he and Richard chatted and laughed.

25—If It Ain't True, It Oughta Be

G ARY AND RICHARD had just returned to New Orleans when the trial
in Richard's lawsuit began. Amsterdam's hotel room was LCDC's
command center for *Sobol v. Perez*. There, surrounded by legal texts, stacks
of motions, and pads of paper piled high alongside the stubs of cheap cigars
and empty cans of Diet Rite, Amsterdam worked the machinery behind the
scenes that would allow Bronstein to focus on the theatrics of the courtroom. During meals and late into the night, Amsterdam would research and
write up new sets of documents, ready for filing if necessary. It was a daunting task—he expected to write as much as a hundred longhand pages a day,
all of which would need to be typed up and made ready.

The case was saturated with lawyers. Every day in the courtroom, at least
eleven attorneys of record would introduce themselves. And because this
was a trial about the law, there were more than forty lawyers scheduled
to give testimony for one side or another. Still more lawyers filled the
courtroom, there because of a connection to the case or simply out of
curiosity.

The newest arrival on Richard's side was Owen Fiss. Tall and owlish, he
was a special assistant to John Doar, who ran the Civil Rights Division of
the Department of Justice. He had been sent from Washington to represent
the United States in the case.

The federal government does not usually join lawsuits like *Sobol v. Perez;*
there needs to be a compelling case such that the nation as a whole has
some stake in the case's outcome. Fiss wrote that the presence of lawyers like
Richard was crucial to "obtaining equal opportunity and equal treatment
for Negroes, and…insuring that all persons receive adequate representation
in legal proceedings." The prosecution of Richard, he argued, violated the

Equal Protection Clause of the Fourteenth Amendment—not Richard's right to equal protection, but that of his clients.

In fact, he added, Richard's prosecution would have a chilling effect on the important work of all out-of-state civil rights lawyers, which would further deny their clients (and future potential clients) equal protection of the laws. The best remedy, Fiss suggested, was to rule that it was unconstitutional to apply Louisiana's law against unlicensed legal practice to civil rights lawyers. In other words, all out-of-state lawyers should be protected from prosecutions like Richard's because that was the only way to make sure that all black Southerners could get their rights. It was a breathtakingly ambitious argument.[1]

Bronstein was glad to see the government join *Sobol v. Perez*. The presence of the United States on his side sent a strong signal about the gravity of the case. Personally, though, he didn't care for Fiss, who was the picture of a government lawyer: brilliant, cautious, buttoned-up. Fiss was the same age as the LCDC lawyers and every bit as sharp, but his style didn't fit in with their improvisatory panache.[2]

On the eve of the trial, preparation intensified. Lolis Elie was selected as Richard's lead-off witness, since he was the best positioned to speak about the difficulties faced by civil rights activists and black lawyers in Louisiana. He was articulate, calm under pressure, and a natural storyteller. Leading with Elie made a statement about the scope of the suit: it was not only about Richard, but about the ability of black people to fully enter Louisiana society.

In the chaotic hotel room, Bronstein and Amsterdam interrogated Elie, simulating the pressures of a hostile cross-examination. For hours they pressured him with questions about his "association" with Richard, his legal practice, and the state of racial equality (Wasn't his very presence in the room a testament to how few barriers blacks actually faced?).

"Wouldn't you agree," Amsterdam shot at him, "that the legal posture of African-Americans in Louisiana has much improved over the past decade?"

Elie fixed Amsterdam with a "warlike stare" for an uncomfortably long time. At last, he said, "They'd better not ask me that question anytime short of two and a half hours before the lunch break."

Everyone laughed, but Elie spoke in earnest—it was a lecture he was eager to give.[3]

———

On the morning of January 22, just five days after Richard's argument before the Supreme Court, lawyers made their way through the damp chill to the dilapidated courthouse on Royal Street. The courtroom was spacious, and it needed to be. More than a dozen men crowded on the far side of the bar, and others filed into the audience. There were reporters from all the local papers and from New York, Washington, and Los Angeles. Important figures in the state's legal community showed up, as did a few staunch Perez supporters. Barbara Sobol's father even came down to watch. Henry Schwarzschild sat near the front, as did Gary Duncan.

A young lawyer named Armand Derfner walked in with his girlfriend. He was just beginning his job running the LCDC office in Mississippi, and his first decision had been to come to New Orleans to observe *Sobol v. Perez,* thinking it would be a good way to learn about the legal world he was stepping into. Derfner was born on the run as his parents fled Hitler from eastern Europe to France and then, on his second birthday, to the United States. That experience had, more or less logically to him, led to his involvement in the civil rights movement, and he was excited to embark on his first full-time job as a movement lawyer.[4]

He was also excited to see several of his role models in action. Amsterdam, Bronstein, and Richard were "elders" by the time Derfner came south, and being in the courtroom with them was invigorating. After he and Mary slid into the back row, Derfner looked to his left, where he saw an older, well-dressed white man with a Panama hat and a cigar, studying a booklet of some sort. He had never seen Leander Perez before, but the Judge's image was famous—compact and intense, the embodiment of everything Derfner reviled. Feeling a little brave, Derfner asked Perez what he was reading and gestured at the booklet in his hand. Without speaking, Perez tilted the cover towards him; it was the latest annual report of the ACLU.[5]

The proceedings opened with a testy back-and-forth—there were a lot of lawyers, and not all of them could get the last word—before Lolis Elie was called to the stand. He testified for hours, covering his professional history, observations of the civil rights movement, and feelings on Gary Duncan's case.

Before long, Bronstein asked whether Elie or his partners had been intimidated or threatened.

"Well, first off, our office was bombed," said Elie, before launching into a litany of abuses he had suffered, from the petty (hearings scheduled on holidays, when the courts were closed) to the monstrous (being tear-gassed in a church by the state police). As he spoke, Bronstein urged him on, guiding him into giving the names of individual members of the legal community whose racist actions had marred his career: Bascom Talley, former president of the Louisiana Bar Association, who refused to shake Robert Collins's hand in public; Robert Reston, who was a known member of the Klan; and John Rarick, the judge whom Perez had helped elect to the US Congress in the previous year, whose mistreatment of Elie was especially poignant.

"My first day in Clinton, Louisiana, Judge Rarick said to me, 'I didn't know they let you coons practice law,'" Elie told the court. "Judge Rarick kept a Ku Klux Klan cross that had been burned in his office." His soft voice rose and fell in a preacherly lilt as he went on to describe how Rarick had laughed at a mock bomb that had been planted on Elie's car during a hearing, calling it a "good practical joke." Elie added that Rarick refused to refer to black people with anything but racial epithets and encouraged policemen on the stand to use slurs in their testimony. Most shockingly, he described how Rarick had "pointed to a tree outside, and he said…that one time there was a Negro sheriff in Clinton, and he had been removed and hanged on that tree outside of his window."

"I went up to a place called Arcadia, Louisiana, in Bienville Parish," Elie continued, describing how he had traveled with two white LCDC attorneys. "We were told to have a seat. In the meantime, they brought out cattle prods. This was quite a display—they put them where we could see them. We knew now that we could expect trouble. I might add that the case we were concerned with was that of a Negro who had been sentenced to six months in jail for drinking out of a white water fountain in the courthouse. We decided that, since I was the only Louisiana lawyer present, I should do the talking. After a half hour, the sheriff said to come in. We went in and I said, 'Sheriff—', and he said, 'Nigger, shut up your mouth.'"

Sidney Provensal tried to cut in, but Elie was not finished. "I was not permitted to open my mouth in that room, and the white lawyers…they had to do the talking. I could not talk, and it was said to me, 'Nigger, don't you come back in here again. Let these white people take care of this.'

"Civil rights workers and other people in that kind of work have no confidence whatsoever in white attorneys in the state of Louisiana," he continued a few minutes later. As for the white community, "The vast majority of them would say that they are completely opposed to any kind of direct action, any kind of marches, any kind of picketing, and that sort of thing…the white people were unadulteratedly opposed to civil rights organizations and people engaged in them."[6]

For Anthony Amsterdam, the moment was revelatory. Elie was giving the lecture he had promised the night before, describing the current state of affairs for black people in Louisiana. It was, Amsterdam thought as the normal time for lunch came and went, the finest speech on civil rights he had ever heard.[7]

When the court at last broke for a midday recess, the LCDC group went out to a late lunch—except Amsterdam, who insisted on working through the break and never ate lunch anyway. Schwarzschild, Collins, Elie, and Bronstein carried on a boisterous conversation; Richard and Nils Douglas were quieter but still clearly pleased with the morning's testimony. Armand Derfner had been mesmerized by Elie's stories, especially about John Rarick. Reporters in the courtroom had scribbled intensely as Elie accused Rarick, a sitting US congressman, of shocking conduct on the bench.[8]

Derfner asked about the story with the black sheriff and the tree. "Is that really true?"

Elie looked at him knowingly and said, "Well, if it ain't, it oughta be!"[9]

———

Elie's testimony encapsulated the main questions of *Sobol v. Perez,* questions that were essential not only to Richard's case, but to an understanding of the changing civil rights movement in the late 1960s. Who counted as a "civil rights lawyer"? What was the role of a civil rights lawyer? Was it simply to enforce the undeniable edicts of the Supreme Court and Congress, or was it broader and less clearly defined than that? Did Northern lawyers need to come into the South to do that work, or would local attorneys suffice? Were civil rights lawyers activists or advocates or just working attorneys with a specialty, like tax lawyers or in-house counsel? And what would constitute harassment of these lawyers? Was an arrest harassment, even if it could be justified under the law? Were threats of prosecution or professional disciplinary action harassment? Was using a slur in court? Or delaying a case?

Lurking under these questions was suspicion: those on Richard's side were suspicious that anything done by the Louisiana establishment was a covert attempt to preserve segregation, and those on Perez's side were suspicious that outside groups were using racial strife to advance a larger agenda that had nothing to do with social justice. Many white Southern lawyers also felt that they had been prejudged, that Richard and his ilk simply assumed that they were all racists and rubes.

It was this last point that had caused the Louisiana Bar Association to intervene in *Sobol v. Perez,* after long months of holding out for fear of association with Perez. In trial, in all its filings, and with the press, the Louisiana Bar took pains to separate themselves from the distasteful named defendant, asserting again and again that they had weighed in "for the sole purpose of defending and protecting two Louisiana statutes" from being thrown out along with Richard's prosecution.[10]

At the root of the questions and suspicions—really, at the root of the entire case—was a single issue: What was a "civil rights case"? Obviously, desegregation and voting cases were quite literally about the legal rights of citizens, which is the textbook definition of "civil rights." Criminal cases could be almost as clear-cut: the defense of an activist arrested for disturbing the peace at a nonviolent demonstration, for instance. But where was the line between case law and advocacy? What was the distinction between incitement and activism, between civil disobedience and mere lawbreaking? Neither Gary Duncan nor Richard Sobol had been arrested as part of a sit-in or a march. In what way were their cases about civil rights? What did people mean when they said "civil rights," anyway?

Lolis Elie spoke for nearly six hours before he was finally released. Though it was very late in the day, Robert Collins took the stand after his partner. Under cross-examination by Provensal, he was ready with his own answer to the lawsuit's central question.

"How in the world does [*Duncan v. Louisiana*] get to be a civil rights case?" asked Provensal.

"The prosecution of Mr. Duncan was for the purpose of depriving him of his equal rights and from the exercise of his rights as a citizen of the United States," Collins explained. "I would make the distinction between the many criminal cases where race is irrelevant—where the question of racial equality is irrelevant—[and] those cases involving race. [*Duncan v. Louisiana*] would be a civil rights case. To us, these cases are cases involving the very heart of our struggle. Our whole system of government is involved here. In other words, it is the vindication of the rights of Gary Duncan."

But Provensal was not listening. "Is it a civil rights case only because Duncan struck a white boy?"

"No." Collins sighed. "As I said, the elements of the civil rights case are to protect and vindicate the equal rights, again, in a racial context."

"What rights of Duncan were you protecting?" Provensal queried. "His right to strike somebody?"

"No. His right not to be frivolously prosecuted on admittedly a very trifling offense," said Collins, theatrically summoning the patience to explain what seemed so obvious. He went on to explain how the presence of Perez and school desegregation and racial tension were underlying every aspect of Gary's prosecution.[11]

A few minutes later, the court finally adjourned for the day. Gary Duncan himself lingered for a moment, reflecting on what he had witnessed. Collins, he thought, had been smooth and articulate, and Elie—he was a fighter and a preacher, black and unafraid of his own blackness in a room full of whites in suits. Gary had never seen anything quite like it.[12]

Even more than the oral argument at the Supreme Court, which had been on foreign soil and strangely distant from the facts of his life and his case, the proceedings on January 22 began to restore his confidence in the legal system. Leander Perez had sat in the audience, just like Gary had, just as much an observer of the court's workings as he was.

———

Afterwards, the lawyers retreated to Anthony Amsterdam's hotel room to strategize. They were exhausted and exhilarated. The testimony of Elie and Collins had gone better than they expected, and both had been able to offer eloquent, coherent explanations of the importance of the LCDC to the civil rights movement and the relevance of racial equality to Gary's case. The next day looked just as promising: Collins would lead off, followed by other civil rights lawyers and a professor from Emory University who had done a statistical study of out-of-state lawyers in civil rights cases.[13]

Amsterdam settled into a nest of soda cans and cigarettes to write up a new Proposed Findings of Fact and Conclusions of Law, based on the developments of the day. Surrounded by briefs, reference books, and notes, he expected to spend at least six or seven hours working on the document, which could run dozens of pages.

This was a Herculean task—really, an unreasonable one. No other lawyer had ever made a regular practice of it, but Amsterdam insisted. The neighboring hotel room had been turned into an ersatz law library, and he would sometimes send a secretary after some obscure volume. He wrote every page longhand, including all citations and references, tearing each page off when he was done with it. "I've filled up this page," he would announce, and someone would come to take it to be typed up. Then he would start on the next page. It would be typed, formatted, and ready to file by the time the other lawyers awoke in the morning.[14]

26—First and Foremost

THE "SOBOL CASE" was big news, partly because of the case's importance, but also because of the clash of outsized personalities. The name of Leander Perez had long sold copies of papers in New Orleans and, for the brief period of his national infamy, around the country. The story had transitioned from merely curious to newsworthy with the involvement of the Department of Justice, the Louisiana Bar Association, and the state. Reporters enjoyed Al Bronstein's aggressive style of advocacy and the gravitas of Owen Fiss.

Most of all, journalists responded to the stories of harassment related by activists, which was a key part of Bronstein's trial strategy. After Elie and Collins had finished, A. Z. Young told the court about Richard's deep involvement with the Bogalusa Voters League and his work on the Crown Zellerbach litigation, which had gained momentum that led to new suits and the involvement of dozens of lawyers in much the same way as Gary's prosecution had. Zelma Wyche, a black organizer and political candidate in Tallulah, testified to a litany of abuses that Richard had helped him overcome. Bronstein led Wyche through a shocking recitation: sixty-one blacks arrested for integrating a café, trumped-up assault and burglary charges at a gas station, arrests after blacks tried to enter the Tri-Parish Fair on "white day," a white man who drove his car into a crowd of black children and escaped without being charged, the many well-documented efforts at voter suppression, and the creation of a "neighborhood school" in the black community to effectively avoid desegregation. After each example, Bronstein asked Wyche who had handled the case, and each time, Wyche responded, "LCDC" or "Dick Sobol."[1]

At last, on the third and fourth days of trial, Bronstein called Gary Duncan and Richard Sobol to deliver the coup de grâce. Richard was calm as Bronstein questioned him and, maddeningly, calmer still on cross-examination, patiently answering Provensal's barbed questions in paragraphs of thought that allowed no space for interruption. He seemed almost lethargic as Provensal hammered on his supposed inadequacies as a lawyer (improbably, one of Perez's arguments was that Richard had provided counsel so deficient that it violated the Constitution). For his part, Gary was nervous about testifying: there were a lot of lawyers in the room, and he had been warned that he could be cross-examined by as many as four hostile lawyers, which he was. But, as before, his mother had insisted that he do the right thing, and she sat with him until his name was called. Once he took the stand, though, he felt secure. From the first question, Bronstein's confidence and authority put Gary at ease, and whenever cross-examination got testy or tricky, Bronstein would rise and strenuously object. Really, Gary reflected as he stepped down, testifying made him feel useful. Just as Richard had worked overtime to defend him from Perez, he could in turn protect Richard.[2]

Where Bronstein had centered his entire trial strategy on proving that Richard Sobol was indispensable to certain people in Louisiana, Owen Fiss, representing the government, focused on demonstrating the larger point that civil rights lawyers in Louisiana could not possibly do all the civil rights cases without outside help, and that Louisiana should be banned—or at least temporarily barred—from excluding out-of-state civil rights lawyers from its courts.

Legendary local civil rights lawyers took the stand as Fiss made his case. A. P. Tureaud and Earl Amedee spoke with authority on the difficulty of being a black lawyer in Louisiana, and they confirmed that they no longer took cases in Plaquemines Parish. Amedee said he had never returned to Plaquemines after Judge Perez told them to "use your damn head" about whether to leave Plaquemines and never return. Perez himself, in his deposition, had grimly recalled the confrontation with Amedee and his partner: "Apparently, they used their own judgment."[3]

As before, the definition of a "civil rights case" was both central and elusive. Virtually every one of the plaintiffs' dozen witnesses was asked to define the term at some point. Each side saw an advantage in this line of inquiry: where the centrality of the "civil rights case" was emphasized by Bronstein, Provensal hammered on its elusiveness. Indeed, Provensal's first question to Richard was "What is your definition of a civil rights case?"

The first part of Richard's answer was easy enough: "A civil rights case is a case that arises out of some effort to achieve racial equality." He knew, though, that this simple definition would not include Gary's case or many of the other cases he had worked on in his year and a half on the job, so he amended it. "Or in which case it is decided to use the courts towards that end."[4] This consequentialist definition was slipperier than it appeared. Any case at all could be a civil rights case, Richard implied, as long as the lawyers were using it to seek racial justice. Provensal, either missing an opportunity or consciously avoiding the issue, moved on to have Richard explain the relation of Gary's case to civil rights. But Richard had offered a flexible, lawyer-centric definition that should have troubled Provensal: a civil rights case is a case about civil rights, and even if it isn't about civil rights, it's a civil rights case if I treat it like one.

Just before Fiss finished calling his witnesses, on February 1, the sixth day of testimony, he produced an impressive array of documentary evidence. He filed depositions of civil rights lawyers and activists who had worked with the LCDC, revealing each one and adding it to a pile on the table in front of him. He filed hundreds of pages of records from the Unauthorized Practice of Law Committee. He filed letters, bus schedules, course catalogs from every law school in Louisiana, the Louisiana Bar Association's criteria for admission, race and socioeconomic census data from Plaquemines Parish and the state of Louisiana, and even a state highway map. Then he stooped over and emerged with three massive volumes of legal paper. The FBI had recovered thousands of pages from the Plaquemines courthouse: detailed "minute entries" and proceedings for every criminal and juvenile case in the parish from January 1, 1966, to December 31, 1967. Fiss filed them all.[5]

Amsterdam and Bronstein tried to stifle their laughter. All six feet and four inches of Fiss had disappeared behind the stack of documents, and, when he spoke to rest his case, his disembodied voice seemed to emanate from the evidence itself.[6]

At last, Provensal took over. His strategy was straightforward: in addition to calling Lea Perez, Darryl Bubrig, and Judge Leon up to defend themselves (he knew better than to risk the scandal of calling Judge Perez as a witness), he had found a collection of local white lawyers who were prepared to say that they had represented black defendants in Plaquemines Parish in the past, or at least that they would happily do so in the future. Each would be on the stand only long enough to affirm his* competency and willingness to take so-called civil rights cases, and then the next one would come up to do the same thing. In all, thirty-three lawyers, excluding the defendants themselves and the Plaquemines court staff, were waiting to testify for the defense. The effect was perhaps intended to be theatrical: a three-day march of eminently qualified lawyers, repeating their commitment to providing excellent legal services to anyone who needed them, regardless of race.

Amsterdam again found himself trying to keep from laughing when he saw a dozen or so of these lawyers, lined up on benches in the anteroom, waiting to testify. "I have never seen such a motley crew of characters in my life," he snickered nearly fifty years later, characterizing them as "of that particular breed of lawyer we once called an 'ambulance chaser.'" Exhausted after two weeks of all-nighters and witness preparation, Amsterdam thought that the collection of self-serious hacks was about as funny as anything he had seen in his life. He leaned in close to Bronstein and, struggling to keep from chuckling too hard at his own joke, said, "You know, if we wanted to clean out the defense's entire case, all we'd need to do is send a guy with a bandaged leg on crutches through here. These guys would follow him like the Pied Piper and hound him down the stairs into tort court!"[†]

Amsterdam did not need to resort to such underhanded tactics. Provensal seemed not to have properly vetted his witnesses, and many turned out to be

---

* They were all men.
† Indeed, many of the lawyers put on the stand by the defense revealed under cross-examination that their primary specialty was plaintiffs' personal injury.

far from ideal. After the lengthy, subtle testimonies given by distinguished attorneys and community leaders that had been the center of the plaintiffs' case, the defense was an embarrassment.[7]

Not all of the lawyers had even been included on the list of witnesses (Provensal admitted that "it didn't even occur to [him]" to call the first one until the night before the trial), and several of them, perhaps unused to being on the witness stand, crumpled in the face of hostile questioning.[8] Richard's lawyers understood this weakness and dug into it. Bronstein, in particular, was infamous for his inquisitorial zeal.

One by one, Fiss and Bronstein picked off the defense witnesses. Most disarmingly, Bronstein had three questions that he repeated to nearly every one of the lawyers: "Have you ever handled a case under Title II of the Civil Rights Act?" (referring to desegregation), "Have you ever handled a case under Title VII of the Civil Rights Act?" (referring to employment discrimination), and "Have you ever handled a case under the Voting Rights Act?"

The answers told the story: "No." "None." "No, I haven't." "I haven't, sir, no." "To my knowledge, no." "No, sir, never." "Not in the true sense of that." "Repeat the question?...No, I have never handled anything under that." "I have not." "Not that I can remember, sir." "I don't understand your question...Oh. No." And so on, for days.

Even those who had touted their civil rights bona fides to Provensal turned out to be misleading. One, who told the court he had been involved with "a civil rights case," clarified on cross-examination that he was referring to working on the *defense* in the grant-in-aid case, to support Perez's system of tuition vouchers. One told the court that he had raised what he considered to be civil rights issues in many cases in Plaquemines and then admitted he would not file any type of civil rights suit, musing that "any lawyer down there that did would be a darn fool."* One talked about his work on a "civil rights case" that turned out to be a dispute between two

---

* The man went on to say that he had specifically refused to bring a suit against the private schools in Plaquemines because he knew that white people in the parish often ran into trouble "if they didn't accede."

whites. Several, who did not claim to have actually handled civil rights cases, insisted that they would willingly take civil rights cases, as long as the clients could pay their hefty fees (every one of the lawyers admitted to accepting only paying clients, and several wondered aloud why no one had approached them with a civil rights case). Not one lawyer could answer honestly that he had practiced anything like civil rights law, and, generally, when asked directly whether he would accept a desegregation case, each lawyer admitted that he would not.[9]

Most memorable was a St. Bernard lawyer who assured the court several times that he did not "distinguish color in [his] law practice" and would willingly take "a case of a Negro who was exercising what he felt was his civil rights."

Bronstein had a single question for him: If civil rights workers came in to protest the segregated drinking fountains at the courthouse, would he represent them?

The man's answer came quick and firm: "I would not. I am a white man first and foremost."[10]

"I have no further questions," said the astonished Bronstein.

27—Workhorse

THERE WAS A tornado warning in Memphis, Tennessee, on April 3, 1968. Rain hammered the windows of Mason Temple, echoing dully in the huge and mostly empty church, as Martin Luther King Jr. pulled himself before the microphone, having seen his movement grow and then shatter, having made unthinkable strides towards racial equality, only now to be stymied by factionalism, fear, and cowardice.

His speech rambled as he recapped his message of economic activism, but he said little that his supporters had not heard before. Just days earlier, Lyndon Johnson had announced that he would not run for reelection, throwing the 1968 presidential campaign into turmoil. King had been disappointed that President Johnson, after aiding with the legislative triumphs of the mid-sixties, seemed as indifferent to arguments about structural inequality as every other white liberal, but King still worried that a wide-open election could free a path for someone far less friendly to King's increasingly socialist beliefs, like George Wallace or Ronald Reagan or Richard Nixon, all of whom had declared their candidacies.

Near the end of his speech, King seemed to grow despondent; he, who so rarely stumbled over a word, struggled to articulate a coherent idea. His thoughts spun like a flywheel. "Now it doesn't matter now," he said, searching. "It really doesn't matter." At last, he confessed to the crowd, "I don't know what will happen now. We've got some difficult days ahead. But it doesn't matter with me now."

Then, at once, the wheel caught. "Because," he said, his voice growing in force against the shaking thunder, "I've been to the mountaintop."

The crowd slowly began to rise to their feet.

"And I've looked over, and I have *seeeeen* the Promised Land!"

King had found his voice again.[1]

Less than twenty-four hours later, Dr. King was shot in the head by a crummy, embittered racist, and the eager tinder of America ignited. The conflagration spread to the Pacific and the Atlantic; it ran from Memphis up the Mississippi River to Minneapolis and down to the end of the river, to lower Plaquemines.

"Nigger in a casket! Nigger in a casket!" sang two girls as they ran down the hallway at Buras High School the next morning.

There was no violence in Plaquemines as there had been in more than a hundred towns and cities around the country. People were plenty angry and desperate, but this was still Perez country, and the threat of retaliatory violence or imprisonment at Fort St. Philip was too real. Members of the black community instead gathered in their churches to mourn, vent, and reaffirm their commitment to organization, empowerment, and equality.

Most Plaquemines whites were cagey about their feelings, but not these girls, who skipped as they sang. They ran up to a black seventh grader. "Nigger in a casket!" they crooned at her, so close she could feel their hot breath and hate.[2]

———

Perez was being introduced on national television: "Judge Leander Perez is the undisputed boss of Plaquemines—"

"Workhorse," corrected Perez.

"Workhorse," allowed William F. Buckley Jr., the show's host, with a grimace.

Buckley was only forty-two but had already spent fifteen years as the cerebral powerhouse behind a conservative intellectual movement that was at last beginning to take hold. He was founder and editor of the *National Review,* writer of a widely syndicated opinion column, and, since 1966, the host of *Firing Line,* on which Perez was his guest.

Even though both men identified as conservatives (and Catholics), Buckley did not bother concealing his disdain for the older man, who represented everything he thought needed to be purged from conservative politics: anti-Semitism, racism, conspiracy theory, Lost Cause mumbo jumbo, and pseudoscience. Buckley was hardly a warrior for racial equality—he had debated James Baldwin in 1965, arguing that the black community was responsible for most of its own problems outside the Jim Crow South—but he hated Perez at least as much as he hated Communism.

Perez's episode of *Firing Line,* titled "The Wallace Movement," was part of a series intended to expose the presidential candidacy of George Wallace for what Buckley saw it to be: the last stand of a failed generation of intellectually bankrupt bigots. That Perez had agreed to spar with the famously quick-witted Buckley was an indication either of the Judge's faith in his own intellect or of heedlessness.

National media outlets at the time were obsessed with trying to explain the appeal of an avowed segregationist like Wallace, who said things that were supposed to be disqualifying for mainstream candidates. The *New York Times Magazine*'s attempt a week before Perez went on *Firing Line* was titled "Wallace Figures to Win Even If He Loses." Buckley, on the other hand, was less interested in explaining Wallace than in discrediting him.[3]

The episode did not go well for Perez. Though his posture and expression were a study of easy confidence, he puffed a little too compulsively on his cigar to keep up the illusion. His face looked as craggy as ever, but jaundiced.

The Judge tried to stick to his talking points: no blacks in Plaquemines Parish had complained about anything; the last time he looked, it was cities in the North that were being burned down by irate mobs. He "guaranteed" that eight black men had been hired for every white man on parish construction projects—Millions of dollars of construction! Tax-free!—and generally avoided talking directly about George Wallace.

Perez put up just enough of a fight for Buckley to seem interested in taking him down. Buckley turned to the Civil Rights Act, the Voting Rights Act, and school desegregation. After bringing up each topic, he would let Perez ramble, predicting correctly that his opponent would be unable to refrain from explaining convoluted theories about Communist agents, the inherent immorality of black people, and the "strictly gestapo-style" incursion of hundreds of federal agents in the South. All the while, the cameras alternated between Perez's unhinged ravings and Buckley's expressive face, contorted into contemptuous grimaces, furrowed brows, and bug-eyed expressions of disbelief.

"Judge Perez," Buckley said in response to a tired point about *Brown v. Board of Education,* "your ignorance is staggering." Perez merely smiled at the insult, but he seemed genuinely unprepared for what followed. The audience, young and urban and intellectual, began to laugh at him.

"It's been said of you," Buckley said at another point, "that you can grudgingly admire his blunt talk. He is honest about his bigotry."

"I am not a bigot, sir," Perez replied, and the audience chuckled. He drew himself up. "I am not a bigot at all!"

The laughter spread and grew, and Buckley waited until it died to deliver his next strike. "Look, whatever you are, Judge Perez—and I'm sure you're a good many things—what you don't have is sovereign power over the English language."

The episode ended with a final round of derisive laughter, and Judge Perez stepped into the fifth and final act of his life. In half a century of public life, he had gone from upstart reformer to builder of dreams to political powerhouse to national symbol of an entire racist ideology and then, at last, to has-been—a sallow, embarrassing reminder of a barbaric past.[4]

28—Profound Judgment

DESPITE THE SOBERING loss of the civil rights movement's most prominent leader, the lawyers could not afford to break stride. Soon after the trial in *Sobol v. Perez* ended, after ten full days of testimony over three weeks, Fiss had returned to Washington, Amsterdam to Philadelphia, and Bronstein went to Cambridge to begin teaching at Harvard. Richard, now the senior lawyer in LCDC, could at last return to his busy docket of cases.

But the attorneys on his team were not done with the case yet. Amsterdam filed an exhaustive brief, the fruit of his all-nighters during the trial, detailing the history of LCDC, Gary Duncan's status as a civil rights client, and a narrative of Richard's triumphant record in civil rights cases. The finished document ran 139 pages, with a hundred footnotes, the last of which sprawled for seven paragraphs. It was, Richard recalled more than fifty years later, "the most incredible intellectual work I have ever seen."[1]

Fiss piled his own work on top of Amsterdam's. Where Amsterdam, as Richard's lawyer, had focused mostly on his client's particular benefit to the community and the specifics of LCDC and Gary's case, Fiss presented the issues with the vision of a wide-angle lens. Methodically, with dozens of citations to cases and laws, Fiss built an argument around the central questions of *Sobol v. Perez,* leading off with a three-part definition of "the civil rights case." He documented the challenges to lawyers taking those cases and how those challenges were met, each point building inexorably to his conclusion: without LCDC, and without Richard, the state of racial justice in Louisiana would have been far worse than it was. But, he wrote, just stopping Perez from prosecuting Richard would not "serve to eliminate the full scope of the chilling effect of the prosecution against Sobol."[2]

What the United States sought, Fiss wrote, was "to prohibit the application of [the unlicensed-practice-of-law statute] to lawyers representing persons in civil rights cases." If adopted, this proposal would provide extraordinary protections to every civil rights lawyer in Louisiana. And because Fiss based his request on the premise that the Louisiana law was unconstitutionally vague without an explicit exception for all civil rights lawyers, there would be no time limit to the order's effectiveness. It would, as Fiss described it, "establish a constitutional safety zone" for civil rights law.[3]

The urgency of *Sobol v. Perez* was redoubled when Ben Dawkins, a cranky federal judge, all but threw Richard out of court on February 20, warning him against returning. Six days later, Dawkins sent a letter to the state's federal judges and to Richard, stating that it was now the official policy of the US District Court for the Western District of Louisiana to require that the primary lawyer on every case in his district be a member of the Louisiana Bar Association. Along with a copy of that letter, Dawkins personally sent Richard a lengthy argument against the necessity of out-of-state lawyers and about his general skepticism about the new breed of civil rights cases.[4]

But even Dawkins could not deny that Richard was on the right side of his cases. Just as he was sabotaging Richard's ability to practice in his district, Dawkins handed down an important victory. In early January, he had ruled against voting officials in Madison Parish for their flouting of the Voting Rights Act, and later that month, during the *Sobol v. Perez* trial, he nullified the entire Madison Parish School Board election from 1966. In the late winter, Dawkins allowed another voting case to go forward against Madison Parish, this time challenging the 1967 election.[5]

As Richard waited for decisions in *Duncan v. Louisiana* and *Sobol v. Perez,* he kept a wary eye on national politics. America remained on edge after Dr. King's assassination. In January, the devastation of the Tet Offensive had reduced confidence in the war effort in Vietnam and exposed a fault line within the Democratic Party between moderate party loyalists and the young, vibrant anti-war movement. George Wallace was continuing his openly racist third-party campaign, aiming to sweep the disgruntled Democrats of the Deep South. And Richard Nixon was surging, having won the first few Republican primaries on his platform of "an all-out, federal-state-local crusade against crime," by which he meant increased surveillance, "full support" of law enforcement, and a war on drugs. Looking at the ongoing (and televised) incidents of civil unrest in cities from coast to coast, it was easy to see why Nixon's message was connecting with people.[6]

Many civil rights workers despaired at the sharp turn in politics. Foreign wars and "law and order" were in; racial equality was out. In the mid-sixties, wrote a longtime movement leader, "most people, if asked to identify the nation's most compelling social problem, would have said 'civil rights.' Today the answer is more likely 'Vietnam.'" And, Richard thought, the movement was continuing the path it had begun the previous year, splintering and giving over to anger. In the meantime, he watched in frustration as "some people [in the North] mistakenly thought that the job was done" and began to turn their attention elsewhere. The lead-up to the 1968 election perfectly encapsulated Richard's observation. Of the candidates, the only one who truly looked like a step forward for racial justice was Robert Kennedy, and that hope ended on June 6, when he was murdered in the kitchen of a hotel in Los Angeles.[7]

Despite the national-level ferment, the spring of 1968 was good for the legal battle over racial equality in Louisiana. In addition to the election lawsuits in Madison Parish, Richard won an order to fully desegregate the faculty in the public schools in Bogalusa, as well as the repeal of the city's latest anti-demonstration ordinance.[8] The white union at the Crown Zellerbach paper mill in Bogalusa had voted to strike when the company made some token concessions to black workers, but a federal court stopped the strike, then declared the concessions themselves so inadequate that they violated the Constitution, and then finally stated that the entire system of separate black and white unions was illegal, all in the space of four months.[9]

In May, Richard won two important appeals in the Fifth Circuit, one that protected criminal defendants and one that fully desegregated a recalcitrant bowling alley that Richard had been suing since he arrived in New Orleans. Most triumphantly, John Minor Wisdom wrote his third and most scathing grant-in-aid opinion, which finally dismantled Perez's system of tuition vouchers. Perez himself had been the attorney for the sneakiest and most recent iteration of grant-in-aid—this time called the Louisiana Education Commission for Needy Children, ostensibly set up to help with "juvenile delinquency"—but Wisdom saw through the ruse. "The purpose of Act 99 of 1967," he wrote, "like the purpose of its predecessors, is to give state aid to private discrimination." With those words, Perez's dream of a dual school system, financed by the state, disappeared.[10]

Then, early in the afternoon of May 20, Richard got a telegram from the clerk of the Supreme Court:

RICHARD B SOBOL LAWYERS CONSTITUTIONAL DE-FENSE COMMITTEE AMERICAN CIVIL LIBERTIES UNION 606 COMMON ST NRLNS (MZ)

JUDGMNT GARY DUNCAN AGAINST LOUISIANA RVERSED TODAY CASE REMANDED OPINION AIR-MAILED[11]

The first thing he did was call Gary.

———

Mazie Duncan's faith had been vindicated. Though it had taken her son almost two years and a trip to the Supreme Court to get justice, God had rewarded the family for its tenacity. Gary had survived the ordeal without so much as losing his job—in fact, he was working as a captain now and making good money. She had been frightened, but her belief in what was right had never wavered.

It made all of the Duncans additionally proud that Gary's name would be affixed to a landmark decision of the highest court. Richard explained to them that *Duncan v. Louisiana* had extended the right to a jury trial to millions of people. The case had changed the accepted interpretation of the Constitution, he told them, and it had created a binding precedent, one that every court and legislature in the United States needed to obey.

In his majority opinion, Justice Byron White was clear about the reasons for applying the jury clause to the states. "The guarantees of jury trial," he wrote for the 7–2 majority, "reflect a profound judgment about the way in which the law should be enforced and justice administered. A right to jury trial is granted to criminal defendants in order to prevent oppression by the Government." But White did not leave it at that; the jury, he continued, was specifically "an inestimable safeguard against the corrupt or overzealous prosecutor and against the compliant, biased, or eccentric judge."

As forceful as the opinion was, it left some questions unanswered. The option of a jury trial was now required for all "serious crimes" but not for "petty offenses." The court stopped short of defining precisely where that line was. White mentioned many times that federal courts gave jury trials when the maximum punishment was greater than six months or $500,[*] but he explicitly declined to impose that interpretation on state courts. It was also unclear how many people needed to make up a jury, whether that jury needed to reach a unanimous verdict, or whether there were any specific rules for how the jury should be selected—those questions were for future courts to answer. But without *Duncan,* there would be no grounds for asking those questions in the first place.[12]

Now that a power higher than Perez had interceded, Mazie Duncan believed, there was nothing any segregationist in Plaquemines or Louisiana or the whole United States could do to bring this injustice back on her son. So it was undoubtedly a surprise when she learned that Lea Perez intended to prosecute Gary again—and, again, without a jury.

---

[*] About $4,000 today. Current federal rules set the bar at six months or $5,000.

29—Tranquility

JUST AFTER THREE o'clock in the afternoon, central time, on July 20, 1969, Neil Armstrong and Buzz Aldrin eased the Apollo 11 lunar module onto the surface of the moon. It was a tense, triumphant moment in the history of a curious species and an emphatic victory in the Cold War proxy battle in space. For more than six hours, the astronauts sat in the cramped capsule before Armstrong finally emerged to take a few awkward steps on the powdery ground. A few moments later, he got a call from President Nixon.

The event was televised. On the split screen, Nixon appeared in profile, the Oval Office phone clamped to his ear. Armstrong looked bulbous and alien beside him.

"For every American this has been the proudest day of our lives," said the president. "As you talk to us from the Sea of Tranquility, it inspires us to redouble our efforts to bring peace and tranquility to Earth. For one priceless moment, in the whole history of man, all the people on this Earth are truly one."

Earth, though, felt fractured. Sixteen thousand Americans had died in Vietnam in 1968, and 1969 was poised to be almost as bloody. A police raid on a gay bar in New York City turned violent and brought another minority group permanently into the broader struggle for equal justice. Racial equality remained elusive; at the moment of Armstrong's first step, a gang of whites in York, Pennsylvania, were chanting "White Power!" Leading the chant was a police officer who, according to several witnesses, also handed out bullets with instructions to kill black people. If anyone thought he was being hyperbolic, the murder of a twenty-seven-year-old black woman by a mob of more than a hundred whites silenced their doubts. The case was dropped for thirty years.[1]

———

On July 22, 1968, the federal court in New Orleans handed down its decision in *Sobol v. Perez;* its unanimous opinion was clear and forceful: Richard's prosecution "can only be interpreted as harassment." The judges went on to echo Al Bronstein's argument from the trial: "The prosecution was meant to show Richard that civil rights lawyers were not welcome in the parish, and that their defense of Negroes…would not be tolerated. It was meant as a warning to other civil rights lawyers and to Negroes in the parish." Richard had won.

But the victory's impact was limited: the court declined to address the constitutional issues raised by Owen Fiss. The charges against Richard had been filed "without basis in law or fact," the court found, and there was no reason to examine the constitutionality of a law when that law had been wrongfully applied.[2] In practice, though, *Sobol v. Perez* set an important precedent: arresting a civil rights lawyer for practicing law without a license would no longer work as a form of harassment or intimidation.[*]

Richard had stated during trial that he intended to leave New Orleans by the end of 1968, and so he did. Before he departed, he tried to leave the office in good order, but that was easier said than done. The successful conclusion of his lawsuit and Gary's Supreme Court case crossed a couple of items off the LCDC docket, but not many. There were dozens of cases pending, including massive undertakings like *Hicks v. Crown Zellerbach,* the groundbreaking employment discrimination suit. There was no way that all

———

[*] This result was soon put to the test. Shortly after the conclusion of Richard's case, Armand Derfner was arrested in Holly Springs, Mississippi, for practicing law without a license. When Derfner was in jail, Al Bronstein called the district attorney and said, "Look, we can try this in federal court again. Last time it took six weeks. We're happy to see you in court." Derfner was released, and the charge was dropped.

of this work would be finished by the end of December. Richard took the biggest cases with him, including *Crown Zellerbach,* but his successor would be coming into a situation not wholly different from the one that Richard encountered in 1966.

Certainly money was no easier to come by. LCDC had always been one step ahead of fiscal ruin, and matters had not improved by late 1968. The year before, LCDC had affiliated itself with the Roger Baldwin Foundation of the ACLU, which covered its overhead and some of its costs. The arrangement made sense; the ACLU had already bailed out LCDC several times with large stopgap donations, and the merger formalized that relationship. But Henry Schwarzschild and Al Bronstein found the ACLU meddlesome as overseers, especially when it came time to name Richard's replacement.

In the end, though, LCDC had no choice but to merge even more fully with the ACLU. This move included letting Schwarzschild go; it no longer made sense to maintain an independent New York office. So 1968, which saw some of LCDC's greatest legal victories, also left the organization with little institutional memory. With Bronstein, Schwarzschild, and Richard gone, there was almost no continuity. In fact, it would take several months to find a full-time replacement to lead the New Orleans office.

Richard didn't like leaving LCDC like that; he just didn't have a choice. He had accepted a professorship at the University of Michigan Law School, where he was to teach two courses: Constitutional Law and Fair Employment Law. (For the latter, the "textbook" was the files from the ongoing *Crown Zellerbach* case.) The Sobols packed their bags for Ann Arbor in December 1968 and said goodbye to their New Orleans life.[3]

Then Richard learned that Lea Perez wanted to prosecute Gary Duncan again.

———

There was nothing illegal about trying Gary a second time. The Supreme Court had overturned the original conviction and sent the case back to

Judge Leon, but it had not protected Gary from the battery charge. Perez had been free to start a new trial, this time with a jury. Practically speaking, no one thought it likely that the parish would waste its time on such a thing. And both Richard and Gary felt confident that a jury would never find him guilty, anyway.

No jury was convened, though. What happened was more sinister: after the Supreme Court's decision in *Duncan,* the Louisiana legislature had quietly reduced the maximum sentence for Simple Battery from two years to six months, the length of time repeatedly cited in Justice White's opinion as a reasonable dividing line between "serious crimes" and "petty offenses." Only then did Perez announce that he intended to prosecute Gary again. With the new, lower penalty, Gary's charge did not entitle him to a jury; he would be tried again in front of Judge Leon. (There is no record of whether Judge Perez, the "third house of the legislature," had anything to do with changing the battery statute.)

Gary's persecution was not limited to the courthouse. He was pulled over for speeding one day by a man in a suit who claimed to be a plainclothes deputy; instead of writing a ticket, though, the man arrested Gary and took him to jail. Another time, Lynn's brother, Calvin Lange, was harassed while borrowing Gary's car. He had stopped at a gas station when the police rolled up, threw him against the side of the car, handcuffed him, and hauled him to the Port Sulphur jail. When he complained, they asked if he was kin to Gary Duncan. He was charged with reckless driving and disturbing the peace and given a citation for "polluting the air." Then, when Gary showed up in the audience section of the courtroom to support a cousin, Judge Leon spied him in the back row and announced with mock reverence that "Mr. Gary Duncan is back there. He is living on a pension, and he has been to Washington, DC—to the Supreme Court!"[4]

Richard was apoplectic. "I said to myself, 'There is no *way* I'm going to let them re-prosecute Gary,'" he recalled. Before he left for Michigan, he filed another lawsuit against Perez, claiming that this further prosecution of Gary could have no purpose other than harassment. The suit, *Duncan v. Perez,* demanded that a federal judge put a permanent end to the battery case, which was beginning to feel like it would never go away. During his time at the University of Michigan, Richard sent regular letters to Gary, updating him on the case.[5]

By mid-1969, Richard was feeling a little bit lost. His time as a professor was not happy. Barbara hated Ann Arbor, and Richard barely spent any time there. His marriage felt like it was falling apart. He found the professors cold, and few of them shared his values. Whenever he could get away, he flew to New Orleans to continue his legal work: many of his lawsuits, including the *Crown Zellerbach* employment-discrimination case, were ongoing. Shortly after the semester began, Richard had already decided to move on, but to where? He had no intention of staying in Ann Arbor, but he couldn't think of a way to go back to New Orleans.[6]

Richard reconnected with Marian Wright, who knew him from the South, where she had worked at the NAACP Legal Defense Fund, right across the street from the Jackson LCDC office. A legendary civil rights lawyer—and the first black woman admitted to the Mississippi Bar—Wright had just founded the Washington Research Project, a law firm that advocated for poor children and families. Wright was a good connection for Richard to have (she would later become famous under her married name, Edelman, as the founder and director of the Children's Defense Fund), and Richard took a job as co-director, though he was still litigating cases in New Orleans. In June, he moved alone into an apartment in Washington. Barbara settled nearby with Joanna and Zachary.[7]

His personal life was not what he had wanted it to be; neither was his job. Richard believed in the mission of the Washington Research Project, but after two years at LCDC, the work felt awfully abstract. Wright wanted to focus on big-picture issues; there was none of the daily interaction with clients that had made Richard's experience with LCDC so invigorating. He was reminded of the difference constantly: when he flew to New Orleans, he worked with Lolis Elie and Nils Douglas, went to court to argue motions, and met with clients, like Gary Duncan, who had become friends. Then he would board a plane to return to Washington, feeling the warm aura of affinity chill as he flew north.[8]

Richard and Al Bronstein worked together on Gary's new case, taking depositions and appearing in court. The judge, Fred Cassibry, had been one of the three assigned to *Sobol v. Perez,* so he was well aware of Gary's situation. Cassibry did not immediately rule in Gary's favor, though, saying he wanted Perez's team to have time to defend themselves. The case dragged on for months. Anthony Amsterdam assured his former colleagues that Perez stood little chance of ultimately winning, but Richard still worried. Gary, for his part, told Richard he'd take him out on a fishing trip in the Gulf when they won.[9]

Despite the disarray in his private life, 1970 was a good year for Richard as a lawyer. He finally went to trial in *Hicks v. Crown Zellerbach,* the groundbreaking employment-discrimination case he had filed back in 1966. It had always been his biggest case. After countless hearings, hundreds of hours of research, and thousands of pages of writing, the case came to a close. The judge (Heebe, who had also been on *Sobol v. Perez*) wrote a sweeping opinion affirming Richard's position on every issue. The court struck down Crown Zellerbach's use of standardized tests and required the company to take affirmative steps to equalize pay and promotions, even if that meant initially giving black employees bigger raises and more chances at advancement than whites.[*] To do otherwise, the opinion stated, was to violate Title VII of the Civil Rights Act.[10]

Richard won Gary's case against Perez, too. In a scathing opinion, Judge Cassibry wrote that the Duncan prosecution had been in bad faith from the beginning; the violation had been "so slight and technical as to be generally reserved for law school hypotheticals rather than criminal prosecutions."[†] At the end of the opinion, Cassibry left no doubt about his take on the case. "Duncan has waged an unprecedented four year fight to avoid conviction

---

[*] Crown Zellerbach dragged its heels on the case. Two months later, Judge Heebe, at Sobol's request, issued a "complete and comprehensive decree" that laid out exactly what the corporation was required to do. He also set an expiration date: the orders were in effect for ten years.

[†] The strong language was no accident; Judge Cassibry adopted almost verbatim the proposed order written by Bronstein and Sobol.

and incarceration on the charges against him," he wrote. "If Duncan were required to face retrial, it could constitute an unmistakable message to Negroes in Plaquemines Parish that it is unprofitable to step outside familiar patterns and to seek to rely on federal rights to oppose the policies of certain parish officials."[11]

By the time *Duncan v. Perez* was decided, "certain parish officials" were not in a position to see themselves so thoroughly rebuked. On March 19, 1969, Leander Perez had died of a heart attack.

———

After the death of a dictator, some societies undergo a period of chaos or backlash or infighting. But in Plaquemines Parish, remarkably, life continued mostly unchanged. Perez had peacefully transferred power to his son Chalin two years prior, and even if Chalin seemed not to have inherited his father's gift for politics, elections and council meetings were no more contested than they had been before. Desegregation continued despite continued heel-dragging, and white students began to return to the public schools. The academies would continue to operate for as long as another twenty years, but they functioned not as a parallel school system but rather as private schools everywhere do: as enclaves of relative privilege that have little real impact on the community. Schools have short memories, and as 1966 receded, more and more of the students who had been in the crucible of desegregation graduated and moved on. Black students joined team sports and student government, especially in the three downriver high schools: Port Sulphur, Buras, and Boothville-Venice. It was no utopia, but Plaquemines Parish had become an improbable success story in the frustrating history of school desegregation.[12]

The bars and restaurants, too, began to break the strict hold of segregation, though the races in such venues rarely mixed very much anywhere. With fewer barriers to getting licenses and permits, black men and women were able to open their own businesses more freely than they had before. Most importantly, the oil industry desegregated at last, and hundreds of black men went to work in the oil fields. There were striking inequalities between black and white workers after the oil companies dropped their racial criteria, but members of the black community could finally direct their tireless work ethic at a single job that paid well enough to comfortably raise a family. Ask a black man older than sixty when Plaquemines took its biggest step towards racial equality, and he will more than likely say it was when Chevron desegregated.[13]

But in the summer of 1969, Plaquemines had a more urgent problem. A hurricane in the Gulf had swung to the west, putting its path directly through the delta.

———

Early in his tenure at the Washington Research Project, Richard knew he needed some time away—from the office and from his life. He had worked almost nonstop for the past five years, and he finally had some time on his hands.

So he left the office, Washington, and the country. He flew with a friend to England, where they rented motorcycles and started to ride.

He had only a vague idea of what he wanted to do. "I wanted to play out the *Easy Rider* story," he recalled fifty years later, referring to the iconic biker film starring Peter Fonda and a very young, rakish Jack Nicholson. He was taken with the freedom embodied in the film: the open road, the chugging engines, the sense of possibility. All of that seemed great.

Richard and his friend rode until they got tired, then they pitched tents on the side of the road. The first day was a little disappointing, if he was honest; riding a motorcycle all day was less romantic than it had seemed in the movie. He slept poorly and awoke early.

"In the morning, the world opened up," he recalled, his eyes growing wide at the memory. "We didn't know where the hell we were, but we knew we were *somewhere*."

From England, the two men made their way to France and Spain and down to North Africa, riding on old roads through little towns and lonely fields.

One day, in Morocco, a local man invited them to stay for a while, so they did. They talked and laughed and took in the scenery. Later that day, the man guided them up to the top of a nearby hill. They could see for miles.

"There it is," the man said, gesturing to the vast landscape around them. "You can go anywhere from here."

And Richard thought to himself that the man just might be right.[14]

30—A Clean Storm

And thou, all-shaking thunder,
Strike flat the thick rotundity o' th' world,
Crack nature's moulds, all germens spill at once
That make ingrateful man!
—Shakespeare, *King Lear*

HURRICANE CAMILLE TOOK a boomerang path, scooting across the Atlantic Ocean from Africa as a wave of low pressure and then intensifying and banking around the westernmost tip of Cuba before making its return leg through the southeastern United States.

Camille was compact, its eye so small it was difficult to see from the air, and meteorologists struggled to make sense of the storm, though they clearly saw the preconditions for rapid intensification: unusually warm water and low wind shear. Sure enough, Camille doubled in strength in twelve hours, becoming a Category 2 hurricane as it rounded Cuba. By the end of the next day, the storm was officially Category 5, headed for somewhere on the Gulf Coast, where it was expected to make landfall on Sunday night, August 17, 1969.[1]

The vote to evacuate lower Plaquemines Parish was made immediately and without debate. By Saturday afternoon, more than twenty-four hours before the storm made landfall and ten hours before the Weather Bureau announced even a hurricane watch in the area, the Plaquemines sheriff had cruisers rolling up and down the road from Empire to Venice, loudspeakers announcing the evacuation warning.[2]

The echoes of Betsy were undeniable to people in Boothville. The droning voice coming from the police cars, the rush ashore of oil workers, even the air was the same. This time, the Duncans did not need to discuss their plan. Lambert and Mazie herded their children and grandchildren together, piled into cars, and set out up the road.[3]

They were joined on the road by their neighbors, black and white, who had crowded into cars to make the slow trek up to New Orleans or Jefferson Parish, escorted by deputies with their lights flashing.

Somewhere among the ten thousand people in the snaking queue with the Duncans was Parnell Latham, who had been named head of the Plaquemines Chamber of Commerce after he finished helping with the creation of Seaway Academy, which was not fated to survive the storm. Wilbur Buras and F. J. Smith, the deputies who had arrested Gary Duncan four times, were among the police escort. Also in the crowd was Darryl Bubrig, the Duncan case a distant memory in a promising early career that would eventually lead him to the office of the district attorney. There, too, were the pastors in Boothville whose political efforts had paid off in the massive voting drives of 1968 and 1969, though it would fall to the next generation to finally change the rigged political system on the peninsula. In with the Duncans was Bert Grant, who was the star of the Boothville-Venice basketball team. Elsewhere was Bernard St. Ann, who had dropped out of school shortly after the incident on the road. Their tormentors on that day three years before were also in line: Herman Landry and Randolph and Wayne Scarabin. Wayne would survive this storm only to die at Port Eads thirty-six years later in Hurricane Katrina.[4]

Gary had changed in the four years since he rode out Betsy in the marina. He was a father now, and a husband. He felt like he had been tested by his ordeal in the courts, and he had survived by relying on his family and Richard Sobol and God. His faith had been tested, too, and there had been some moments so low that even thinking of them caused a black knot to gather in his gut—he could still feel the sensation of sinking through the courtroom floor after hearing the guilty verdict, and he could call up the terrifying emptiness that bloomed inside him during his late-night arrest.

But just as indelible in his memory were moments of joy and victory: the births of his children, eating lunch in the Supreme Court cafeteria, watching Al Bronstein demolish Perez's witnesses on the stand, hearing from Richard that they had won his case. In the car with him were his family, and there was nothing Perez could do anymore to hurt them.

The Duncans passed over the canal that divided Plaquemines Parish from the mainland, and the convoy of their neighbors broke up. Evacuees scattered to motels and the homes of family and friends, leaving behind only a few stragglers.

———

Camille's winds were unprecedented. They seemed to change the laws of physics, creating a new, horizontal force for which neither human structures nor living things were prepared. The winds were never measured with complete accuracy, since they broke most of the gauges they contacted at their peak. What is undoubted is that Camille is the second most intense storm to hit the mainland United States and one of only two such hurricanes to make landfall at full Category 5 strength.

Camille sideswiped Plaquemines Parish before smashing the Mississippi coast, where it killed 137 people. As the storm boomeranged back towards Africa, it dumped thirty inches of rain on the Blue Ridge Mountains; another one hundred people died in floods and landslides there.

At the height of the flood, parts of Plaquemines were under sixteen feet of water. At Pass Christian, Mississippi, the surge reached 24.6 feet, far higher than Betsy's worst, and a record not exceeded until Katrina in 2005.[*]

Only three people died in Plaquemines Parish, a fact attributed to the

---

[*] Despite Katrina's record storm surge, Camille was far more intense.

unprecedented mobilization by parish authorities. In all, nearly eighteen thousand people successfully vacated the precarious land at the end of the Mississippi River. In lower Plaquemines, the evacuation was almost 100 percent effective.[5]

———

Camille left a clear, hot day in its wake, and the survivors began to investigate the damage. Where evacuees had spent the night, the storm had not seemed especially intense, and as they drove back down the road, what they saw confirmed their perceptions: up the road, Plaquemines Parish was untouched from Belle Chasse to the Empire bridge.

Down the road, there was nothing. Camille's fist had been tightly clenched. Empire was gone. Sunrise was leveled. In all of Buras, only six structures remained intact. Little was left of Boothville or Venice.

Gary returned once the floodwaters had receded to find that his trailer was gone. So was his brother's house, and his parents', which had survived Betsy without so much as moving from its blocks. There weren't even the fields of debris—the heaps of mud and matted marsh grass that usually washed up in a hurricane. Nothing was left of the Duncan property but the concrete slabs.

"Camille cleaned us out. Down in Boothville and Venice, there wasn't nothing to clean up," recalled a cousin of Gary's. "After Betsy, you could rebuild your home with all the lumber. After Camille, you couldn't find enough wood to start a fire."

"It was like looking at the desert," remembered a woman who lived nearby. "I mean, it looked like absolutely virgin land. Land that no person had set foot on before."[6]

Gary looked across the empty property, his home. It was as if he were one of those mad French explorers who landed there four hundred years ago, taking one first step out of his boat and onto the end of the earth. It was a good place to build, a good place to grow up and raise a family, a good place to work and grow old, even if it offered little protection. The almighty forces of destruction, Gary believed, were part of a scheme much bigger than he could comprehend, but he also knew they had the power to renew in equal proportion to their ruin—because there are two kinds of storms in Plaquemines Parish, Louisiana: there are dirty storms, and there are clean storms.

Epilogue

In late July 1970, Richard returned to the United States, having completed his motorcycle sojourn. Life wasn't bad. He went back to work at the Washington Research Project, where he was comfortable and friendly with everyone. He met and fell in love with a law student named Anne Buxton. Cases kept coming, and he kept working on them, including his litigation from Louisiana, so he shuttled back and forth between Washington and New Orleans.

The civil rights scene was beginning to shift. The days of filing boilerplate desegregation lawsuits were mostly over. Funding for LCDC and similar organizations had dried up, and the Nixon administration began walking back the role of Civil Rights Division attorneys in the South. Many of the lawyers who had done civil rights work moved into equal employment practice, which seemed to be the next legal front in the battle for social justice.[1]

There was also a new generation of black lawyers. Thanks to the effects of desegregation at every level, more and more black people were graduating from southern law schools. These young lawyers would be mentored by the trailblazers who came before—Robert Collins, Nils Douglas, and Lolis Elie would be role models for these men and women—and they would end up taking on the labor of the civil rights movement in the decades to come.[2]

In 1971, Richard moved back to New Orleans. He and some former LCDC colleagues started a private firm that could continue the work they had started in the sixties. Al Bronstein was on board, as was Lolis Elie, and they would be joined by two other ex-LCDC lawyers.

The idea behind the firm was as simple as it was quixotic: they worked together to find a way of doing civil rights law outside of the context of big civil rights institutions. For a time, it worked, and Richard took on a number of significant, innovative lawsuits in the early seventies. Anne moved down to join him in 1972, and they worked on several big cases together.

Nationally, there were some dark clouds gathering on the horizon. The civil rights movement was effectively over. Nixon was president. Chief Justice Earl Warren, the author of *Brown v. Board of Education* and steward of the most progressive era in Supreme Court history, had resigned. The court's new appointees, including future chief justice William Rehnquist, were far more conservative. A new legal theory, which would later be labeled "originalism," was being developed in law schools by the conservative Federalist Society. Championed by influential young professors like Antonin Scalia, originalism threatened the underpinnings of Richard's life's work.

That was all in the future, though. For now, Richard resumed his runs with Nils Douglas. He and Anne were often over at Lolis Elie's house for dinner or just to talk and relax. He even made a second *Easy Rider* trip, this time to Denmark. It wasn't LCDC, but it was an exciting time of life.

As often happens, personal differences between the law partners broke up the firm within a few years. In 1974, Richard and Anne moved back to Washington, DC, to be closer to Richard's children.[3]

Richard and Gary stayed in touch, mostly about his case, which refused to die completely for more than a year after the initial decision. Lea Perez tried to take it all the way to the US Supreme Court, which, at last, refused it. On November 9, 1971, more than five years after Gary was first arrested for touching Herman Landry, Richard wrote a letter saying simply,

EPILOGUE

Dear Gary:

The Supreme Court refused to hear Perez' appeal of the decision in your favor by the Court of Appeals. The case is therefore over for all time.

Sometime later, the two friends got together to celebrate.

———

Gary's Supreme Court case was one of the most important moments in what became known as the "criminal procedure revolution." During the 1960s, the Warren Court created everything from the Miranda warning ("You have the right to remain silent…," named for the case that created it, *Miranda v. Arizona*) to the first public defenders (*Gideon v. Wainwright*). Compared to those cases, the immediate human impact of *Duncan v. Louisiana* was limited, despite its enormous legal importance. *Duncan* did not, as some had feared, invalidate every previous nonjury trial. Nor did it require jury trials for every petty offense, which would have brought the criminal-justice system to a standstill.* But it forced changes in the laws of many states, and it provided a new foundation for the extension of criminal defendants' rights.

The problem was that *Duncan* answered fewer questions than it raised. All trials for serious offenses required juries, but what was a "serious offense"? And what was a "jury"? Did it mean twelve people? How would those people be chosen? Did they need to reach a unanimous verdict? In fact, Richard Sobol found himself back in the Supreme Court in 1972 arguing that last issue. The case, *Apodaca v. Oregon,* seemed simple to Richard: four years earlier, he had convinced seven justices that juries were an indispensable safeguard against oppression, but several states, including

---

* Actually, the most important damper on *Duncan's* impact was unforeseeable in 1968. In the long term, all of the effects of *Duncan* were muted by plea bargaining, which now decides the outcomes of more than 95 percent of criminal cases, effectively gutting the jury system that *Duncan* was written to uphold.

Louisiana and Oregon, did not require juries to be unanimous. (Their conviction rates were predictably high.) But the court in 1972 was very different from the one Richard addressed in 1968, and he lost *Apodaca.* Oregon still allows convictions by a 10–2 vote.

Despite its limitations, *Duncan* opened the way for changes in criminal procedure that have affected the outcomes of millions of cases. Immediately after the court's decision in 1968, dozens of cases went through the courts, including the arrests of nine hundred anti-war demonstrators at Columbia University that year. To avoid these challenges, most states rewrote their jury laws to come in line with the court's mandate.

Apodaca did not spell the end of *Duncan*'s life in the Supreme Court. *Duncan* was central to *Taylor v. Louisiana,* which in 1975 barred the systematic exclusion of any portion of the community from jury service (unless there is a "compelling state interest" in keeping them out). And the right spelled out in *Duncan* was crucial to the court's 1986 landmark decision in *Batson v. Kentucky,* which outlawed the practice of striking potential jurors because of their race. More recently, *Duncan* was the basis of a series of cases in the early 2000s that barred judges from adding "sentencing enhancements"—hallmarks of the golden age of mass incarceration—without first putting the underlying facts before a jury. In 2019, the court heard arguments in a case, based on *Duncan,* that could overrule *Apodaca* and require all juries to reach unanimous verdicts.[*]

Gary Duncan's name continues to echo through courthouses and litter the footnotes of law reviews. An intervention on the side of the road turned into a junky, Jim Crow misdemeanor—unjust but less egregious than hundreds of others that year all over the South and the nation. That case, through Gary's tenacity and Richard's vision, changed American law. The story of the state of Louisiana against Gary Duncan did not end in the Plaquemines Parish courthouse, or even in the Supreme Court.

---

[*] *Ramos v. Louisiana* was argued on October 7, 2019. Richard Sobol deadpanned to me that, if the court demands unanimous juries, he's going to start saying that he won *Apodaca* "retroactively."

Afterword

Anthony Amsterdam became a pioneer of experiential legal education. He taught for decades at New York University School of Law, where he is a professor emeritus. He has argued several times before the US Supreme Court. Most famously, he convinced the court, in *Furman v. Georgia,* that the death penalty was unconstitutional. (The court later reversed itself.)

Al Bronstein spent the rest of his career advocating for America's prisoners. He was instrumental in founding Penal Reform International, and he directed the ACLU National Prison Project for twenty-five years. In 1989, he won a MacArthur Foundation grant (the so-called genius prize) in recognition of his work. He died in 2015.

Darryl Bubrig became a prominent attorney in Plaquemines Parish in private practice and public service, including four terms as district attorney. He lives in Plaquemines.

Robert Collins was nominated by Jimmy Carter to a seat on the United States District Court for the Eastern District of Louisiana in 1978. He was the first black judge to sit on a federal court in the Deep South, and he served there until his resignation in 1993. He died in 2018.

The Deacons for Defense and Justice mostly disappeared by the end of the 1960s as the threat of Klan violence began to lessen. In recent years, the Robert Hicks Foundation (named for the leader of the Deacons, who sued Crown Zellerbach with Richard Sobol) has been raising funds for a museum dedicated to the struggle for equal rights in Bogalusa—there is, as of this writing, no civil rights museum in the state of Louisiana.

Nils Douglas went on to co-found the Southern Organization for Unified Leadership (SOUL), which sought to aid black political candidates by registering and mobilizing black voters. His political career took him from the Louisiana Board of Highways to the Board of Ethics for Elected Officials, and he was inducted into the National Bar Association Hall of Fame. He died in 2003.

Gary Duncan left Plaquemines Parish shortly after Hurricane Camille to join the navy, returning a few years later to take over his father's charter fishing business. Since then, he has worked as a commercial fisherman and tugboat captain while simultaneously maintaining various side businesses—everything from a trucking company to a beauty supply store. Decades after his trip to the Supreme Court, Gary returned to Washington, DC, to lobby on behalf of commercial fishermen. Following Hurricane Katrina, he and Fay, his second wife, moved to a suburb of New Orleans, but he returns to Boothville every Sunday to attend Mt. Olive Missionary Baptist Church, where he is a deacon. Gary is semi-retired and enjoys spending time with his numerous grandchildren and great-grandchildren.

Lolis Elie continued his work as an activist and advocate. Fiercely independent, he mostly eschewed traditional positions of power and prestige, but his legendary house parties were a hub of New Orleans intellectual life for decades. For his accomplishments, he was inducted into the National Bar Association Hall of Fame and received the Martin Luther King Lifetime Achievement Award. He died in 2017.

The Lawyers Constitutional Defense Committee dissolved in 1972 due to lack of funds (but "having eliminated racial discrimination in Louisiana," as staff attorney Stanley Halpin deadpanned in a letter). Many of its former lawyers have gone on to be prominent in academia, civil rights and equal-employment law, and private practice.

Lea and Chalin Perez held on to the power granted to them by their father until they started feuding in the late 1970s. The brothers launched public investigations of each other and, in a few years, were both driven out of politics. At the same time, a lawyer stumbled upon an old legal document that revealed the extent of their father's land theft and graft. The so-called Rosetta Stone of Perez resulted in the family returning $12 million to the parish, along with all of the oil-rich land stolen by Judge Perez. Both brothers were out of power by 1984, never to serve in elected office again. Lea died in 1988. Chalin died in 2003.

Henry Schwarzschild spent the rest of his career at the American Civil Liberties Union, including fifteen years as head of its Capital Punishment Project. He was a driving force behind the National Coalition to Abolish the Death Penalty, which he directed until his death in 1996.

Richard Sobol became an expert in civil rights law, especially labor law. In his wide-ranging practice, he wrote Supreme Court briefs for the AFL-CIO and represented agricultural workers, bus drivers, longshoremen, and many others. He wrote an award-winning nonfiction book, *Bending the Law,* which told the story behind a massive corporate bankruptcy. Anne, his wife, practiced for many years in civil rights, welfare, and financial law. In her long and varied career, she worked for the Carter administration, the Civil Division of the Department of Justice, the Federal Deposit Insurance Corporation, and others, and she worked with Richard on many important cases. In 1991, Richard and Anne returned to New Orleans, where they stayed for more than twenty years. They now live in Northern California.

Acknowledgments

Writing this book has been one part solo effort and nine parts team sport—no word between these covers belongs to me alone.

More than anyone, these words belong to Gary Duncan. Gary, my friend, I wish I had a tenth of your work ethic and moral fiber. Someday, if I can earn it, I hope to have a tenth of your wisdom. And to the Duncan clan: Fay, Vivian, Robert, Mancil, Calvin, Augerine, Gaynelle, Reverend Samuel, Flora Mae, Cheryl, Stanley, Janice, Darius, and all the others. Theirs is a rowdy sort of love, so different from anything I encountered in my staid family. They made me feel instantly at home, and their open hearts mask an iron will that carries them through dark times.

I had no idea what I was doing the first time I spoke to Richard Sobol, but he patiently talked me through his life and the case. Those interviews were richer with meaning than I could have understood at the time. Richard, without your brilliance and truly unreasonable devotion to justice, so many people would be worse off. I am also indebted to Anne Buxton Sobol, a brilliant lawyer in her own right. Anne works behind the scenes, and her stewardship of Richard and his legacy is a profound act of love. This is no Wikipedia entry, Anne, but I hope it will suffice.

All of the lawyers who spoke to me about their civil rights work have my gratitude. Special mention must be made of Owen Fiss and Tony Amsterdam (who has the fastest email reply this side of the Mississippi). Thomas Hilbink was generous with his research materials, including interviews with people who died before I started my work.

I planted a little piece of myself down the road—not in the soil, but in the people who inhabit it. Dominick Scandurro was my window into Plaquemines: my travel guide, my lifeline, my fixer, my encyclopedia, and a fine family man. I learned a great deal from Alice and the whole Scandurro family: Tim, Steve, and especially Dewey and Michelle.

Laverne and Harold Jones spent hours telling me, in incredible detail, about life before and after integration. This book would have been impoverished without their memories and those of their friends, who are too numerous to list here, but whose names fill the endnotes.

Reverend Theo Turner and his wife, Henrietta, welcomed me into Mt. Olive Missionary Baptist Church with an enthusiasm that staggers me still, and they had this Quaker boy swaying and clapping in no time. To the entire Mt. Olive community—your faith and perseverance is beautiful. Glory be.

I could not have written this book without my family away from family in my home away from home, New Orleans. I will always be grateful to Jay Sones for his generosity and seemingly limitless interest in whatever I was working on. And my task would have been dull indeed without Andrew Farrier, Guy Feltenstein, Savannah and Eric Strachan, David and Adair Faust, and all of the others.

It is rare to find a friend with whom you can be absolutely yourself, rarer still for that person to be a fellow artist whose ambition and creativity spur your own. Lucy Faust is both of those things, as well as a lovely person and a talented actress. You're my role model, Lucy, and you're in these pages as much as any of the subjects.

A succession of mentors at Columbia gave me the faith in myself I needed to embark on this journey. Patty O'Toole gave me all five of the best pieces of advice I've ever received. Brenda Wineapple challenged me to reexamine my assumptions. Daniel Bergner always called out my bullshit.

Sam Freedman never, ever let me off the hook. Lis Harris always knew how to give me what I needed, from the first time we spoke on the phone to just a few days before I sent off this manuscript. Somehow, I have no words to describe my feelings for Ian Port and Constanza Martínez. Guys, we made an unlikely trio, but I have grown as a writer, reporter, and human because of you.

I have special affection for all the people who carried me through the painful early days of birthing this book: Marsha Pechman, Bill Fitzharris, Jillian Husman, Dylan Hoover, Jean Garnett, Paul Shechtman, and Lucia Savchick. And for the people who supported me through the day-to-day work of writing the damn thing: Walter and Ava Butzu, Frannie Shepherd-Bates, Eleanore Johnstone, Linda West, and Gabrielle Paluch.

Kris Dahl has countered my impatience with patience, my fantasies with practicality, my complacency with urgency, and my anxieties with confidence. She's a woman of action and a damn fine agent. Vanessa Mobley, my editor, is possessed of a powerful heart and a hurricane-force intellect. There are so few people like Vanessa, and she was exactly what the book—and I—needed.

This book would not be what it is without the spiritual and emotional education I have received from the members of my prison ensemble. My colleagues on the inside, men and women, model radical bravery and empathy for me, and they have taught me how to be a *man*—not a stereotype or a reaction against that stereotype, but fully myself. I cannot print their names, but they are my heroes and they know who they are.

The story of my life would be very different without Colleen Fitzharris. She is a brilliant attorney and a fearsome advocate, and I am in awe of the moral clarity with which she views the world. Her passion glows in her like a vein of radium, fueling her work and lending its light to the people around her. Thank you.

My parents made me who I am, and their firm but quiet support is, more than anything else, what enabled me to do what I do. They are people of rare insight and dignity, and I owe them no less than everything.

Notes

CHAPTER 1

1 *Gemini V Air-to-Ground Transcription,* 549.

2 *Report on Hurricane Betsy,* plate 2.

3 Interviews with Gaynelle Duncan, Geralyn Lewis, and Vivian Taylor.

4 *Report on Hurricane Betsy.* Even the "one football field an hour" analogy doesn't capture the pace of the loss. That image first appeared in a 2011 report by Brady Couvillion for the US Geological Survey, referring to the average rate of coastal wetland loss over the twenty-five-year period from 1985–2010, which was 16.6 square miles per year, or roughly 57,000 square feet—the size of a football field—per hour. The limitations of the analogy are obvious: wetland loss is neither constant nor linear, and hurricanes account for an outsized share of the damage. Still, the number is broadly accurate, even conservative: the current rate of loss is much, much faster. See Tristan Baurick, "Is Louisiana Really Losing a Football Field of Land per Hour?" *New Orleans Times-Picayune,* May 29, 2017. Also, Couvillion et al., *Land Area Change in Coastal Louisiana from 1932 to 2010.*

5 Interview with Pam Dickenson.

6 Interviews with Augerine Duncan, Gary Duncan, and Robert Duncan.

7 Interviews with Gary Duncan, Lucretia Hunter, and Harold Jones. The memory about the job seekers was from a Plaquemines Parish resident who declined to give her name. The quote about oil-field work is from Rev. Theodore Turner, who worked for Chevron after the company desegregated.

8 Interviews with Calvin Duncan, Gary Duncan, Mancil Duncan, Robert Duncan, Harold Jones, and Rev. Theodore Turner.

9 Roth, *Louisiana Hurricane History,* 6.

10 *Hearings Before the Special Subcommittee to Investigate Areas of Destruction of Hurricane Betsy; Investigation of the Performance of the New Orleans Flood Protection Systems in Hurricane Katrina;* Rogers, "Development of the New

Orleans Flood Protection System prior to Hurricane Katrina"; Roth, *Louisiana Hurricane History*, 7.

11 "Hurricane Veers From Coast, Pauses 350 Miles Off Florida," *New York Times,* September 5, 1965; "Hurricane Turns Toward Bahamas," *New York Times,* September 6, 1965; "Hurricane Winds Lash At Bahamas," *New York Times,* September 7, 1965; Cuchiara, *A Hurricane Called Betsy.*

12 Interviews with Darryl Bubrig, Pam Dickenson, Gary Duncan, and Dominick Scandurro; Howard, "Home at the Mouth of the Mississippi," 77; Zebrowski and Howard, *Category 5,* 44–46.

13 "Thousands Flee Inland," *New Orleans States-Item,* September 9, 1965; *Report on Hurricane Betsy,* 7; Zebrowski and Howard, *Category 5,* 48.

14 "'Hard-Headed' Residents of Perez's Parish Tell How They Clung to Life in the Hurricane," *New York Times,* September 15, 1965. Buras had told a *New York Times* reporter a few days after the hurricane, "We have some kind of hard-headed people down here."

15 Interviews with Calvin Duncan, Gary Duncan, and Mancil Duncan; "'Hard-Headed' Residents of Perez's Parish Tell How They Clung to Life in the Hurricane," *New York Times,* September 15, 1965.

16 "City Won't Forget Betsy's Eery [*sic*] Voice," *New Orleans States-Item,* September 10, 1965.

17 Interview with Gary Duncan.

18 "'Hard-Headed' Residents of Perez's Parish Tell How They Clung to Life in the Hurricane," *New York Times,* September 15, 1965.

19 Ibid.; interviews with Gary Duncan, Harold Jones, and Laverne Jones; Buras, *Betsy & Camille,* 22–24.

20 Interviews with Calvin Duncan and Gary Duncan.

21 "Tour by 'Copter Reveals Scars," *New Orleans Times-Picayune,* September 25, 1965; Shallat in Colten, *Transforming New Orleans and Its Environs,* 124.

22 Interviews with Laverne Jones and Rev. Theodore Turner.

23 Interviews with Gary Duncan, Harold Jones, and Laverne Jones; Conaway, *Judge,* 158. The "parish official," as Laverne recalls it, was Leander Perez.

24 "FBI Report Airs Clean-Up Clash," *New Orleans Times-Picayune,* October 6, 1965; Conaway, *Judge,* 158.

CHAPTER 2

1 "Plaquemines Assessments Top $100 Million," *New Orleans States-Item,* January 28, 1966; see image on front page of *Plaquemines Gazette,* September 17, 1965.

2 "Plaquemines Assessments Top $100 Million," *New Orleans States-Item,* January 28, 1966; Goudeau and Connor, "Storm Surge Over the Mississippi River Delta Accompanying Hurricane Betsy, 1965," 124.

3 *Hearings Before the Special Subcommittee to Investigate Areas of Destruction of Hurricane Betsy.*

4 "New Dial Unit to Go Into Use," *New Orleans Times-Picayune*, February 12, 1966; "New Buras Phone Exchange Is Cut Over for Service," *Plaquemines Gazette*, May 13, 1966; "Swim Pools Make News In Lower End," *Plaquemines Gazette*, June 17, 1966; "Council OK's Port Sulphur Sewer Work, Studies Other Bids," *Plaquemines Gazette*, June 17, 1966. Louisiana's GDP for 1965 was a bit over $11 billion, according to the Bureau of Economic Analysis. See "Regional Economic Accounts: Gross domestic product (GDP) by state (millions of current dollars)," US Department of Commerce, Bureau of Economic Analysis, accessed April 16, 2018, https://www.bea.gov/iTable/index _nipa.cfm.

5 "Perez Asks Plaquemines Industry to Aid in Relief," *New Orleans States-Item*, October 7, 1965; "Speedup in Hurricane Protection," *New Orleans Times-Picayune*, March 3, 1966.

6 Interview with Stanley Gaudet; "Progress So Rapid in Parish That Parishioners Are Asked to Return to Rehabilitate Their Homes and Businesses," *Plaquemines Gazette*, October 8, 1965; "Seventy-five Percent of People Returned to Parish to Rebuild," *Plaquemines Gazette*, November 26, 1965; "Hurricane-Hit Area Improves," *New Orleans Times-Picayune*, December 11, 1965.

7 "FBI Report Airs Clean-Up Clash," *New Orleans Times-Picayune*, October 6, 1965; untitled report, FBI file for Leander Perez, part 3, document no. 44-30670-15, October 28, 1965, https://vault.fbi.gov/Leander%20 Perez%2C%20Sr./Leander%20Perez%2C%20Sr.%20Part%203%20of%204 /view.

8 "Break in Levee," *St. Bernard Voice*, May 29, 1920.

9 "Perez Gives Lie to Dymond Claim," *New Orleans States*, October 13, 1923.

10 "Ouster Hearing Against Judge Perez Is Continued Until Tuesday by Court," *New Orleans Item*, May 16, 1924; Jeansonne, *Leander Perez*, 16–31.

11 "Spring Surprise on Perez," *New Orleans Item*, May 15, 1923; "Dymond Files Another Suit Against Perez," *New Orleans States*, December 14, 1923; "Factions Clasp Hands as Perez Suit Is Dropped," *New Orleans Times-Picayune*, June 5, 1924; "The True Story of Leander Perez, Chapter Seven," *New Orleans Item*, June 18, 1950.

12 "The True Story of Leander Perez: Chapter Eight," *New Orleans Item*, June 18, 1950; "The True Story of Leander Perez: Chapter Fifteen," *New Orleans Item*, June 26, 1950; Meyer, *Plaquemines: The Empire Parish*, 51, 71.

13 "The True Story of Leander Perez: Chapter Three," *New Orleans Item*, June 18, 1950.

14 Davis and Place, *The Oil and Gas Industry of Coastal Louisiana*, 18; Plaquemines Parish Government, *Primary Government Financial Statements*, 10.

15 "Troops Oust Slater, Put Blaize in Sheriff Office," *New Orleans Times-Picayune*, October 10, 1943; Jeansonne, *Leander Perez*, 141.

16 This litany of improvements comes from too many sources to cite expeditiously,

but it is largely represented in Jeansonne, *Leander Perez*, 113–20, citing many of the same sources. "The True Story of Leander Perez: Chapter Two," *New Orleans Item*, June 18, 1950, includes improvements made before its publication in 1950. The final anecdote comes from an interview I did with Darryl Bubrig and Dominick Scandurro.

17 See, generally, *Plaquemines Parish Government v. Getty Oil Company*, 673 So. 2d 1002 (1996); *Plaquemines Parish Commission Council v. Delta Development Co.*, 502 So. 2d 1034 (1987); *Richardson & Bass v. Board of Commissioners of the Orleans Levee District*, 359; "The Complete Story May Never Be Known," *New Orleans Times-Picayune and States-Item*, June 1, 1986; Jeansonne, *Leander Perez*, 75–81.

18 "Parish Fighting to Find Out Who Paid What to Whom," *New Orleans Times-Picayune and States-Item*, June 3, 1986; "Perez Made Millions from Public Land," *New Orleans Times-Picayune and States-Item*, June 1, 1986. That $78 million figure includes only Delta Development lands, and only those associated with the leases uncovered by this revelation. The true total is likely much higher. These leases continued to pay out for years.

19 This account is based on dozens of interviews, but especially with Gary Duncan and Dominick Scandurro; "The True Story of Leander Perez: Chapter Two," *New Orleans Item*, June 18, 1950; "Louisiana Parish Fights Pentagon," *New York Times*, September 5, 1963.

20 Jeansonne, *Leander Perez*, 220, citing the *New Orleans States*; Read and McGough, *Let Them Be Judged*, 111.

21 Untitled teletype to J. Edgar Hoover, name of author redacted, FBI file for Leander Perez, part 2, document no. 44-9732 (unrecorded serial), January 31, 1956, https://vault.fbi.gov/Leander%20Perez%2C%20Sr./Leander%20Perez%2C%20Sr.%20Part%202%20of%204/view.

22 "Segregation Planner," *New York Times*, November 28, 1960; "Plan to Shift Pupils Bared," *New Orleans Times-Picayune*, November 23, 1960; Louisiana State Advisory Committee, *The New Orleans Crisis*, 14; Bass, *Unlikely Heroes*, 129; Conaway, *Judge*, 114; Fairclough, *Race & Democracy*, 224; Wall and Rodrigue, *Louisiana*, 380.

23 Transcript of interview with Leander Perez on *Working Press*, June 13, 1961, WYES, b1, f1, Save Our Schools Collection, ARC.

CHAPTER 3

1 "5 Integrate Buras Parochial School," *New Orleans States-Item*, August 28, 1962; "Pickets on Hand, Five Buras Mix Pupils Absent," *New Orleans States-Item*, August 30, 1962; "Negro Children Fail to Appear," *New Orleans Times-Picayune*, August 31, 1962; "Some Scenes of Buras Integration Try," *Plaquemines Gazette*, September 7, 1962; "Week-Old Buras Boycott Still

On," *New Orleans States-Item,* September 9, 1962; "New Orleans Area Catholic Schools Integrated 2 Years after the City's Public Schools," *New Orleans Times-Picayune,* November 15, 2010; Conaway, *Judge,* 126.

2 Rather, *CBS Reports,* "The Priest and the Politician"; Jeansonne, *Leander Perez,* 269.

3 "Satan and Segregation," *Newsweek,* April 30, 1962; Conaway, *Judge,* 122; Fairclough, *Race & Democracy,* 259.

4 "Perez Denounces Bid to Integrate Catholic Schools," *Chicago Daily Tribune,* April 26, 1962; "Caesar of the Bayous Rules with Iron Fist," *Los Angeles Times,* May 3, 1964; "Catholics Protest Integration Ruling," *Plaquemines Gazette,* May 4, 1962; Endres, "Judge Leander Perez and the Franciscans of Our Lady of Good Harbor," 19; Conaway, *Judge,* 122; Jeansonne, *Leander Perez,* 266.

5 Interviews with Gary Duncan and Bernard St. Ann; "Pickets on Hand, Five Buras Mix Pupils Absent," *New Orleans States-Item,* August 30, 1962; "Negro Children Fail to Appear," *New Orleans Times-Picayune,* August 31, 1962; Rather, *CBS Reports,* "The Priest and the Politician"; Jeansonne, *Leander Perez,* 266–268.

6 "Pickets on Hand, Five Buras Mix Pupils Absent," *New Orleans States-Item,* August 30, 1962; "Negro Children Fail to Appear," *New Orleans Times-Picayune,* August 31, 1962.

7 "Calm Settles Over Buras Mixing Scene," *New Orleans States-Item,* September 1, 1962; Zebrowski and Howard, *Category 5,* 42.

8 "Buras School Shut; FBI Opens Probe," *New Orleans States-Item,* August 31, 1962; "Calm Settles Over Buras Mixing Scene," *New Orleans States-Item,* September 1, 1962; "School Shuts; FBI Inquiry On," *New Orleans Times-Picayune,* September 1, 1962; "Segregated Fiefdom," *Christian Science Monitor,* September 11, 1962.

9 "Blast, Fire Hit Boycotted Catholic School in Buras," *New Orleans States-Item,* August 28, 1962; "Gasoline Used in School Blast, Says Deputy," *New Orleans States-Item,* August 28, 1963; "Blast Severely Damages Buras Parochial School," *New Orleans Times-Picayune,* August 28, 1963.

10 "Gasoline Used in School Blast, Says Deputy," *New Orleans States-Item,* August 28, 1963; "School Fire Probers Find No Good Leads," *New Orleans States-Item,* September 5, 1963.

11 Rather, *CBS Reports,* "The Priest and the Politician."

12 Interview with Buddy Cossé; Fairclough, *Race & Democracy,* 260; Zebrowski and Howard, *Category 5,* 43.

13 "Plaquemines Negotiation on Storm Losses Is Told," *New Orleans Times-Picayune,* June 30, 1966.

14 *Plaquemines Parish School Board v. US,* memo from Joe Gladden, law clerk, to Judges Godbold, Simpson, and McRae, March 4, 1968, memoranda, 2–3, RG 3192, NARA-SW.

15 Wolters, *The Burden of Brown,* 82–87, 106.

16 *Plaquemines Parish School Board v. US,* testimony of Luke Petrovich, February 27, 1967, vol. 1, 331–42, and testimony of Harold Smith, August 5, 1966, vol. 1, 194, RG 3192, NARA-SW; *US v. Plaquemines Parish School Board,* Findings of Fact and Conclusions of Law, August 26, 1966, vol. 1, 178, RG 1637, NARA-SW; "US Rests Plaquemines Integration Case," *New Orleans States-Item,* August 11, 1966.

17 *US v. Plaquemines Parish School Board,* affidavit of Emelda Mae Griffin, September 12, 1966, vol. 2, 271–72, RG 1638, NARA-SW; "Plaquemines School Registers 5 Negroes," *New Orleans Times-Picayune,* September 1, 1966.

18 "Plaquemines White Pupils Stage Boycott," *Baton Rouge Morning Advocate,* September 1, 1966; "Plaquemines School Registers 5 Negroes," *New Orleans Times-Picayune,* September 1, 1966.

19 "Plaquemines School Chief Steps Down," *New Orleans States-Item,* September 1, 1966; "Patti Named Head of Independent Schools," *Plaquemines Gazette,* September 26, 1966.

20 Interview with Ray Terry; "Plaquemines Schools Stay Open to Enroll," *Baton Rouge Morning Advocate,* September 6, 1966; "Plaquemines Schools' Top Administration Collapses," *New Orleans States-Item,* September 8, 1966.

21 "Plaquemines Economy Is Oil, Gas; Society Is Segregation," *Baton Rouge Morning Advocate,* September 11, 1966.

22 Interview with Buddy Cossé; "Whites Bust Plaquemines Class Boycott," *Baton Rouge Morning Advocate,* September 13, 1966; "4 Plaquemines Schools Mixed," *New Orleans Times-Picayune,* September 13, 1966; Edwards, *The Forgotten People,* 150–54.

23 *US v. Plaquemines Parish School Board,* affidavits of Alberta Anderson, Emelda Mae Griffin, Shirley Mae Sylvester, and Bertha Williams, September 12, 1966, vol. 2, 269–80, RG 1638, NARA-SW; *Plaquemines Parish School Board v. US,* testimony of Thelma Louis Watson, September 15, 1966, vol. 1, 698–717, RG 3192, NARA-SW; "4 Plaquemines Schools Mixed," *New Orleans Times-Picayune,* September 13, 1966.

24 "Whites Jeer Negro Pupils at Chalmette," *Baton Rouge Morning Advocate,* September 14, 1966; "Whites Spit at, Stone Negroes at St. Bernard," *Baton Rouge Morning Advocate,* September 14, 1966; "5 Arrested at Gym Fire in Chalmette," *Baton Rouge Morning Advocate,* September 15, 1966.

25 "Integration Comes to Plaquemines," *Chicago Daily Defender,* September 15, 1966; "Integrate Public Schools of Perez' Plaquemines Parish," *Louisiana Weekly,* September 17, 1966.

26 "4 Plaquemines Schools Mixed," *New Orleans Times-Picayune,* September 13, 1966.

27 Interviews with Lucretia Hunter, Laverne Jones, and Henrietta Turner; Edwards, *The Forgotten People,* 151–52.

28 Interviews with Lucretia Hunter, Laverne Jones, Carolyn Parker, Henrietta Turner, and Rev. Theodore Turner.

29 Interview with Harold Jones.

30 Interviews with Rev. Tyronne Edwards, Bernard St. Ann, and Rev. Theodore Turner.

31 Interview with Laverne Jones.

32 Interviews with Carolyn Parker, Henrietta Turner, and Rev. Theodore Turner.

33 Interview with Lucretia Hunter.

34 Interview with Harold Jones.

35 Interviews with Harold Jones and Bernard St. Ann; *Plaquemines Parish School Board v. US,* memo from Joe Gladden, law clerk, to Judges Godbold, Simpson, and McRae, March 4, 1968, memoranda, 2–3, RG 3192, NARA-SW.

36 Interview with Carolyn Parker.

CHAPTER 4

1 Interviews with Gaynell Crum, Gary Duncan, Lynn Duncan, Robert Duncan, and Geralyn Lewis.

2 Interviews with Gary Duncan, Lynn Duncan, Robert Duncan, and Bernard St. Ann; Baker, *The Second Battle of New Orleans,* 13; Powell, *Black Monday's Children,* 126. For a lively and nuanced description of the kaleidoscopic racial scene in New Orleans, see Spear, *Race, Sex, and Social Order in Early New Orleans,* and Gill, *Lords of Misrule: Mardi Gras and the Politics of Race in New Orleans.*

3 Interview with Gary Duncan; *Duncan v. Perez,* report of Probation Officer Edward Nolan, February 21, 1969, r21, LCDC.

4 Interview with Gary Duncan.

5 *Sobol v. Perez,* testimony of Gary Duncan, vol. IV, 209, b679 f1, ACLU; *Duncan v. Perez,* deposition of Parnell Latham, March 13, 1970, 3–5, r21, LCDC.

6 Interview with Gary Duncan; *Duncan v. Perez,* deposition of Parnell Latham, March 13, 1970, 11, LCDC. Latham does not spell out the details of the penultimate sentence (what is meant by "trouble"), but his language is pulled so completely—almost verbatim—from racist op-eds in the *Plaquemines Gazette* and from Judge Perez's speeches and articles that it is safe to say that "trouble" was for him the same shorthand it was for Perez, who had no qualms about detailing his terror of race mixing.

7 *Duncan v. Perez,* deposition of Feltus Smith, March 12, 1970, 3, r21, LCDC.

8 Interview with Gary Duncan.

9 *Sobol v. Perez,* testimony of Gary Duncan, vol. III, 210, b679 f1, ACLU; *Duncan v. Perez,* handwritten report of statement by Feltus Smith, March 22, 1969, r21, LCDC; *Duncan v. Perez,* deposition of Feltus Smith, March 12, 1970, 4, r21, LCDC.

10 *State v. Duncan,* statement of Herman Landry Jr., November 4, 1966, r20, LCDC; *Duncan v. Perez,* deposition of Feltus Smith, March 12, 1970, 4, r21, LCDC.

11 *Duncan v. Perez,* deposition of Feltus Smith, March 12, 1970, 5, r21, LCDC.

12 Interview with Gary Duncan; *Sobol v. Perez,* testimony of Gary Duncan, vol. III, 211, b679 f1, ACLU; *Duncan v. Perez,* deposition of Feltus Smith, March 12, 1970, 5 and 9, r21, LCDC. In 1970, F. J. denied remembering Westley McKinney's statement or even McKinney's presence on the scene. He also claimed to have lost his contemporaneous notes.

13 Interview with Gary Duncan; *Duncan v. Perez,* deposition of Feltus Smith, March 12, 1970, 9, r21, LCDC.

14 *Duncan v. Perez,* deposition of Herman Landry Jr., April 28, 1970, NARA-SW; *Duncan v. Perez,* deposition of Feltus Smith, March 12, 1970, 5, r21, LCDC.

15 *Duncan v. Perez,* deposition of Herman Landry Sr., April 28, 1970, 4–6, b2186, NARA-SW; *Duncan v. Perez,* deposition of Mrs. Herman Landry, April 28, 1970, 3–5 and 9, b2186, NARA-SW.

16 *Duncan v. Perez,* deposition of Herman Landry Sr., April 28, 1970, 5, b2186, NARA-SW.

17 La. Rev. Stat. § 14:93. The statute has been amended several times since 1966. Ten years of hard labor was the maximum penalty at the time, and the crime did not then have three well-defined degrees. For these reasons, Collins and Sobol, in their motion to quash, also suggested that the statute might be un-constitutionally vague.

18 *Duncan v. Perez,* deposition of Wayne Scarabin, March 12, 1970, 3, r21, LCDC.

19 *State v. Duncan,* statement of Parnell Latham, Randolph Scarabin, and Wayne Scarabin to Arthur Cope, November 4, 1966, r20, LCDC.

20 *State v. Duncan,* statement of Herman Landry Jr. to Arthur Cope, November 4, 1966, r20, LCDC.

21 *Duncan v. Perez,* deposition of Mrs. Herman Landry, April 28, 1970, 6, b2186, NARA-SW.

22 Interview with Gary Duncan.

CHAPTER 5

1 Interview with Richard Sobol; "Mixers' Safety Ordered, Says Bogalusa Official," *New Orleans Times-Picayune,* July 27, 1965; Richard Sobol in Spriggs, *Voices of Civil Rights Lawyers,* 214; Hewitt, *Political Violence and Terrorism in Modern America,* 21. No one was ever charged or even arrested in the attack, and it barely made the local news.

2 Interview with Richard Sobol; interview of Richard Sobol by Joseph Mosnier, May 26, 2011, CRHP; Warren, *Who Speaks for the Negro?,* 28–9.

3 Interview with Richard Sobol.

4 Interview with Richard Sobol, October 29, 2015; interview of Richard Sobol by Joseph Mosnier, May 26, 2011, CRHP; Rogers, *Righteous Lives,* 137.

5 This, and subsequent facts in this chapter about Sobol's life through summer

1965 (unless otherwise noted): Interviews with Richard B. Sobol, October 29, 2015, and February 10, 2016; interview of Richard Sobol by Joseph Mosnier, May 26, 2011 (CRHP).

6 "Bronx Science Teacher Requests Reinstatement," *Observation Post*, April 22, 1953.

7 Interview with Richard Sobol.

8 "Legal Problems of the Poor Get Increasing Attention," *Law Quadrangle* 13 (1969): notes 9–10.

9 Ibid.; Richard Sobol's application for position as US District Court judge, May 1979, Sobol's personal papers (copy in possession of author).

10 Interview with Daniel Rezneck.

11 Temple, *Life, Liberty, and the Pursuit of Happiness*, 9.

12 *Butler v. District of Columbia*.

13 Interview with Daniel Rezneck.

14 Watson, *Freedom Summer*, 53–54.

15 Interview of Henry Schwarzschild by Thomas Hilbink, August 31, 1992.

16 Ibid.

17 Hilbink, "Filling the Void," 45.

18 Letter from J. Edgar Hoover to Leo Pfeffer, June 30, 1964, r17, ACLU.

19 Interview of Richard Frank by Thomas Hilbink, September 30, 1992; Larry Aschenbrenner in Spriggs, *Voices of Civil Rights Lawyers*, 109 (Aschenbrenner worked for the Lawyers' Committee for Civil Rights Under Law, but he describes the conditions generally); Carol Weisbrod, "Report to the Lawyers Constitutional Defense Committee," August 7, 1964, Lukas.

20 Interview of Alan Levine by Thomas Hilbink, September 18, 1992; "Report Covering Period June 11–July 14, 1964," r17, ACLU; "New Orleans LCDC List," August 5, 1964, r17, ACLU; "Report of [CORE] General Counsel," July 1965, r21, ACLU; Hilbink, "Filling the Void," 77–78.

21 Interview of Elsbeth Levy Bothe by Thomas Hilbink, October 9, 1992; interview of Richard Frank by Thomas Hilbink, September 30, 1992; interview of Jeremiah Gutman by Thomas Hilbink, September 1, 1992; interview of Peter Marcuse by Thomas Hilbink, September 17, 1992; Hilbink, "Filling the Void," 83, citing Bronstein, "A Trip to the South," 15.

22 Interview with Richard Sobol; Richard Sobol in Spriggs, *Voices of Civil Rights Lawyers*, 213–14.

CHAPTER 6

1 "Levee Inspection Reveals Litter Clutters West Bank," *Plaquemines Gazette*, November 25, 1966.

2 "Vote 'NO' to Added Taxes for Federal Operation of Schools, Sat. December 10," *Plaquemines Gazette*, December 2, 1966.

3 Advertisement for rally, *New Orleans Times-Picayune,* October 4, 1966; "Need of Organization of Southern States Cited by Judge Perez," *Plaquemines Gazette,* October 14, 1966.

4 "Treatise on 14th Amendment by Judge Perez Hopes to Awaken People and the United States Congress," *Plaquemines Gazette,* October 14, 1966.

5 "New River Oaks Academy Dedicated at Belle Chasse," *New Orleans Times-Picayune,* October 17, 1966; "First Newly Built Independent School Dedicated Sunday," *Plaquemines Gazette,* October 21, 1966.

6 "Belle Chasse Teachers Resign," *Plaquemines Gazette,* October 21, 1966.

7 *Plaquemines Parish School Board v. US,* testimonies of Loren Humphrey, Louise Walsh, and Suzanne Trahant, 37–53, 967–75, and 975–1001, b3192, NARA-SW.

8 "Judicial Tyranny to Reopen Belle Chasse Public High School," *Plaquemines Gazette,* October 28, 1966; *US v. Plaquemines Parish School Board,* motion to recuse, April 17, 1967, 9, NARA-SW. The testimony from the hearings on October 20 speaks for itself. The motion cited contains a description of the reaction to Tinsley's testimony.

9 "3 New Schools Are Dedicated," *New Orleans Times-Picayune,* November 7, 1966; "Three New Independent Schools in Parish Dedicated," *Plaquemines Gazette,* November 11, 1966; "Housewives Take Over Public School Classes," *Plaquemines Gazette,* November 11, 1966; "School Board 'Undermines Morale' at Belle Chasse," *New Orleans Times-Picayune,* November 25, 1966; "Superior Educational System Planned By Plaquemines' Private School Officials and Faculties," *Plaquemines Gazette,* November 25, 1966.

10 "Construction, Levee Debris Removal, Permits Acted On," *Plaquemines Gazette,* January 27, 1967.

CHAPTER 7

1 Richard Sobol in Spriggs, *Voices of Civil Rights Attorneys,* 217.

2 Interview with Richard Sobol; interview by Thomas Hilbink with Richard Sobol, November 9, 1992; *Sobol v. Perez,* testimony of Richard Sobol, vol. V, 44, b679 f3, ACLU.

3 Interview with Robert Collins Jr.; Rogers, *Righteous Lives,* 51–53.

4 Interviews with Hazell Boyce, Lolis Eric Elie, Vaughn Fauria, Calvin Johnson, Anne Sobol, and Richard Sobol; Rogers, *Righteous Lives,* 53–55.

5 Interviews with Robert Collins Jr., Anne Sobol, and Richard Sobol.

6 Interview with Richard Sobol.

7 Richard Sobol in Spriggs, *Voices of Civil Rights Attorneys,* 216.

8 Interview with Richard Sobol, May 7, 2015; Richard Sobol in Spriggs, *Voices of Civil Rights Attorneys,* 216–17.

9 Interviews with Richard Sobol; *Sobol v. Perez,* testimony of Richard Sobol, vol.

IV, 114–15, b679 f2, ACLU; Richard Sobol in Spriggs, *Voices of Civil Rights Attorneys*, 217.

10 *Sobol v. Perez*, deposition of Richard Sobol, August 11, 1967, 4, b1743, NARA-SW.

11 Interview with Richard Sobol; letter from Jeremiah Gutman to Richard Sobol, July 5, 1966, r97 LCDC; letter from Richard Sobol to Jeremiah Gutman, July 7, 1966, r168 LCDC; "Civil Rights Program Summer 1966," r97 LCDC; "Jeremiah S. Gutman, 80, a Fighter for Free Speech," *New York Times*, February 26, 2004; Richard Sobol in Spriggs, *Voices of Civil Rights Attorneys*, 218.

12 "Contributions to LCDC for 1966 Operational Year," November 1965, b648 f3, ACLU; "Projected Cash Flow and Budget Revisions, 1966," memo from Henry Schwarzschild to Edwin Lukas, March 8, 1966, b648 f3, ACLU; letter from Henry Schwarzschild to Bronstein, Farmer, Jelinek, and Sobol, August 29, 1966, b666 f11, ACLU.

13 Letter from Richard Sobol to Henry Schwarzschild, September 16, 1966, r81, LCDC.

14 There are several such letters just from Sobol's first months, though usually not from the reserved Sobol himself. The best example is Al Bronstein, who asked to sit in on board meetings for this reason. Letter from Al Bronstein to Henry Schwarzschild, November 28, 1966, b666 f11, ACLU.

15 Memo by Peter Honigsberg, August 18, 1966, b674 f2, ACLU; letter from Richard Sobol to Henry Schwarzschild, September 2, 1966, b674 f2 r36, ACLU.

16 *Sobol v. Perez*, testimony of Gary Duncan, vol. III, 200, b649 f1, ACLU; *Sobol v. Perez*, testimony of Richard Sobol, vol. IV, 152, b649 f2, ACLU.

17 *State v. Duncan*, testimony of Gary Duncan, 92, r20, LCDC.

18 Interview with Gary Duncan.

19 *Sobol v. Perez*, testimony of Richard Sobol, vol. IV, 153, b679 f2, ACLU; *Duncan v. Perez*, testimony of Gary Duncan, 46–47, r21, LCDC; *Duncan v. Perez*, report of Probation Officer Edward Nolan, February 21, 1969, r21, LCDC.

20 Interviews with Gary Duncan and Richard Sobol; letter from Henry Schwarzschild to Lolis Elie and Jeremiah Gutman, June 29, 1966, b674 f2, ACLU.

21 *Sobol v. Perez*, testimony of Robert Collins, vol. I, 231–32, b648 f5, ACLU.

22 Interview with Gary Duncan; *Sobol v. Perez*, testimony of Gary Duncan, vol. III, 201, b649 f1, ACLU.

23 Interview with Gary Duncan.

CHAPTER 8

1 *Sobol v. Perez*, testimony of Lolis Elie, vol. I, 106, b648 f5, ACLU; *Sobol v. Perez*, testimony of Robert Collins, vol. I, 231, b648 f5, ACLU.

2 "Turn Old Fort Dungeons into Jail for Race Rioters," *Chicago Tribune*, October

24, 1963; "Perez's Fort St. Phillip Prison Is Uncomfortable," *Baton Rouge Morning Advocate,* October 24, 1963 (a delightfully understated headline); "Swampland Fort Is Set Aside For Racial Prisoners," *Washington Post,* October 25, 1963; "Perez Seeks Stockade for Racial Foes," *Times Herald,* October 12, 1963; "Heart of Louisiana: Fort St. Phillip," Fox 8 News, New Orleans, accessed December 1, 2015, www.fox8live.com (no stable link available); Jeansonne, *Leander Perez,* 279.

3 Interview with Richard Sobol; *Sobol v. Perez,* testimony of Richard Sobol, vol. IV, 153, b679 f2, ACLU.

4 *Sobol v. Perez,* testimony of Nils Douglas, vol. XI, 102, b1746, NARA-SW; *Sobol v. Perez,* testimony of Richard Sobol, vol. V, 75, b679 f3, ACLU.

5 *Sobol v. Perez,* testimony of Lolis Elie, vol. I, 108, b648 f5, ACLU; Rogers, *Righteous Lives,* 133.

6 *Sobol v. Perez,* testimony of Lolis Elie, vol. I, 105, b648 f5, ACLU.

7 *Sobol v. Perez,* testimony of Earl Amedee, vol. V, 135–42, b679 f3, ACLU.

8 Interview with Richard Sobol; *Sobol v. Perez,* testimony of Earl Amedee, vol. V, 135–42, b679 f3, ACLU.

9 La. Rev. Stat. § 14:93.

10 *Sobol v. Perez,* deposition of Eugene Leon, August 11, 1967, 13, b1744, NARA-SW; *Duncan v. Perez,* testimony of Nils Douglas, 97–98, r21, LCDC.

11 *Sobol v. Perez,* testimony of Robert Collins, vol. I, 232, b678 f5, ACLU; *Sobol v. Perez,* testimony of Robert Collins, vol. II, 15, b678 f6, ACLU.

12 *Sobol v. Perez,* testimony of Darryl Bubrig, vol. VII, 116–17; *Sobol v. Perez,* testimony of Robert Collins, vol. I, 233, b678 f5, ACLU.

13 Interview with Darryl Bubrig; *Sobol v. Perez,* deposition of Eugene Leon, August 11, 1967, 6–7, 13, and 24–25, b1744, NARA-SW; "Parish Mourns Death of Judge Rudolph M. McBride," *Plaquemines Gazette,* July 29, 1966; "Independent Schools Open in November," *Plaquemines Gazette,* October 7, 1966; "D.A. & Judge Are Sworn In," *Plaquemines Gazette,* December 30, 1966; "Son of Former Political Chief Indicted in Louisiana," *New York Times,* August 19, 1982. Leon was indicted along with Lea Perez for malfeasance, a sign of Leon's future trajectory.

14 Interview with Darryl Bubrig; *Sobol v. Perez,* testimony of Darryl Bubrig, vol. VII, 113, b680 f1, ACLU.

15 *Sobol v. Perez,* deposition of Eugene Leon, August 11, 1967, 11, b1744, NARA-SW; *Sobol v. Perez,* testimony of Robert Collins, vol. I, 233–36, b678 f5, ACLU.

16 Interview with Darryl Bubrig; *Sobol v. Perez,* testimony of Darryl Bubrig, vol. VII, 116, b680 f1, ACLU; *Sobol v. Perez,* testimony of Robert Collins, vol. I, 237–39, b678 f5, ACLU; *Sobol v. Perez,* deposition of Eugene Leon, August 11, 1967, 34, b1744, NARA-SW; *Sobol v. Perez,* testimony of Richard Sobol, vol. IV, 155, b679 f2, ACLU. Darryl Bubrig, for the record, testified that either Collins or Sobol mentioned that the charge "should have been" battery, though no one else corroborated this.

17 *Sobol v. Perez,* testimony of Robert Collins, vol. I, 249, b678 f5, ACLU.

18 Interview with Gary Duncan.

19 Interview with Gary Duncan; *Duncan v. Perez,* deposition of Parnell Latham, March 13, 1970, 16, r21, LCDC.

20 *Duncan v. Perez,* deposition of Mrs. Herman Landry, April 28, 1970, 4–8, b2186, NARA-SW. I am reading into her (very demure, polite, and deferential) testimony a bit and drawing on that of her husband.

21 *Duncan v. Perez,* deposition of Parnell Latham, March 13, 1970, 17, r21, LCDC.

22 *Duncan v. Perez,* deposition of Darryl Bubrig, March 13, 1970, 13–14, r21, LCDC; *Duncan v. Perez,* deposition of Eugene Leon, March 11, 1970, 33, r21, LCDC; *Duncan v. Perez,* deposition of Randolph Scarabin, March 13, 1970, 7–9, r21, LCDC; *Duncan v. Perez,* deposition of Wayne Scarabin, March 12, 1970, 6–8, r21, LCDC.

23 Interview with Gary Duncan.

CHAPTER 9

1 *Sobol v. Perez,* testimony of Richard Sobol, vol. IV, 156–57, b1745, NARA-SW.

2 Ibid., 156; Richard Sobol in Spriggs, *Voices of Civil Rights Attorneys,* 255.

3 *Sobol v. Perez,* testimony of Richard Sobol, vol. IV, 156, b1745, NARA-SW.

4 Interview with Richard Sobol; *Duncan v. Perez,* suggested opinion by Al Bronstein, 2, r21, LCDC.

5 Paul Good, "Klantown USA," *The Nation,* February 1, 1965, 110–12; Fairclough, *Race & Democracy,* 350–56.

6 "Crown-Zellerbach in Bogalusa," memo dated March 31, 1964, series 2, box 652, folder 12, ACLU; Fairclough, *Race & Democracy,* 348.

7 Bell, *CORE and the Strategy of Nonviolence,* 170–71; Fairclough, *Race & Democracy,* 356–57; Harding, *There is a River,* 107; Hill, *The Deacons for Defense,* 2–8, 100; Wendt, "'Urge People Not to Carry Guns,'" 262–70.

8 Fairclough, *Race & Democracy,* 357.

9 Interview with Richard Sobol.

10 42 U.S.C. § 2000e-2.

11 Interview with Richard Sobol; *Sobol v. Perez,* testimony of Lolis Elie, vol. I, 101, b678 f5, ACLU; "Tabulation of Test Results," 3, r30, LCDC. See also *Hicks v. Crown Zellerbach,* 321 F. Supp. 1241, and several other same-named cases, and "Minutes of Meeting between Representatives of Crown-Zellerbach and Representatives of the Bogalusa Voters League," July 15, 1965, r30, LCDC.

12 Interview with Richard Sobol; *Sobol v. Perez,* testimony of Richard Sobol, vol. IV, 123, b649 f2, ACLU; press release on *Hicks v. Crown Zellerbach* by Henry

Schwarzschild, July 21, [1967], Civil Rights Litigation Clearinghouse, accessed May 25, 2018, https://www.clearinghouse.net/chDocs/public/EE-LA-0119-0001.pdf. As Sobol aptly put it to me: "[The idea of indirect discrimination] is not in Title VII. You can read Title VII and you don't see anything about that. It was *developed*."

13 Louisiana Constitution of 1921, Art. VII, § 41 (superseded by 1974).

CHAPTER 10

1 Interview with Gary Duncan.
2 This, and all subsequent quotes in this chapter unless otherwise cited, are from *State v. Duncan,* Transcript of Proceedings, r20, LCDC.
3 Interview with Darryl Bubrig.
4 Interview with Gary Duncan.
5 Interview with Bernard St. Ann.
6 Interview with Richard Sobol.
7 Interview with Gary Duncan.
8 Interview with Darryl Bubrig; *Sobol v. Perez,* deposition of Leander Perez Jr., August 11, 1967, 38, b1744, NARA-SW.
9 Interview with Richard Sobol.
10 Interview with Gary Duncan.

CHAPTER 11

1 Interview with Gary Duncan.
2 Interview with Richard Sobol.
3 Interview with Gary Duncan. The text of both Sobol's and Perez's closing arguments are, frustratingly, lost. The official transcript merely reports, "(Argument by counsel)," and the official record of *State v. Duncan* was destroyed by a fire, along with all court documents in Plaquemines Parish. The broad strokes of the statement are clear in Leon's reply, and I asked Bubrig, Duncan, and Sobol for their best recollections (which were understandably hazy).
4 Interview with Gary Duncan.

CHAPTER 12

1 This passage is based on extensive archival research, broad reading of articles by and about both Leander Perezes, and interviews with people who knew them.

Especially helpful were Glen Jeansonne's biography of the elder Perez, my wide-ranging interviews with Dominick Scandurro and his family, the FBI's Perez file, and the New Orleans Public Library's Perez collection. The extent to which Lea Perez did or did not buy into his father's tinfoil-hat worldview can be intuited from the record in *Sobol v. Perez, Duncan v. Perez,* and *Rousselle v. Perez* and in some of the documents that came to light during the Perez scions' power struggle in the 1980s—a tale that, one part *King Lear* and one part *Confederacy of Dunces,* deserves its own book.

2 See previous note, although this paragraph draws particularly heavily on Leander Perez Jr.'s revealing depositions in *Sobol v. Perez* and *Duncan v. Perez.*

3 *Sobol v. Perez,* deposition of Eugene Leon, 48, b1744, NARA-SW; *Sobol v. Perez,* deposition of Leander Perez Jr., August 11, 1967, 60–63, b1744, NARA-SW. Actually, Leon and Perez denied a few of the details of the account I have constructed, including their collusion and (sometimes) Perez's presence in the room. Their denials are neither convincing nor consistent. Most tellingly, Perez was present at Duncan's sentencing on February 1, though it was not "his day" to be in Pointe à la Hache (a custom anyway more honored in the breach than in the observance), and he reported Sobol to the Louisiana Bar Association that morning, before sentencing. How would he have known to call? Leon insisted that it did not "dawn on him" until a week later that Douglas had given up incriminating information (if, as I believe, he did), which strains credulity. Lea Perez was unable to offer a satisfactory explanation of what compelled him to check Sobol's status. It is hard to think of a situation other than the one I have described that explains the timing of Lea Perez's call to Baton Rouge.

4 *Sobol v. Perez,* testimony of Leander Perez Jr., vol. VII, 189, b680 f1, ACLU. He may also have told his father at this point, though he denied it.

5 *Sobol v. Perez,* testimony of Leander Perez Jr., vol. VII, 190, b680 f1, ACLU; *State of Louisiana v. Richard B. Sobol,* Number 1967–00014948, 25th District Court, Parish of Plaquemines.

6 *Sobol v. Perez,* testimony of Leander Perez Jr., vol. VII, 190, b680 f1, ACLU.

7 Ibid., 193. For general information about the fishing trips, I have relied on Perez's biographies and on an interview with Darryl Bubrig and Dominick Scandurro, November 2, 2016.

8 *Sobol v. Perez,* deposition of Leander Perez Jr., August 11, 1967, 66, b1744, NARA-SW.

9 Ibid., 64–65; *Sobol v. Perez,* testimony of Leander Perez Jr., vol. VII, 189, b680 f1, ACLU.

10 *Sobol v. Perez,* testimony of Leander Perez Jr., vol. VII, 193, b680 f1, ACLU.

11 Interview with Richard Sobol; *Sobol v. Perez,* deposition of Leander Perez Jr., August 11, 1967, 60–65, b1744, NARA-SW; *Sobol v. Perez,* deposition of Richard Sobol, August 11, 1967, 7–8, b1744, NARA-SW; *Sobol v. Perez,* testimony of Leander Perez Jr., vol. VII, 190–94, b680 f1, ACLU.

CHAPTER 13

1 Interview with Gary Duncan.

2 Interviews with Gary Duncan, Lynn Duncan, and Geralyn Lewis. Gregory Louis Taylor, it should be noted, petitioned successfully to have his name changed to Gary Duncan Jr., which was the name on his death certificate when he was killed in a head-on collision on the way home from a Martin Luther King Jr. Day parade in 1992, twenty-eight days short of his twenty-fifth birthday. Lynn Duncan still has a memorial to him in her home.

3 This paragraph was broadly informed by many hours of interviews with more than a dozen members of the extended Duncan family. I have spent considerable time figuring out and confirming the legal relationships between the Duncans and their kin, but it is important to note that I did this mostly because of my own cultural background, in which such distinctions are important, and to avoid confusing readers. The Duncans do not think about their family in these terms and were often frustrated or confused by my insistence on grilling them about it. This does not include only fathers. Three women list Gregory among their children without qualification: Adrian Taylor, Lynn Duncan, and Fay Duncan.

4 Interviews with Lynn Duncan, Cheryl Lange, and Stanley Lange.

5 Interview with Gary Duncan.

6 Interviews with Calvin Duncan, Gary Duncan, Laverne Jones, Harold Jones, Geralyn Lewis, and Vivian Taylor.

7 Interviews with Vivian and Robert Duncan. This was, of course, long before such activities were afforded the protection of publicity and the involvement of Northern whites. The Amistad Research Center has a fascinating collection of documents from the Prince Hall Grand Lodge going back to 1857. A hint of this Masonic lodge's vital importance to a century and a half of struggle for racial equality can be gleaned from this excellent note on the Amistad Research Center's website: http://amistadresearchcenter.tulane.edu/archon /?p=collections/findingaid&id=246&disabletheme=1. The lodge in Baton Rouge alone has several books' worth of stories waiting to be told about it.

8 Interview with Gary Duncan, May 18, 2017; *Sobol v. Perez,* testimony of Lambert Duncan, vol. VII, 43–46, b680 f1, ACLU.

CHAPTER 14

1 Interviews with Armand Derfner, David Fathi, Stanley Halpin, Warren Kaplan, and Richard Sobol; interview with Al Bronstein by Thomas Hilbink, September 24, 1992.

2 Interview with Jan Elvin; interview with Al Bronstein by Jack Bass, January 16,

1979, f9, JB; interview with Al Bronstein by Thomas Hilbink, September 24, 1992; Emily Langer, "Alvin Bronstein, Civil Rights Lawyer Who Pursued Prison Reform, Dies at 87," *Washington Post,* October 30, 2015.

3 Interviews with Jan Elvin and Mac Farmer; interview with Al Bronstein by Thomas Hilbink, September 24, 1992; interview with Al Bronstein by Jack Bass, January 16, 1979, f9, JB.

4 Interviews with Armand Derfner and Mac Farmer.

5 Ibid.; Emily Langer, "Alvin Bronstein, Civil Rights Lawyer Who Pursued Prison Reform, Dies at 87," *Washington Post,* October 30, 2015; Walker, *In Defense of American Liberties,* 266.

6 Interview with Armand Derfner.

7 Interview with Daniel Rezneck; letter from Al Bronstein to Henry Schwarzschild, February 13, 1967, LCDC; letter from Richard Sobol to Daniel Rezneck, February 13, 1967, LCDC.

8 Letter from Richard Sobol to Daniel Rezneck, February. 13, 1967, LCDC.

9 *State v. Duncan,* order denying writ of certiorari by Louisiana Supreme Court, February 20, 1967, r20, LCDC; *State v. Duncan,* affidavit of Richard Sobol, February 24, 1967, r21, LCDC.

10 *Sobol v. Perez,* testimony of Richard Sobol, vol. IV, 162–64, b679 f2, ACLU.

11 Ibid.; *Sobol v. Perez,* deposition of Eugene Leon, August 11, 1967, 27–28, b1744, NARA-SW; *State v. Duncan,* affidavit of Richard Sobol, February 24, 1967, r20, LCDC.

12 *Sobol v. Perez,* testimony of Richard Sobol, vol. IV, 165, b679 f2, ACLU.

13 Interview with Richard Sobol; email from Richard Sobol, September 3, 2016.

CHAPTER 15

1 *US v. Plaquemines Parish School Board,* report to the court, 1–5, b1638, NARA-SW.

2 *US v. Plaquemines Parish School Board,* testimony of Donald Gros, vol. II, 85, b1637, NARA-SW.

3 School board advertisement, *Plaquemines Gazette,* October 7, 1966; independent school advertisement, *Plaquemines Gazette,* October 14, 1966.

4 *US v. Plaquemines Parish School Board,* report to the court, 3, b1638, NARA-SW; *US v. Plaquemines Parish School Board,* testimony of John Baker, vol. II, 40, b1638, NARA-SW; *Plaquemines Parish School Board v. US,* brief of the United States on appeal, 11–17, b3771, NARA-SW.

5 Interview with Harold Jones; *US v. Plaquemines Parish School Board,* testimony of Loren Humphrey, vol. 1, 40–1, b1638, NARA–Ft. Worth. *US v. Plaquemines Parish School Board,* testimony of Henry Aymond, vol. 2, 92, b1638, NARA-SW; *Plaquemines Parish School Board v. US,* brief of the United

States on appeal, 13, b3771, NARA-SW; *Plaquemines Parish School Board v. US,* 415 F. 2d 817 (1969), 829.

6 *US v. Plaquemines Parish School Board,* testimony of Donald Gros, vol. II, 83, b1637, NARA-SW; *US v. Plaquemines Parish School Board,* testimony of Charles Simmons, vol. IV, 48, b1637, NARA-SW.

7 *US v. Plaquemines Parish School Board,* testimony of Hubert Stephens, vol. II, 60–61, b1637, NARA-SW.

8 *US v. Plaquemines Parish School Board,* testimony of Loren Humphrey, vol. I, 29–36, b1638, NARA-SW; *US v. Plaquemines Parish School Board,* testimony of Allen Deem, vol. I, 60–63, b1638, NARA-SW; *US v. Plaquemines Parish School Board,* testimony of Bert Taylor, vol. I, 70–72, b1638, NARA-SW; *US v. Plaquemines Parish School Board,* testimony of Henry Aymond, vol. I, 84, b1638, NARA-SW; *US v. Plaquemines Parish School Board,* testimony of Mrs. Andree Lawrence, vol. I, 89–92, b1638, NARA-SW; *US v. Plaquemines Parish School Board,* testimony of Hubert Stephens, vol. II, 60–64, b1638, NARA-SW; *US v. Plaquemines Parish School Board,* testimony of Charles Simmons, vol. III, 33–48, and vol. IV, 47–52, b1638, NARA-SW. See also *Plaquemines Parish School Board v. US.*

9 *US v. Plaquemines Parish School Board,* testimony of Charles Simmons, vol. III, 34, b1638, NARA-SW.

10 "Mrs. Perez Funeral Rites Are Scheduled," *New Orleans States-Item,* February 11, 1967.

CHAPTER 16

1 *Sobol v. Perez,* testimony of Lambert Duncan, vol. VII, 45, b680 f1, ACLU.

2 Interviews with Gary Duncan and Robert Duncan.

3 Proceedings in Open Court, February 21, 1967, 25th District Court, Parish of Plaquemines, r65, LCDC; *Sobol v. Perez,* deposition of Eugene Leon, August 11, 1967, 29–51, b1744, NARA-SW; *Sobol v. Perez,* deposition of Leander Perez Jr., August 11, 1967, 51, b1744, NARA-SW; *Sobol v. Perez,* testimony of Darryl Bubrig, vol. VII, 128–30, b1746, NARA-SW; *Sobol v. Perez,* testimony of Darryl Bubrig, vol. VII, 130, b1746, NARA-SW.

4 Interview with Richard Sobol; arrest report, February 21, 1967, r65, LCDC; *Sobol v. Perez,* testimony of Richard Sobol, vol. IV, 166, b1745, NARA-SW.

5 *Sobol v. Perez,* testimony of Richard Sobol, vol. IV, 165, b1745, NARA-SW.

6 Interview with Richard Sobol.

7 *Sobol v. Perez,* testimony of Richard Sobol, vol. IV, 165–66, b1745, NARA-SW.

8 Ibid., 165; interview with Richard Sobol, October 29, 2015; "New Jail, Model Penal Institution," *Plaquemines Gazette,* January 29, 1960.

9 Oral history with Don Jelinek by Bruce Hartford, 2005, Civil Rights Movement Archive, Tougaloo College, http://www.crmvet.org/nars/jelinek.htm; "Donald Jelinek, Lawyer for Attica Prisoners, Dies at 82," *New York Times,* July 3, 2016.

10 Interview with Richard Sobol; oral history with Richard Sobol by Joseph Mosiner, May 26, 2011, CRHP; Sobol in Spriggs, *Voices of Civil Rights Lawyers,* 191.

11 Interviews with Calvin Duncan, Gary Duncan, and Robert Duncan.

12 *Sobol v. Perez,* deposition of Eugene Leon, August 11, and testimony of Richard Sobol, vol. IV, 166, b1745, NARA-SW.

13 Interview with Gary Duncan; *Sobol v. Perez,* testimony of Richard Sobol, vol. IV, 168, b1745, NARA-SW.

14 Interview with Richard Sobol; email from Richard Sobol, September 3, 2016.

15 Interview with Gary Duncan.

16 Interviews with Gary Duncan and Robert Duncan; *Sobol v. Perez,* testimony of Richard Sobol, vol. IV, 168, b1745, NARA-SW.

CHAPTER 17

1 Interviews with Gary Duncan and Lynn Duncan.

2 Interview with Gary Duncan; *Sobol v. Perez,* testimony of Lambert Duncan, vol. VII, 43, b680 f1, ACLU. Wilbur Buras denied having been present that evening, which is odd not only because Duncan clearly remembers him, but also because his signature appears on the arrest report from that evening. Both Smith and Buras are now deceased, so I could not ask them. See *State v. Duncan,* arrest report, February 23, 1967, LCDC, and *Duncan v. Perez,* deposition of Wilbur Buras, April 28, 1970, r21, LCDC.

3 Interviews with Calvin Duncan and Gary Duncan; *Duncan v. Perez,* testimony of Gary Duncan, 35, r21, LCDC.

4 Interview with Gary Duncan; *Duncan v. Perez,* deposition of Ralph Ferranto, April 28, 1970, 13–15, r21, LCDC. Ferranto denied remembering much of this.

5 Interview with Gary Duncan; *State v. Duncan,* arrest report, February 23, 1967, r20, LCDC; *Duncan v. Perez,* testimony of Gary Duncan, 36–37, r21, LCDC. Gary repeated this story many times to me over two years; it haunts him.

6 Interview with Vivian Taylor.

CHAPTER 18

1 *State v. Duncan,* Testimony and Notes of Evidence, February 23, 1967, r65, LCDC.

2 Memo by Donald Juneau, February 24, 1967, r21, LCDC.

CHAPTER 19

1 "People Would Not Believe It Could Happen in Parish," *Plaquemines Gazette,* April 28, 1967.

2 "Private School Funds Studied," *New Orleans Times-Picayune,* October 6, 1966; "$1.5 Million Deficit in Budget Expected," *Plaquemines Gazette,* March 3, 1967; Jeansonne, *Leander Perez,* 304–5.

3 Interview with George Singlemann, 12, March 15, 1973, b1 f24, Reverse Freedom Rides, ARC.

4 Salisbury and Lartigue, *Educational Freedom in Urban America,* 21 and 46; *Poindexter v. Louisiana Financial Assistance Commission* (II).

5 *Poindexter v. Louisiana Financial Assistance Commission* (II), 835.

6 "Water Plant Expansion at Belle Chasse Underway," *Plaquemines Gazette,* March 3, 1967; "Parish Authorizes Bids for Two Pollution-Free 25-Ton Incinerators," *Plaquemines Gazette,* March 31, 1967.

7 "All Parish Private Schools Accredited by State Dept. of Ed." and "HEW Guidelines Adopted by Christenberry in Court Order," *Plaquemines Gazette,* April 7, 1967; "Parish Independent Schools Receive Eight Thousand Books," *Plaquemines Gazette,* April 14, 1967.

8 *US v. Plaquemines Parish School Board,* testimony of Dallas Picou, April 17, 1967, 138, b1638, NARA-SW.

9 "Tiny Tots in Rose Patti's Kindergarten Class," *Plaquemines Gazette,* April 28, 1967.

10 Letter by Leander Perez Sr., April 3, 1967, b1 f24, Reverse Freedom Rides ARC; Halberstam, "White Citizens Councils"; "Judge Perez Opens 'Save Our Children Crusade,'" *Plaquemines Gazette,* May 17, 1967.

11 "Judge Perez Opens 'Save Our Children Crusade,'" *Plaquemines Gazette,* May 17, 1967.

12 "Fifty-Four Graduates at River Oaks," *Plaquemines Gazette,* June 6, 1967; "Delta Heritage Graduates 23," *Plaquemines Gazette,* June 6, 1967; "Graduates Are Urged to Safeguard Their Liberties with Determined Resolution," *Plaquemines Gazette,* June 9, 1967.

13 "Chalin Perez Named to Replace His Father on Parish Council," *Plaquemines Gazette,* July 14, 1967.

CHAPTER 20

1 "Lawyer Seeks to Avoid Trial," *New Orleans Times-Picayune,* February 23, 1967; "Oral Argument Due in Review," *New Orleans Times-Picayune,* February 23, 1967.

2 Branch, *Parting the Waters,* 508.

3 This entire scene, unless otherwise indicated, is from an interview with Al Bronstein by Jack Bass, January 16, 1979, f9, JB.

4 Interview with Owen Fiss; email from Anthony Amsterdam, July 27, 2017.

5 Interview with Anthony Amsterdam; email from Anthony Amsterdam, July 27, 2017. I heard several different versions of the misbound-volume story from people who knew and worked with Amsterdam over the years. The most complete ones were from my interviews with Mac Farmer, Stanley Halpin, and Richard Sobol. The "real" version appears in Labi, "A Man Against the Machine," 15.

6 Interview with Owen Fiss; Labi, "A Man Against the Machine," 14–15.

7 Interviews with Mac Farmer and Owen Fiss; interview with Al Bronstein by Jack Bass, January 19, 1979, f10, JB; Labi, "A Man Against the Machine," 14–16.

8 Interview with Anthony Amsterdam. His correspondence with Schwarzschild is largely preserved in the ACLU Archive.

9 Report of meeting by Anthony Amsterdam, March 25, 1967, r166, LCDC; "Yankee Lawyer Go Home," *New York Times,* March 12, 1967.

10 Report of meeting by Anthony Amsterdam, March 25, 1967, r166, LCDC; letter from Louis Lusky to Anthony Amsterdam, March 30, 1967, r166, LCDC.

11 Report of meeting by Anthony Amsterdam, March 25, 1967, r166, LCDC (Amistad); letter from Anthony Amsterdam to Louis Lusky, March 28, 1967, r166, LCDC.

12 Letter from Thomas Collins to Robert Collins and Nils Douglas, March 7, 1967, r65, LCDC; report of meeting by Anthony Amsterdam, March 25, 1967, r166, LCDC. Amsterdam brings up this issue urgently in the early correspondence in *Sobol v. Perez.*

13 Interview with Anthony Amsterdam; report of meeting by Anthony Amsterdam, March 25, 1967, r166, LCDC; letter from Anthony Amsterdam to Louis Lusky, March 28, 1967, r166, LCDC; letter from Anthony Amsterdam to Al Bronstein, April 13, 1967, r166, LCDC.

CHAPTER 21

1 Interview with Jan Elvin in Conaway, *Judge,* 175. Conaway quotes Bronstein describing this feeling.

2 Here, and for the rest of this scene unless otherwise noted: *Sobol v. Perez,* deposition of Leander Perez Sr., August 11, 1967, b1744, NARA-SW.
3 Interview with Anthony Amsterdam.
4 Interview with Richard Sobol.

CHAPTER 22

1 Memo from Henry Schwarzschild to LCDC Board and Personnel, August 2, 1967, r81, LCDC.
2 "CORE and Bogalusa Civic and Voters' League, July 7, 1965, 0104–0103," KZSU, https://purl.stanford.edu/hh384ch2927.
3 Email from Richard Sobol, September 2, 2016.
4 Cal. Pen. Code 25850; Adam Winkler, "The Secret History of Guns," *The Atlantic,* September 2011. The causes of violence in the summer of 1967—or in 1965 or any other year—are complex and so indelibly politicized that it is probably impossible to find a truly unbiased accounting of them. The closest thing is Thomas Sugrue's *The Origins of the Urban Crisis.* Sugrue's book is about Detroit, but what happened in the Motor City is simply a more extreme version of what happened all over the northern and western urban cores of the nation.
5 Oral history with Cynthia Anderson by Joseph Mosiner, May 27, 2011, CRHP; Honigsberg, *Crossing Border Street,* 139.
6 Pfeifer, *Rough Justice,* 83–85.
7 Oral history with Chuck Jenkins by Joseph Mosiner, May 28, 2011, CRHP.
8 "15 Whites Attack Louisiana Negroes on Rights March," *New York Times,* August 16, 1967.
9 "Attack by Whites on March Halted," *New York Times,* August 17, 1967.
10 Oral history with A. Z. Young by Jackson Sailor, October 15, 1992, LDMA, http://ladigitalmedia.org/video_v2/asset-detail/OH-0060; oral history with Chuck Jenkins by Joseph Mosiner, May 28, 2011, CRHP; "Attack by Whites on March Halted," *New York Times,* August 17, 1967. Peter Honigsberg, who was there, has a somewhat different recollection in *Crossing Border Street.*
11 Oral history with A. Z. Young by Jackson Sailor, October 15, 1992, LDMA, http://ladigitalmedia.org/video_v2/asset-detail/OH-0060; oral history with Fletcher Anderson by Joseph Mosiner, May 27, 2011, CRHP; "Attack by Whites on March Halted," *New York Times,* August 17, 1967; Honigsberg, *Crossing Border Street,* 140.
12 Oral history with A. Z. Young by Jackson Sailor, October 15, 1992, LDMA, http://ladigitalmedia.org/video_v2/asset-detail/OH-0060; "Armed Force Protects Negroes in Rights March through Louisiana," *New York Times,* August 19, 1967.

13 Interview with Richard Sobol; Honigsberg, *Crossing Border Street,* 140–41.

14 "Armed Force Protects Negroes in Rights March through Louisiana," *New York Times,* August 19, 1967.

15 "Guard to Protect Louisiana Negroes," *New York Times,* August 18, 1967; "Armed Force Protects Negroes in Rights March through Louisiana," *New York Times,* August 19, 1967; Fairclough, *Race & Democracy,* 413; Honigsberg, *Crossing Border Street,* 142.

16 "Armed Force Protects Negroes in Rights March through Louisiana," *New York Times,* August 19, 1967.

17 *Crossing Border Street,* 142.

18 "Louisiana March Nears Its Climax," *New York Times,* August 20, 1967.

19 Ibid.; Honigsberg, *Crossing Border Street,* 142.

20 "Louisiana March Nears Its Climax," *New York Times,* August 20, 1967.

21 "Blazes Erupt in Baton Rouge," *New Orleans Times-Picayune,* August 21, 1967.

22 Interview with Richard Sobol. Peter Honigsberg described this scene (and his feelings) similarly in *Crossing Border Street,* 144–46.

23 Carmichael, *Black Power,* 35, 41, and 83.

24 "Dr. King Stresses Pride in His Race," *New York Times,* August 19, 1967.

25 Interview with Deb Millenson, September 8, 2017. Armand Derfner also told me about a similar meeting, in which LCDC lawyer Don Jelinek told Carmichael, "Well, I guess you don't need me now." Carmichael responded, "Don't move an inch."

26 Fairclough, *Race & Democracy,* 414.

CHAPTER 23

1 John Woolley and Gerhard Peters, "Presidential Job Approval," the American Presidency Project, University of California, Santa Barbara, accessed August 20, 2018, http://www.presidency.ucsb.edu/data/popularity.php?pres=36.

2 Interview with Richard Sobol. Also see *Brown v. Post* and letter from Richard Sobol to Henry Schwarzschild, October 5, 1967, r81, LCDC. The letter describes Sobol's "lousy Louisiana docket," including several voting cases around the state, as well as concerns that the 1967 election will bring still more.

3 "The Turning Point," *Time,* October 7, 1966; The 14th Amendment—Equal Protection Law or Tool of Usurpation, H.R. 7161, 90th Cong. (1967).

4 Testimony of Mary Fox, September 27, 1961, in *Hearings Before the United States Commission on Civil Rights,* 228.

5 Constitutional Test for Registration, Form No. 2, in *Hearings Before the United States Commission on Civil Rights,* 804.

6 Testimony of Edgar Brown, September 27, 1961, in *Hearings Before the United States Commission on Civil Rights,* 243–6.

7 Constitutional Test for Registration, Form No. 9, in *Hearings Before the United States Commission on Civil Rights,* 807.

8 Testimony of Mary Fox, September 27, 1961, in *Hearings Before the United States Commission on Civil Rights,* 221. She was corrected by the chairman on p. 234.

9 Testimony of Edgar Brown, September 27, 1961, in *Hearings Before the United States Commission on Civil Rights,* 243–4; Application for Voter Registration of Miroslaw Slavich, in *Hearings Before the United States Commission on Civil Rights,* 637; Application for Voter Registration of Mrs. Donald Wolf, in *Hearings Before the United States Commission on Civil Rights,* 636; *US v. Louisiana,* 225 F. Supp. *353,* 383–84 (1963); Jeansonne, *Leander Perez,* 248. This does not include twelve people who declined to state their race.

10 Interview with Vivian and Robert Duncan.

11 Testimonies of Percy Griffin, Elizabeth Taylor, and Joseph Taylor, in *Hearings Before the United States Commission on Civil Rights,* 101, 103, and 109.

12 Testimony of Joseph Taylor, September 27, 1961, in *Hearings Before the United States Commission on Civil Rights,* 108.

13 Testimony of Mary Fox, September 27, 1961, in *Hearings Before the United States Commission on Civil Rights,* 219–20; Irene Pansy in Edwards, *The Forgotten People,* 109–10.

14 See, generally, testimonies of Percy Griffin, Elizabeth Taylor, and Joseph Taylor, in *Hearings Before the United States Commission on Civil Rights;* Edwards, *The Forgotten People,* 109.

15 Interview with Vivian and Robert Duncan; Angelina and Robert Jones, August Tinson, Carolyn Sapps, Irene Pansy, and Viola Piquet in Edwards, *The Forgotten People,* 109–13.

16 See *US v. Fox.*

17 Edwards, *The Forgotten People,* 136.

18 Lyndon Johnson, "Annual Message to the Congress on the State of the Union" (speech, Washington, DC, January 4, 1965); *US v. Louisiana,* 225 F. Supp. 353.

19 *US v. Louisiana,* 265 F. Supp. 703.

20 "Voting Rights Bill Passage; Influence By Reds Is Shown: Complete Text of Television Talk by Judge Perez over WWL-TV, Channel 4, August 17," *Plaquemines Gazette,* August 27, 1965; Jeansonne, *Leander Perez,* 252.

21 Berman, *Give Us the Ballot,* 45.

22 Tucker, "The Power of Observation," 237–38.

23 Report of special agents, FBI file for Leander Perez, part 3, document no. 44-37688-3, November 8, 1967, https://vault.fbi.gov/Leander%20Perez%2C %20Sr./Leander%20Perez%2C%20Sr.%20Part%203%20of%204/view. The names of the observers, alas, were redacted. NB: The observers primly wrote "(obscene)" in lieu of even the mildest curse words. There is a key later in the file.

CHAPTER 24

1 Interviews with Gary Duncan and Lynn Duncan.

2 Interview with Lynn Duncan; interview with Gary Duncan by Nancy Buirski, July 18, 2018.

3 Interview with Gary Duncan.

4 Letter from John Davis to Richard Sobol, October 10, 1967, LCDC; "The Supreme Court 1967–68—The Term in Review."

5 Interviews with Gary Duncan and Lynn Duncan.

6 Interview with Gary Duncan.

7 Obituary for Dorothy Dowling Wolbrette, January 10, 2013, TheAdvocate .com, accessed August 24, 2018, https://obits.theadvocate.com/obituaries /theadvocate/obituary.aspx?n=dorothy-dowling-wolbrette&pid=162272340 &fhid=5630; "Tulane Law School Hall of Fame—2014 Inductees," Tulane University Law School, accessed August 24, 2018, https://law.tulane.edu/alumni /hall-fame.

8 *Duncan v. Louisiana,* oral argument, Oyez.org, accessed May 30, 2015, https://www.oyez.org/cases/1967/410.

9 Interview with Gary Duncan.

CHAPTER 25

1 *Sobol v. Perez,* brief of the United States, 1–4, b1743, NARA-SW; memo from Owen Fiss to John Doar, September 12–13 (date illegible), Civil Rights Litigation Clearinghouse, University of Michigan Law School, accessed August 22, 2018, https://www.clearinghouse.net/chDocs/public/PA-LA-0001-0031 .pdf; letter from John Doar to Ralph Spritzer, September 13, 1967, Civil Rights Litigation Clearinghouse, University of Michigan Law School, accessed August 22, 2018, https://www.clearinghouse.net/chDocs/public/PA-LA-0001 -0031.pdf.

2 Interview with Al Bronstein by Jack Bass, January 19, 1979, f10, JB.

3 Interview with Anthony Amsterdam.

4 Interview with Armand Derfner; "Armand Derfner Recalls Late 1960s in Mississippi as Civil Rights Lawyer," *Post and Courier* (Charleston, SC), June 24, 2017.

5 Interview with Armand Derfner.

6 Interview with Anthony Amsterdam; *Sobol v. Perez,* testimony of Lolis Elie, vol. I, 106–9, 116, 118, b1745, NARA-SW.

7 Amsterdam has referred to this several times, including in interviews with me and in Elie's obituary in *The Advocate.* The trial transcript does not include the unbroken speech that Amsterdam vividly remembers, but the effect of

Elie's eloquent testimony was noted by many. The transcript does not note a change in lunch recess time, exactly, but the day's proceedings do seem lopsided—far more testimony before lunch than after—when compared with the other days of trial in this case.

8 Interviews with Anthony Amsterdam, Armand Derfner, and Richard Sobol; interview with Al Bronstein by Jack Bass, January 19, 1979, f10, JB; "State Lawyers Said Bypassed," *New Orleans Times-Picayune,* January 23, 1967.

9 Interview with Armand Derfner. Despite Elie's winking implication, much of what Elie said about Rarick was documented. Elie's friend, attorney Calvin Johnson, told me that "what's recorded about Rarick doesn't come close."

10 "Bar Group, U.S. Opponents in Lawyer's Suit," *New Orleans States-Item,* January 22, 1967.

11 *Sobol v. Perez,* testimony of Robert Collins, vol. I, 253–55, b1745, NARA-SW; "State Lawyers Said Bypassed," *New Orleans Times-Picayune,* January 23, 1967.

12 Interview with Gary Duncan.

13 Interviews with Anthony Amsterdam, Armand Derfner, and Richard Sobol. Elie's unshakable nerve and persuasive testimony, in particular, have attained mythic status among civil rights lawyers in New Orleans and elsewhere. Calvin Johnson called the first day of *Sobol v. Perez* "one of Lolis's classic moments."

14 Interviews with Anthony Amsterdam, Owen Fiss, and Richard Sobol.

CHAPTER 26

1 *Sobol v. Perez,* testimony of Zelma Wyche, vol. III, 160–70, b1745, NARA-SW. A note on the last in the list of outrages: The creation of strategically placed school districts was (and is) the favorite tactic for separating the races in the North and in Southern counties with geographically segregated populations. Because of the relative integration of Plaquemines housing (and the parish's unusual shape), it would have been almost impossible to effectively segregate public schools using this method, which led Perez to the much more onerous and expensive option of creating a parallel private-school system. This "segregation academy" model, which never worked as well as race-based redistricting, was struck down by the Supreme Court in *Runyon v. McCrary,* 427 U.S. 160 (1976). There has never been an effective challenge mounted against the system of district-based segregation that increasingly drives Americans' decisions about where to live.

2 Interview with Gary Duncan.

3 *Sobol v. Perez,* deposition of Leander Perez Sr., August 11, 1967, 81, b1744, NARA-SW; *Sobol v. Perez,* testimony of Earl Amedee, vol. V, b1745, NARA-SW.

4   *Sobol v. Perez,* testimony of Richard Sobol, vol. IV, 180–81, b679 f2, ACLU.

5   *Sobol v. Perez,* transcript of proceedings, vol. VI, 76–106, b679 f4, ACLU.

6   Interview with Anthony Amsterdam.

7   Interview with Anthony Amsterdam.

8   *Sobol v. Perez,* transcript of proceedings, vol. VI, 129, b679 f4, ACLU.

9   *Sobol v. Perez,* testimony of John Slavich, vol. VI, 138, b679 f4, ACLU; *Sobol v. Perez,* testimony of Joseph Defley, vol. VI, 156–57, 159, b679 f4, ACLU; *Sobol v. Perez,* testimony of Edward Baldwin, vol. VII, 11–12, b680 f1, ACLU.

10 *Sobol v. Perez,* testimony of Thomas McBride III, vol. VI, 188, b679 f4, ACLU.

CHAPTER 27

1   "Johnson Says He Won't Run," *New York Times,* April 1, 1968; Branch, *At Canaan's Edge,* 720–22, 754–58; Ralph Abernathy, Jesse Jackson, Bill Lucy, and James E. Smith in Hampton and Fayer, *Voices of Freedom,* 463–64; Perelstein, *Nixonland,* 255.

2   Interviews with Gary Duncan, Robert Duncan, Rev. Tyronne Edwards, Harold Jones, and Laverne Jones. The memory from Buras High School is Laverne's.

3   "Wallace Figures to Win Even If He Loses," *New York Times Magazine,* April 7, 1968.

4   Buckley, *Firing Line,* "The Wallace Movement."

CHAPTER 28

1   Interviews with Anthony Amsterdam, Armand Derfner, Owen Fiss, and Richard Sobol; *Sobol v. Perez,* plaintiffs' post-trial brief, April 8, 1968, Civil Rights Litigation Clearinghouse, University of Michigan Law School, accessed September 3, 2018, https://www.clearinghouse.net/chDocs/public/PA-LA-0001-0035 .pdf.

2   *Sobol v. Perez,* government's post-trial brief, April 12, 1968, 114, Civil Rights Litigation Clearinghouse, University of Michigan Law School, accessed May 12, 2017, https://www.clearinghouse.net/chDocs/public/PA-LA-0001-0001.pdf.

3   Ibid., 124, 132.

4   Letter from John Fournet to Ben Dawkins, February 22, 1968, LCDC; letter from Ben Dawkins to Richard Sobol, February 26, 1968, LCDC; letter from Ben Dawkins to John Fournet, February 26, 1968, LCDC.

5   *Brown v. Post* and *Wyche v. Post. Wyche* did not result in an opinion; its case files can be found on reel 74 of the LCDC papers. Also see "Voting Rights: A Case Study of Madison Parish, Louisiana," 726–87.

6 "Republican Party Platform of 1968" in Gerhard Peters and John T. Woolley, the American Presidency Project, University of California, Santa Barbara, http://www.presidency.ucsb.edu/ws/?pid=25841.

7 Interview with Richard Sobol; Rustin, *Down the Line,* 195–97.

8 *Sobol v. Perez,* plaintiffs' post-trial brief, April 8, 1968, 26, Civil Rights Litigation Clearinghouse, University of Michigan Law School, accessed September 3, 2018, https://www.clearinghouse.net/chDocs/public/PA-LA-0001-0035.pdf.

9 *Sobol v. Perez,* plaintiffs' post-trial brief, April 8, 1968, 26, Civil Rights Litigation Clearinghouse, University of Michigan Law School, accessed September 3, 2018, https://www.clearinghouse.net/chDocs/public/PA-LA-0001-0035.pdf. The case was *US v. Local 189,* but the case summary is best found in Judge Wisdom's opinion in the appeal, *Local 189 v. US,* 985–88.

10 *Poindexter v. LFAC* (III), 688. *Griffin v. Louisiana* and *Adams v. Fazzio Real Estate* were the bowling alley cases.

11 Telegram from John Davis to Richard Sobol, May 20, 1968, r20, LCDC.

12 *Duncan v. Louisiana,* 155–56; 18 U.S.C. § 19 indicates that "petty offense" comprises infractions and class B or C misdemeanors, as defined by 18 U.S.C. § 3559 and § 3571.

CHAPTER 29

1 William Bunch, "Handcuffed by History," *New York Times Magazine,* September 2, 2001; "York Ex-Mayor Acquitted, Two Men Are Convicted in the 1969 Race-Riot," *Philadelphia Inquirer,* October 20, 2002.

2 *Sobol v. Perez,* 289 F. Supp. 392, 401–2 (1968).

3 Interview with Deb Millenson; Richard Sobol's application for position as US District Court judge, May 1979, Sobol's personal papers (copy in possession of author); minutes of LCDC board meeting, June 17, 1968, r17, ACLU; letter from Richard Sobol to John de J. Pemberton, May 19, 1969, r81, LCDC; letter from Richard Sobol to George Forman, December 20, 1969, r81, LCDC.

4 *Duncan v. Perez,* testimony of Calvin Lange and Gary Duncan, 27–50, r163, LCDC; memo from Al Bronstein to Richard Sobol, Anthony Amsterdam, and George Strickler, June 11, 1970, 4, r163, LCDC.

5 Interviews with Gary Duncan and Richard Sobol. Some of this correspondence is scattered throughout the LCDC papers.

6 Interviews with Deb Millenson and Richard Sobol.

7 Interview with Richard Sobol.

8 Ibid.

9 Letter from Richard Sobol to Gary Duncan, June 29, 1970, r163, LCDC.

10 *Hicks v. Crown Zellerbach Corp.,* 319 F. Supp. 214 (E.D. La. 1970); *Hicks v. Crown Zellerbach Corp.,* 321 F. Supp. 1241 (E.D. La. 1971).

11 *Duncan v. Perez,* 321 F. Supp 181, 184–85 (1970).

12 This account is based on interviews with more than a dozen Plaquemines natives, but special thanks to the Scandurros, Stanley Gaudet, Buddy Cossé, Bernard St. Ann, Lucretia Hunter, and, especially, Harold and Laverne Jones.

13 As before, this is based on more than a dozen interviews. Special thanks to Gary and Robert Duncan, Rev. Theodore Taylor, Harold Jones, Stanley Lange, and Rev. Tyronne Edwards (who, I suspect, disagrees somewhat with the description).

14 Interviews with Anne and Richard Sobol.

CHAPTER 30

1 *Report on Hurricane Camille,* 2–3; Zebrowski and Howard, *Category 5,* 52–53.

2 Zebrowski and Howard, *Category 5,* 72–73.

3 Interview with Gary Duncan.

4 Interviews with Darryl Bubrig, Gary Duncan, Rev. Tyronne Edwards, and Bernard St. Ann; "Port Eads: A Family Remembers," *Plaquemines Gazette,* June 18, 2013.

5 *Report on Hurricane Camille,* 3, 8, 13, 31, and 75; Keiper, Landsea, and Beven, "A Reanalysis of Hurricane Camille," 382; Simpson, Sugg, et al., "The Atlantic Hurricane Season of 1969," 299; Zebrowski and Howard, *Category 5,* 73.

6 Interviews with Gary Duncan, Harold Jones, and Laverne Jones.

EPILOGUE

1 Interviews with Armand Derfner, Brian Landsberg, Deb Millenson, and Ray Terry.

2 Interviews with Robert A. Collins, Lolis Eric Elie, Ernest Jones, and Calvin Johnson.

3 Interviews with Anne and Richard Sobol; letter from Anthony Amsterdam to Al Bronstein, October 27, 1970, r163, LCDC.

Sources

INTERVIEWS

Anthony Amsterdam, October 28, 2015.

Janice Andry, *daughter of Vivian Duncan Taylor,* November 30, 2016, and August 6, 2017.

Hazell Boyce, *friend of Lolis Elie,* July 24, 2018.

Darryl Bubrig, December 17, 2015, and November 2, 2016.

Barbara Hicks Collins, *daughter of Robert Hicks,* November 28, 2018.

Kathy Collins, *daughter-in-law of Justice Department lawyer Hugh Fleischer,* July 18, 2017.

Robert A. Collins, *son of Robert F. Collins,* July 25, 2018.

Buddy Cossé, *coach at Port Sulphur High School and Delta Heritage Academy and recreation director for Plaquemines Parish,* May 19, 2017.

Gaynell Crum, *née Duncan,* November 30, 2016, and August 6, 2017.

Rev. Samuel Crum, *Zion Hill Christian Church, Boothville, LA, and husband of Gaynell Duncan Crum,* August 6, 2017.

Armand Derfner, *LCDC staff attorney, 1967–1970,* August 27, 2017.

Brian Dickenson, *Buras High School '68,* March 28, 2017.

Pam Dickenson, *attended Delta Heritage Academy,* March 28, 2017.

Calvin Duncan, November 30, 2016, August 6, 2017, and July 19, 2018.

Darius Duncan, *grandson of Gary Duncan,* November 6, 2016.

Fay Duncan, *wife of Gary Duncan,* November 4 and 30 and December 3 and 5, 2016; May 8 and 18 and August 4 and 6, 2017; May 2 and 6, 2018; and March 1, 2019.

Flora Mae Duncan, November 30, 2016, and August 6, 2017.

Gary Duncan, November 4, 7, and 30 and December 3 and 5, 2016; May 6, 8, and 18 and August 4 and 6, 2017; January 27 and 28, May 2 and 6, June 10, and July 15–17 and 19, 2018; and March 1, 2019.

Lynn Duncan, June 18, 2017.

Mancil Duncan, November 30, 2016, and August 6, 2017.

Robert Duncan, November 30, 2016, and August 6, 2017.

Rev. Tyronne Edwards, *Zion Traveler Baptist Church, Phoenix, LA,* August 4, 2017.

Lolis Eric Elie, *son of Lolis Edward Elie,* June 26, 2018.

Jan Elvin, *wife of Al Bronstein,* June 25, 2018.

Augerine Encalade, *née Duncan,* November 30, 2016, and August 6, 2017.

Ansley Erickson, *Teacher's College, Columbia University,* February 25, 2016.

Malcolm Farmer III, *LCDC staff attorney, 1965–1967,* August 31, 2017.

Vaughn Fauria, *friend of Lolis Elie,* July 25, 2018.

Bethany Fayard, *Ocean Springs Seafood, Inc.,* February 7, 2017.

Earl Fayard, *Ocean Springs Seafood, Inc.,* February 7, 2017.

Owen Fiss, August 11, 2016, and August 1, 2017.

Lanie Fleischer, *wife of Hugh Fleischer,* July 19, 2017.

Stanley Gaudet, *principal of Boothville-Venice High School, 1987–1989,* March 28, 2017.

Hewitt Gauthier, *Plaquemines resident,* May 3, 2018.

Mike Gauthier, *Plaquemines resident,* May 3, 2018.

Stanley Halpin, *LCDC staff attorney, 1969–1972,* July 29, 2017.

Valeria Hicks, *wife of Robert Hicks,* November 28, 2018.

Peter Honigsberg, *LCDC intern, 1966–1968,* August 30, 2016.

Lucretia Hunter, *Buras High School '70,* August 7, 2017.

Calvin Johnson, *friend of Lolis Elie,* July 26, 2018.

Ernest Jones, *civil rights attorney, former law partner of Lolis Elie,* July 19, 2018.

Harold Jones, *Boothville-Venice High School '69,* March 29 and August 3 and 5, 2017.

Laverne Jones, *Buras High School '73,* March 29 and August 3 and 5, 2017.

Warren Kaplan, *LCDC volunteer, 1965,* August 5, 2016.

Betsy Kuhn, *worked with Al Bronstein at National Prison Project,* June 28, 2018.

Brian Landsberg, *Civil Rights Division of the US Department of Justice,* August 2, 2017.

Cheryl Lange, *cousin of Gary Duncan,* August 6, 2017, and June 10, 2018.

Stanley Lange, August 6, 2017, and June 10, 2018.

Geralyn Lewis, *née Duncan,* June 18, 2017.

Karry Merricks, *cousin of Gary Duncan,* June 3, 2018.

Suzie Merricks, *wife of Karry Merricks,* June 3, 2018.

Deb Millenson, *LCDC staff attorney, 1969–1972,* September 8, 2017.

Lawrence Miller, *LCDC volunteer, 1965,* August 5, 2016.

Carolyn Parker, *Buras High School '72,* August 7, 2017.

Robert Rachlin, *LCDC volunteer, 1965,* August 17, 2016.

Daniel Rezneck, *worked with Richard Sobol at Arnold, Fortas & Porter,* July 28, 2017.

Alice Scandurro, *Plaquemines resident,* December 10, 2016; June 16 and December 2, 2017; and July 24, 2018.

Dewey Scandurro, *attended Delta Heritage Academy,* February 8 and December 2, 2017.

Dominick Scandurro, *Plaquemines resident,* November 2 and December 10, 2016; February 4 and 8, June 16, and December 2, 2017; and July 24, 2018.

Michelle Scandurro, *wife of Dewey Scandurro,* December 2, 2017.

Tim Scandurro, *attended Delta Heritage Academy,* February 8, 2017.

SOURCES

Steve Scandurro, *attended Delta Heritage Academy,* February 8, 2017.

Sara Shreve, *historic preservationist,* August 27, 2017.

Carol Ruth Silver, *LCDC volunteer, 1965,* August 3, 2016.

Anne Sobol, October 28, 2015, and August 21 and 22, 2019.

Richard Sobol, May 7 and October 28, 2015; February 10, 2016; and August 21 and 22, 2019.

Bernard St. Ann, August 2, 2017.

Vivian Taylor, *née Duncan,* November 30, 2016, and August 6, 2017.

Ray Terry, *Civil Rights Division of the US Department of Justice,* July 28, 2017.

Henrietta Turner, *Buras High School '73,* August 7, 2017.

Rev. Theodore Turner, *Mt. Olive Missionary Baptist Church,* August 7, 2017.

Donald Walter, *Senior US District Court Judge (W.D. La.),* June 20, 2018.

Herman Landry and Barbara Sobol did not respond to multiple interview requests.

BOOKS

Baker, Liva. *The Second Battle of New Orleans: The Hundred-Year Struggle to Integrate the Schools.* New York: HarperCollins, 1996.

Bass, Jack. *Unlikely Heroes.* New York: Simon & Schuster, 1981.

Bell, Inge Powell. *CORE and the Strategy of Nonviolence.* New York: Random House, 1968.

Berman, Ari. *Give Us the Ballot: The Modern Struggle for Voting Rights in America.* New York: Picador, 2015.

Branch, Taylor. *At Canaan's Edge: America in the King Years, 1965–1968, Vol. III.* New York: Touchstone, 2006.

———. *Parting the Waters: America in the King Years, 1954–1963, Vol. I.* New York: Touchstone, 1988.

Buras, Janice P. *Betsy & Camille: Sisters of Destruction.* Belle Chasse, LA: Down the Road Publishing, 1995.

Carmichael, Stokely (Kwame Ture), and Charles V. Hamilton. *Black Power: The Politics of Liberation in America.* New York: Vintage, 1967.

Carson, Clayborne, David J. Garrow, Gerald Gill, Vincent Harding, and Darlene Clark Hine, eds. *The Eyes on the Prize Civil Rights Reader.* New York: Penguin, 1991.

Colten, Craig E., ed. *Transforming New Orleans and Its Environs: Centuries of Change.* Pittsburgh, PA: University of Pittsburgh Press, 2000.

Conaway, James. *Judge: The Life and Times of Leander Perez.* New York: Knopf, 1973.

Edwards, Tyronne. *The Forgotten People: Restoring a Missing Segment of Plaquemines Parish History.* Self-published, Xlibris, 2017.

Fairclough, Adam. *Race & Democracy: The Civil Rights Struggle in Louisiana, 1915–1972.* Athens, GA: University of Georgia Press, 1995.

Gill, James. *Lords of Misrule: Mardi Gras and the Politics of Race in New Orleans.* Jackson, MS: University Press of Mississippi, 1997.

Hampton, Henry, and Steve Fayer. *Voices of Freedom: An Oral History of the Civil Rights Movement from the 1950s through the 1980s.* New York: Bantam Books, 1990.

Harding, Vincent. *There Is a River: The Black Struggle for Freedom in America.* San Diego, CA: Harcourt Brace, 1981.

Hewitt, Christopher. *Political Violence and Terrorism in Modern America: A Chronology.* Westport, CT: Greenwood Publishing Group, 2005.

Hill, Lance E. *The Deacons for Defense: Armed Resistance and the Civil Rights Movement.* Chapel Hill, NC: University of North Carolina Press, 2004.

Honigsberg, Peter Jan. *Crossing Border Street: A Civil Rights Memoir.* Berkeley, CA: University of California Press, 2000.

Jeansonne, Glen. *Leander Perez: Boss of the Delta.* Baton Rouge, LA: Louisiana State University Press, 1977.

Meyer, J. Ben. *Plaquemines: The Empire Parish.* New Orleans, LA: Laborde Printing Co., 1981.

Perlstein, Rick. *Nixonland: The Rise of a President and the Fracturing of America.* New York: Simon and Schuster, 2010.

Pfeifer, Michael. *Rough Justice: Lynching and American Society, 1874–1947.* Urbana, IL: University of Illinois Press, 2004.

Powell, Gloria. *Black Monday's Children: A Study of the Effects of School Desegregation on Self-Concepts of Southern Children.* New York: Appleton-Century-Crofts, 1973.

Read, Frank T., and Lucy S. McGough. *Let Them Be Judged: The Judicial Integration of the Deep South.* Metuchen, NJ: Scarecrow Press, 1978.

Rogers, Kim Lacy. *Righteous Lives: Narratives of the New Orleans Civil Rights Movement.* New York: New York University Press, 1993.

Rustin, Bayard. *Down the Line: Collected Writings.* Chicago: Quadrangle Books, 1971.

Salisbury, David, and Casey Lartigue. *Educational Freedom in Urban America: Brown v. Board after Half a Century.* Washington, DC: Cato Institute, 2004.

Spear, Jennifer M. *Race, Sex, and Social Order in Early New Orleans.* Baltimore: Johns Hopkins University Press, 2009.

Spriggs, Kent, ed. *Voices of Civil Rights Lawyers: Reflections from the Deep South, 1964–1980.* Gainesville, FL: University Press of Florida, 2017.

Sugrue, Thomas. *The Origins of the Urban Crisis: Race and Inequality in Postwar Detroit.* Princeton, NJ: Princeton University Press, 1996.

Temple, Ralph. *Life, Liberty, and the Pursuit of Happiness.* Brooklyn: Akashic Books, 2011.

Walker, Samuel. *In Defense of American Liberties: A History of the ACLU.* Carbondale, IL: Southern Illinois University Press, 1990.

Wall, Bennett H., and John C. Rodrigue, eds. *Louisiana: A History, Sixth Edition.* West Sussex, UK: John Wiley & Sons, 2014.

Warren, Robert Penn. *Who Speaks for the Negro?* New York: Random House, 1965.

Watson, Bruce. *Freedom Summer: The Savage Season That Made Mississippi Burn and Made America a Democracy.* New York: Viking, 2010.

Wolters, Raymond. *The Burden of Brown: Thirty Years of School Desegregation.* Knoxville, TN: University of Tennessee Press, 1984.

Zebrowski, Ernest, and Judith A. Howard. *Category 5: The Story of Camille, Lessons Unlearned from America's Most Violent Hurricane.* Ann Arbor, MI: University of Michigan Press, 2005.

ARTICLES

NB: Newspaper and magazine archives can be found on the websites of the respective publications or on NewsBank. There are two exceptions: the archives of the *Plaquemines Gazette* and the *Louisiana Weekly* are kept on microfilm in the New Orleans Public Library, Louisiana Division.

Amsterdam, Anthony G. "Criminal Prosecutions Affecting Federally Guaranteed Civil Rights: Federal Removal and Habeas Corpus Jurisdiction to Abort State Court Trial." *University of Pennsylvania Law Review* 113, no. 6 (1965): 793–912.

Bennett, Dale F. "The 1966 Code of Criminal Procedure." *Louisiana Law Review* 27, no. 2 (1967): 175–230.

"Dialogue on the American Jury: Part I—The History of Trial by Jury." Washington, DC: American Bar Association Division for Public Education, n.d. https://www.americanbar.org/content/dam/aba/administrative/public_education/resources/dialoguepart1.pdf.

Elie, Lolis E. "Niggertown Memories." *Black River Journal* 1, no. 1 (1977).

Endres, David J. "Judge Leander Perez and the Franciscans of Our Lady of Good Harbor: A School Integration Battle in Buras, Louisiana, 1962–1965." *Catholic Southwest* 27 (2016).

Fiss, Owen M. "Dombrowski." *Yale Law Journal* 86 (1977): 1103–64. Accessed August 22, 2018. http://digitalcommons.law.yale.edu/fss_papers/1222.

Goudeau, D. A., and W. C. Connor. "Storm Surge Over the Mississippi River Delta Accompanying Hurricane Betsy, 1965." *Monthly Weather Review* 96, no. 2 (1968): 118–24.

Hill, Rickey. "The Bogalusa Movement: Self-Defense and Black Power in the Civil Rights Struggle." *Black Scholar* 41, no. 3 (2011): 43–54.

"The Honorable Judge Robert F. Collins." *National Black Law Journal* 11, no. 2 (1989): 280–81.

Howard, Judith A. "Home at the Mouth of the Mississippi." *Southern Cultures* 14, no. 2 (2008): 69–88.

Keiper, Margaret, Christopher Landsea, and John Beven. "A Reanalysis of Hurricane Camille." *Bulletin of the American Meteorological Society* 97, no. 2 (2016): 367–84.

Labi, Nadya. "A Man Against the Machine." *NYU Law Magazine,* Autumn 2007.

Latham, Mark D. "Plaquemines Parish Commission Council v. Delta Development Co.: Contra Non Valentem Applied to Fiduciaries." *Louisiana Law Review* 48, no. 4 (1988): 967–83.

Rogers, J. D. "Development of the New Orleans Flood Protection System Prior to Hurricane Katrina." *Journal of Geotechnical and Geoenvironmental Engineering* 135, no. 5 (2008): 602–17.

Simpson, R. H., Arnold L. Sugg, et al. "The Atlantic Hurricane Season of 1969." *Monthly Weather Review* 98, no. 4 (1970): 293–306.

Sugg, Arnold L. "The Hurricane Season of 1965." *Monthly Weather Review* 94, no. 3 (1966): 183–91.

Tucker, James. "The Power of Observation: The Role of Federal Election Observers Under the Voting Rights Act." *Michigan Journal of Race and Law* 13 (2007): 227–76.

"Voting Rights: A Case Study of Madison Parish, Louisiana." *University of Chicago Law Review* 38, no. 4 (1971): 726–87.

Wendt, Simon. "'Urge People Not to Carry Guns': Armed Self-Defense in the Louisiana Civil Rights Movement and the Radicalization of the Congress of Racial Equality." *Louisiana History* 45, no. 3 (2004), 261–86.

REPORTS

Couvillion, Brady, John Barras, et al. *Land Area Change in Coastal Louisiana from 1932 to 2010.* Reston, VA: US Geological Survey, 2011.

Gemini V Air-to-Ground Transcription. Houston, TX: NASA Manned Spacecraft Center, October 1965.

Gemini V PAO Mission Commentary Transcription. Houston, TX: NASA Manned Spacecraft Center, October 1965.

Hearings Before the Special Subcommittee to Investigate Areas of Destruction of Hurricane Betsy of the Committee on Public Works, New Orleans; Sept. 25, 1965. Washington, DC: US House of Representatives, 89th Congress, 1st session, 1965.

Hearings Before the United States Commission on Civil Rights, New Orleans; Sept. 27, 1960, Sept. 28, 1960, May 5, 1961, May 6, 1961. Washington, DC: US Commission on Civil Rights, 1961.

Hurricane Camille: A Report to the Administrator. Rockville, MD: US Department of Commerce, Environmental Science Services Administration, September 1969.

Lopez, John, Theryn Henkel, et al. *Bohemia Spillway in Southeastern Louisiana: History, General Description, and 2011 Hydrologic Surveys.* New Orleans: Lake Pontchartrain Basin Foundation, 2013.

Louisiana's Comprehensive Master Plan for a Sustainable Coast. Baton Rouge, LA: Coastal Protection and Restoration Authority of Louisiana, 2017.

The New Orleans School Crisis: Report of the Louisiana State Advisory Commission to the United States Commission on Civil Rights. Washington, DC: US Commission on Civil Rights, 1961.

Preliminary Report on Hurricane "Hilda," September 26 to October 5, 1964. Washington, DC: National Weather Bureau, 1964. Accessed March 29,

2018. https://www.nhc.noaa.gov/archive/storm_wallets/atlantic/atl1964/hilda/prenhc/.

Report on Hurricane Betsy, 8–11 September 1965, in the U.S. Army Engineer District, New Orleans. New Orleans: US Army Corps of Engineers, November 1965.

Report on Hurricane Camille, 14–22 August 1969, in the U.S. Army Engineer District, Mobile. Mobile, AL: US Army Corps of Engineers, May 1970.

Roth, David. *Louisiana Hurricane History.* Camp Springs, MD: National Weather Service, April 2010.

"The Supreme Court 1967–68—The Term in Review" in *CQ Almanac 1968, 24th ed.* Washington, DC: Congressional Quarterly, 1969.

DISSERTATIONS AND THESES

Hilbink, Thomas. "Filling the Void: The Lawyers Constitutional Defense Committee and the 1964 Freedom Summer." Columbia University, 1993.

FILM AND TELEVISION

Buckley, William F, presenter. *Firing Line.* Episode 95, "The Wallace Movement." Aired April 15, 1968, on WOR-TV.

Cuchiara, Joseph D., dir. *A Hurricane Called Betsy.* US Department of Defense, 1966.

Rather, Dan, presenter. *CBS Reports.* Episode "The Priest and the Politician." Aired September 18, 1963, on CBS.

UNPUBLISHED PAPERS

Hilbink, Thomas. Transcripts of interviews by Thomas Hilbink with Elsbeth Levy Bothe, Al Bronstein, Richard Frank, Jeremiah Gutman, Peter Marcuse, Henry Schwarzschild, and Richard Sobol. Copies in possession of author.

Kaplan, Warren. "Bogalusa Diary." Unpublished manuscript, 1965. Copy in possession of author.

Sobol, Richard. Richard Sobol's application for position as US District Court judge. Sobol's personal papers, May 1979. Copy in possession of author.

COURT CASES

(* denotes Richard Sobol as attorney)

SOURCES

Adams v. Fazzio Real Estate Co. 268 F. Supp. 630 (E.D. La. 1967).*
Apodaca v. Oregon. 406 U.S. 404 (1972).*
Brown v. Post. 279 F. Supp. 60 (W.D. La. 1968).*
Butler v. District of Columbia. 346 F.2d 798 (D.C. Cir. 1965).*
Carter v. West Feliciana Parish School Board. 349 F.2d 1020 (5th Cir. 1969).*
Cox v. Louisiana. 379 U.S. 536 (1965).
Duncan v. Louisiana. 391 U.S. 145 (1968).*
Duncan v. Perez. 321 F. Supp. 181 (E.D. La. 1970).*
Griffin, et al. v. Louisiana. 395 F.2d 991 (5th Cir. 1968).*
Hicks v. Crown Zellerbach Corp. 310 F. Supp. 536 (E.D. La. 1970).*
Hicks v. Crown Zellerbach Corp. 321 F. Supp. 1241 (E.D. La. 1971).*
Hicks v. Knight. Civ. Ac. No. 15, 727 (E.D. La. 1965).*
Hicks v. Weaver. 302 F. Supp. 619 (E.D. La. 1969).*
Local 189, United Papermakers and Paperworkers v. United States. 416 F.2d 980 (5th Cir. 1969).*
Plaquemines Parish School Board v. United States. 415 F.2d 817 (5th Cir. 1969).
Poindexter v. Louisiana Financial Assistance Commission. (I), 258 F. Supp. 158 (E.D. La. 1966).
Poindexter v. Louisiana Financial Assistance Commission. (II), 275 F. Supp. 833 (E.D. La. 1967).
Poindexter v. Louisiana Financial Assistance Commission. (III), 296 F. Supp. 686 (E.D. La. 1968).
Sobol v. Perez. 289 F. Supp. 392 (E.D. La. 1968).
State v. Duncan, No. 1967–14643 (La. 25th D. 1967).
State v. Sobol, No. 1967–14948 (La. 25th D. 1967).
United States v. Fox. 211 F. Supp. 25 (E.D. La. 1962).
United States v. Louisiana, 265 F. Supp. 703 (E.D. La. 1966).
United States v. Plaquemines Parish School Board. 291 F. Supp. 841 (E.D. La. 1967).

ARCHIVES

American Civil Liberties Union Records, Public Policy Papers, Seeley G. Mudd Manuscript Library, Princeton University (ACLU). *NB: Where indicated, I used the microfilm versions at Tulane University and Wayne State University.*
Amistad Research Center, Tulane University (ARC).
Civil Rights History Project, American Folklife Center, Library of Congress (CRHP).
Edwin J. Lukas Papers, Balch Institute for Ethnic Studies, Historical Society of Pennsylvania (Lukas).
Jack Bass Oral History Collection, Law Library, Tulane University (JB).
KZSU Project South Interviews, Stanford University (KZSU).
Louisiana Digital Media Archive, Louisiana State Archives (LDMA).
National Archives and Records Administration—Southwest Region (NARA-SW).

SOURCES

NB: Records of the US Court of Appeals for the Fifth Circuit are labeled "5th Cir." Records of the US District Court for the Eastern District of Louisiana are labeled "E.D. La."

Papers of the Lawyers Constitutional Defense Committee, Southern Civil Rights Litigation Records for the 1960s (microfilm edition), Amistad Research Center, Tulane University (LCDC).

Index

Act 3 of 1960, 138
Act 99 of 1967, 139, 207
Act 147 of 1962, 138, 139
Act 258 of 1958, 138
Ainsworth, Robert, 144
Aldrin, Buzz, 209
Amedee, Earl, 72–73, 154, 195
American Civil Liberties Union
    (ACLU), 53, 55–56, 112–13, 125,
    151–52, 156, 188, 211
Amistad Research Center, 252n8
Amsterdam, Anthony
    on Al Bronstein, 150
    and civil rights cases, 146
    at New York University School of
        Law, 227
    and Lea Perez's prosecution of Gary
        Duncan, 214
    personality of, 144–46, 257n5
    and Henry Schwarzschild, 146, 257n8
    and Richard Sobol's arrest, 144
    and *Sobol v. Perez*, 146–48, 185,
        186–87, 189, 192–93, 196–97,
        204, 257n12, 261–62n7
Anti-Communist Christian Association,
    79
Apodaca v. Oregon (1972), 225–26, 226n
Apollo 11, 209
Armstrong, Joyce, 91
Armstrong, Neil, 209
Army Corps of Engineers, 11, 12
Arnold, Fortas & Porter, 52–54, 57,
    58, 105

Arnold & Porter, 64, 66–67, 113, 147,
    159
Aschenbrenner, Larry, 245n19
Asevedo, Harold "Dutch," 17–18, 17n,
    130
Aycock, C. C., 63

Baldwin, James, 202
Batson v. Kentucky (1986), 226
Bell, Murphy, 49, 50n
Belle Chasse, Louisiana, 16, 19–20,
    26–27, 74
Belle Chasse High School, 35, 36, 37,
    61–63, 117, 119, 137
Belle Chasse School Association, 61
Bienville Parish, Louisiana, 188–89
Bill of Rights, 84–85
Birmingham, Alabama, 102
Black, Hugo, 182–83
black Americans. *See also* segregation
    as attorneys, 48, 65, 72–73, 154, 155,
        167, 186, 195, 223–24
    as candidates in Louisiana election of
        1967, 169
    and desegregation of Catholic
        schools, 29–30
    and desegregation of public schools, 3,
        4–5, 36–39
    and elusive nature of racial equality,
        209–10
    forced labor in cleanup for Hurricane
        Betsy, 17–18, 21
    in oil industry, 117

rights asserted by, 161
risks of being black in South, 107,
    109–10
standardized tests for employment,
    82, 82n, 214
unions of, 80, 160, 165, 206
and voter registration, 55, 56–57, 59,
    141, 164, 169, 173–75, 176, 177,
    219
voting rights of, 26n, 28, 80, 81, 113,
    170, 186, 194
and workplace discrimination, 81–83,
    82n, 159, 164
Black Power movement, 164, 166–68,
    169
Bogalusa, Louisiana
    Ku Klux Klan in, 79–81
    Richard Sobol's cases in, 79, 81–83,
        104, 159–60, 206
    and A. Z. Young's march to Baton
        Rouge, 160–66, 168
Bogalusa Voters League, 80, 81, 159–60,
    164, 165, 194
Boothville, Louisiana
    Gary Duncan's home in, 8, 41
    evacuation from Hurricane Betsy, 12
    evacuation from Hurricane Camille,
        219
    living standards in, 11
    Mississippi River mouth at, 9
    trawling in, 10
Boothville Drifters (baseball team), 108
Boothville-Venice High School, desegre-
    gation of, 3, 36, 38, 42, 62, 89, 117,
    119, 119n, 120, 215
Boothville-Venice Private School Associ-
    ation, 42
Bradley, Gregory, 37
Bronstein, Al
    on Stokely Carmichael, 167
    as civil rights lawyer, 113, 125
    and Armand Derfner, 210n
    and Gary Duncan case, 181
    and finances of LCDC, 247n14

founding of Penal Reform Inter-
    national, 227
at Harvard's Kennedy School of
    Government, 159, 204
intimidation faced by, 112–13
and LCDC work, 111, 112, 143, 159,
    211
and Leander H. Perez's deposition in
    Sobol v. Perez, 149–57, 158
and Lea Perez's prosecution of Gary
    Duncan, 214, 214n
personality of, 111, 112
and Richard Sobol's arrest, 124,
    143–44
and Richard Sobol's lawsuit, 127
and Sobol v. Perez, 146–48, 149, 185,
    186, 187, 188, 189, 194–97, 198,
    199, 204, 210
and work with Richard Sobol, 224
Bronstein, Kate, 111–12
Brown v. Board of Education (1954),
    26–27, 32–33, 155–56, 203, 224
Bubrig, Darryl
    as assistant district attorney, 75, 76, 91
    as district attorney, 227
    and Gary Duncan case, 75, 76–77,
        77n, 78, 86–91, 92, 94, 96, 97, 99,
        115, 248n16
    and Hurricane Camille, 219
    on Leander H. Perez, 240n16
    Lea Perez on, 102
    and Richard Sobol's arrest, 122–23,
        124
    as witness in Sobol v. Perez, 197
Buckley, William F., Jr., 201–3
Buras, Louisiana
    Buras High School, 37, 38–39, 117,
        119, 215
    and offshore oil industry, 10
    Our Lady of Good Harbor school,
        29–31, 34
Buras, Wilbur, 77, 128–31, 219, 238n14,
    255n2

California State Assembly, march on, 161
Carmichael, Stokely, 166–67, 259n25
Carter v. West Feliciana Parish School Board (1969), 50n
Cassibry, Fred, 214–15, 214n
Catholic Church, 26–27, 29–30
Chaney, James, 144
Chaplin, Charlie, 26n
Cheney, James, 56
Chicago Defender, 36
Chicken Shack case, 72–73
Children's Defense Fund, 213
Christenberry, Herbert, 117–19
Citizens' Councils, 140–41, 141n
Civil Rights Act (1964), 32, 82, 155, 159, 202
civil rights movement
  and Black Power movement, 166–67
  and civil rights lawyers, 5, 55, 64n, 72, 73, 79, 113, 125, 137, 146, 148, 155, 186, 190, 192, 195, 196, 205, 210, 213
  and Armand Derfner, 187
  ending of, 224
  and Freedom Summer, 54–55, 56, 57, 64, 112
  and LCDC, 54–58, 64
  and Richard Sobol, 53–54
  and *Sobol v. Perez,* 147, 186, 190–91
  and summer of 1967, 160–61, 164, 258n4
  victories of, 32
  vision of, 80, 200, 206
  E. Gordon West on, 49
Collette, Herb, 69, 126–27, 129
Collins, Douglas & Elie
  black workers in Bogalusa hiring, 80, 81
  bombing of office, 48, 48n, 72, 188, 244n1
  on Chicken Shack case, 73
  as civil rights lawyers, 64n
  and Gary Duncan case, 71–72
  intimidation faced by, 72, 72n, 188

Lea Perez's attempts to disqualify from Gary Duncan case, 102–3
  and Richard Sobol, 48–49, 66, 67, 69, 83, 123
  threats of disbarment, 147
Collins, Robert
  as civil rights lawyer, 64n, 65, 223–24
  and Gary Duncan case, 71, 73, 74, 95
  Gary Duncan case motion to quash, 75, 244n17, 248n16
  and Gary Duncan's arraignment for battery, 78
  and Gary Duncan's arraignment for Cruelty to Juveniles, 75–76, 248n16
  Gary Duncan's initial meeting with, 69–70
  education of, 65
  and election of 1967, 169
  intimidation faced by, 72, 72n
  and Richard Sobol, 50, 65, 114
  and *Sobol v. Perez,* 189
  as US District Court judge, 227–28
  as witness in *Sobol v. Perez,* 191–92, 194
Collins, Thomas, 103
Commission on the Unauthorized Practice of Law, 147
Congress of Racial Equality (CORE)
  and Bogalusa Voters League, 80
  and Al Bronstein, 111
  Ku Klux Klan's murder of workers, 56
  and LCDC office, 69
  and Leander H. Perez, 104, 153
  and Plaquemines Parish, 71
  and Carl Rachlin, 55
  and A. Z. Young's march to Baton Rouge, 164–65
constitutional-interpretation test, 170–73, 171n, 174, 175
Cooper, Gordon, 7
Cope, Arthur, 45–46
Councilor, The, 140
Couvillion, Brady, 237n4
Cox, William Harold, 143–44

Creoles, 40, 40n
Crown Zellerbach, 80–82, 82n, 160,
165, 194, 206, 214, 214n
Cruelty to Juveniles statute, 45, 68–69,
77, 244n17

Dawkins, Ben, 205
Deacons for Defense and Justice, 80–81,
161, 162, 165, 228
Delta Bank, 135
Delta Development Company, 25,
240n18
Delta Heritage Academy, 63, 142
Democratic Party, as the Ring, 21, 22
Derfner, Armand, 187, 189–90, 210n,
259n25
Devitt, T. K., 123
Doar, John, 185
Douglas, Nils R.
as civil rights lawyer, 64n, 65–66,
223–24
on Gary Duncan case, 71–72, 73, 74,
78, 95, 251n3
and election of 1967, 169–70
intimidation faced by, 72, 72n
and Eugene Leon, 75
and Richard Sobol, 49, 65, 66, 213,
224
and *Sobol v. Perez,* 189
and Southern Organization for Unified Leadership, 228
Duncan, Calvin, 12–16, 43, 128–29,
175
Duncan, Fay, 228, 252n3
Duncan, Gary
agriculture work of, 10
arraignment on battery charges, 78
arraignment on Cruelty to Juveniles
charge, 75, 76–77, 77n
and arrest of Richard Sobol, 122
arrests of, 43, 45, 47, 69, 77, 78, 86,
107, 122, 128–32, 133, 134, 179,
191, 212, 255nn2, 5
birth of son Gregory, 107–8

bonds of, 69, 75, 79, 79n, 100, 109,
113, 114–15, 122, 123, 124, 125,
126–27, 133, 134–36
as commercial fisherman, 228
Cruelty to Juveniles charge against,
68–69, 71, 73–74, 78, 79
on desegregation of public schools,
40, 41
family background of, 8
guns of, 15
and Hurricane Betsy, 12–16, 40, 219
and Hurricane Camille, 219–22
and Herman Landry, Jr. encounter,
4–5, 6, 42, 43–45, 46, 68–70,
73–74, 79, 87–89, 98
marriage of, 4, 40–41, 47, 108, 109, 131
Lea Perez's prosecution of, 208,
211–12, 214
Plaquemines Parish as home of, 8–9,
10
and preliminary proceedings, 74–76
sentencing hearing of, 103–4
Simple Battery charges against, 77, 78,
83–84
and Richard Sobol's arrest, 125–26
Richard Sobol's friendship with, 213,
224
and *Sobol v. Perez,* 187, 192
trawling for shrimp, 8, 10, 41, 97, 108
at trial for battery, 86, 90, 91, 94–95,
96, 97–98, 99, 100
and Washington, DC trip, 179–82,
184
as witness in *Sobol v. Perez,* 179, 194,
195
work on crew boats, 10, 41, 69, 97,
108, 127, 128
work on tugboats, 4, 41, 97, 108
Duncan, Gary, Jr., 252n4
Duncan, Gaynelle, 175
Duncan, Geralyn, 4, 41, 47, 108, 131
Duncan, Lambert (Gary's father)
arrest of, 129
boats of, 13, 110, 179

dog of, 12, 16
and Gary Duncan's arraignment for
  battery, 78
and Gary Duncan's arrest, 128–29,
  131, 134
and Gary Duncan's bail bond, 109,
  126–27
and Gary Duncan's trial, 95, 98, 99
as Freemason, 110, 252n8
and Hurricane Betsy, 12, 16
and Hurricane Camille, 219, 221
and NAACP, 109
on responsibilities of fatherhood, 018,
  40
on risks of being black in South, 107,
  109–10
and F. J. Smith, 43
and Richard Sobol's arrest, 125, 126
success of, 107
traffic violations of, 122
and voter registration, 174, 175
work ethic of, 8
Duncan, Lynn Lange
  and Gary Duncan's trial, 86
  marriage to Gary Duncan, 4, 40–41,
    47, 108, 109, 131
  and Gregory Taylor, 252nn3, 4
  and Washington, DC trip, 179–82,
    184
Duncan, Mancil, 12–16, 43
Duncan, Mazie (Gary's mother)
  and Gary Duncan's arraignment for
    battery, 78
  and Gary Duncan's arrest warrants,
    47, 69, 128–29, 131
  and Gary Duncan's testimony in *Sobol
    v. Perez,* 195
  and Gary Duncan's trial, 86, 95, 96,
    98, 99
  and Gary Duncan's work, 10
  and Hurricane Betsy, 12, 16
  and Hurricane Camille, 219, 221
  on risks of being black in South, 107,
    110

and F. J. Smith, 43
and Richard Sobol, 68, 76, 207
and voter registration, 173, 175
work ethic of, 8
Duncan, Robert, 122, 125, 134–36, 173,
  175, 221
Duncan, Vivian, 107, 131–32, 173, 175
Duncan family
  in Boothville, 8
  and Lynn Lange Duncan's family, 41,
    108–9
  and evacuation for Hurricane Betsy,
    12, 16
  extended family, 108, 179, 221,
    252n3
  and rebuilding after Hurricane Betsy,
    40
  and F. J. Smith, 43
  traffic violations for, 122
Duncan v. Louisiana (1968), 180–82,
  191–92, 205, 207–8, 212, 225–26,
  225n
Duncan v. Perez (1970), 212–15, 251n1

Easy Rider (film), 216, 224
Edelman, Marian Wright, 213
education. *See* public schools; white
  segregation academies
Education Expense Grant Fund, 138
Elie, Lolis
  as civil rights lawyer, 64n, 65, 223–24,
    228–29
  on Gary Duncan case, 73, 74, 95, 102,
    188
  education of, 65
  and election of 1967, 169
  intimidation faced by, 72, 72n,
    188–89
  and Eugene Leon, 75
  on Plaquemines Parish's reputation,
    71, 72
  as prosecutor in Orleans Parish, 102–3
  and Richard Sobol, 65, 66, 83, 213,
    224

and Richard Sobol's arrest, 123–24
as witness in *Sobol v. Perez,* 186–90, 191,
    192, 194, 261–62n7, 262nn9, 13
equal employment cases, 223
Equal Protection Clause, 186

Farmer, James, 72
FBI
    investigation of forced labor for blacks
        in Hurricane Betsy cleanup, 21
    investigation of Our Lady of Good
        Harbor fire, 31
    investigation of Plaquemines Parish
        court cases, 196
    Leander H. Perez investigated by,
        26–27, 34, 36, 120, 155, 251n1
Federalist Society, 224
Ferranto, Ralph, 130–31, 136
Ferranto, Mrs. Ralph, 136
Fifth Amendment, 85
Firing Line, 201, 202
First Amendment, 84
Fiss, Owen, 145, 185–86, 194–98,
    204–5, 210
Fitzgerald's Bar, Venice, 110
Fleischer, Hugh, 64n
Fonda, Peter, 216
Fortas, Abe, 52, 58, 64, 85, 105, 181–84
Fort Jackson, 38–39
Fort St. Philip, Leander H. Perez's prison
    camp for "racial agitators" at, 71, 135,
    153, 201
Fourteenth Amendment, 60–61, 85n,
    155, 170, 186
Fourth Amendment, 85
Frankfurter, Felix, 146
Franklin, Cheryl, 108
Franklin, Paula, 108
Freedom Summer, 54–55, 56, 57, 64, 112

Gemini V, 7–8
Gideon, Clarence, 52, 58
Gideon v. Wainwright (1963), 52, 85, 225
Gitlow v. New York (1925), 84n

Goodman, Andrew, 56, 144
Grant, Bert
    and Gary Duncan's trial, 86, 89–90,
        94, 96, 98
    and Highway 23 incident, 3, 4–5, 43,
        46, 70
    and Hurricane Camille, 219
grant-in-aid statutes, 138, 139, 198,
    206–7
Griffin, Percy, 175
Gutman, Jeremiah, 67

Hébert, F. Edward, 61, 63
Heebe, Frederick, 144, 214, 214n
Hicks, Bob, 81–82, 165
Hicks v. Crown Zellerbach Corp. (1970),
    82, 82n, 159, 210–11, 213, 214
Highway 23
    black drivers stopped on, 110
    and evacuation for Hurricane Betsy, 12
    and incident with Gary Duncan and
        Herman Landry, 3, 4–5, 42,
        43–44, 68–70, 73–74, 79, 87–89
    and oil industry, 10
    Leander H. Perez's supervision of
        construction of, 121
    in Plaquemines Parish, 9, 24
Hitler, Adolf, 187
Honigsberg, Peter, 161, 163
Hoover, J. Edgar, 27, 56
Hotz, Ronald, 154
House Committee on Un-American
    Activities, 51
Hunter, Lucretia, 37–39
Hurricane Betsy
    cleanup following, 17–18, 20–21,
        118
    and Gary Duncan, 12–16, 40, 219
    evacuation of Plaquemines Parish,
        11–12
    forced labor of blacks in clearing
        debris from, 17–18, 21
    Hurricane Camille compared to, 219
    path of, 11, 13–14

and Leander H. Perez, 19–21, 59, 141, 176
and Plaquemines Parish, 7, 12–16, 219
refugees in Scottville School, 17–18
Hurricane Camille, 218–22, 220n
Hurricane Katrina, 36n, 219, 220, 228
Hurricane Rita, 36n
Hurtado v. California (1884), 84n

Irwin, Woodrow, 104

Jeansonn, Glen, 251n1
Jefferson Parish, Louisiana, 9n, 114, 135, 219
Jelinek, Don, 125, 147, 259n25
Johnson, Calvin, 262nn9, 13
Johnson, Lyndon B., 32, 169, 175–76, 200
Jones, Harold, 38–39
Jones, Laverne, 38
Jump, The (levee), 12–13, 14
Juneau, Don, 125–26, 133–36, 147, 161, 181
jury trial, right to, 84, 85, 85n, 86–87, 93, 95, 115, 182–84, 207–8, 225–26, 225n

Katzenbach, Nicholas, 176
Kennedy, Robert, 206
King, Martin Luther, Jr., 53–54, 71, 80, 153–54, 160, 166–67, 200–201, 204–5
Ku Klux Klan
on Black Power movement, 167
in Bogalusa, 79–81
Al Bronstein threatened by, 112
murder of CORE workers, 56
Leander H. Perez on, 156
Lea Perez on, 102
and A. Z. Young's march to Baton Rouge, 163, 164

Landry, Gloria, 45–46, 76–77, 77n, 86, 98, 249n20

Landry, Herman, Jr.
and Gary Duncan case, 76–77, 77n
and Gary Duncan encounter, 4–5, 6, 42, 43–45, 46, 68–70, 73–74, 79, 87–89, 98
and Gary Duncan's trial, 86–87, 94, 99
and Hurricane Camille, 219
statement for justice of peace, 46
Landry, Herman, Sr., 45–46, 86, 98, 249n20
Lange, Calvin, 108–9, 212
Lange, Stanley, 108–9
Latham, Parnell "Bud," 42–44, 46, 76–77, 94, 98–99, 219, 243n6
Lawyers' Committee for Civil Rights Under Law, 245n19
Lawyers Constitutional Defense Committee (LCDC)
and Anthony Amsterdam, 146, 204
and Al Bronstein, 111, 112, 143, 159, 211
budget of, 67–68, 67n, 211, 223, 247n14
Stokely Carmichael on, 167, 259n25
and civil rights movement, 54–58, 64
dissolution of, 229
field office of, 112
intimidation tactics against, 72
and Don Jelinek, 125
and Henry Schwarzschild, 55–56, 57, 67, 211
and Richard Sobol, 57–58, 64–68, 104, 111, 159, 166, 180, 210–11, 213, 247n14
and *Sobol v. Perez*, 185, 186, 189, 192, 194, 196, 204
state challenges to, 147
volunteer lawyers working for, 55–57, 64–65, 66
and voting rights, 170
and A. Z. Young's march to Baton Rouge, 161, 163, 164
Leon, Eugene
as assistance district attorney, 75

deposition in *Sobol v. Perez,* 157

and Gary Duncan's arrest, 133, 134, 136

indictment for malfeasance, 248n13

as judge in Gary Duncan case, 74–75, 77, 77n, 86–87, 90, 92–95, 96, 98–99, 212, 250n3, 251n3

and Don Juneau, 126

and Leander H. Perez's deposition in *Sobol v. Perez,* 149

and Lea Perez's attempt to disqualify Richard Sobol, 103

and Richard Sobol's arrest, 123, 124

Richard Sobol's bond application to, 113, 114–15, 122, 123

Richard Sobol's lawsuit against, 127

as witness in *Sobol v. Perez,* 197

Lewis, Anthony, 52

literacy tests, 170–71

Little Fish bar, 3, 4–5, 43

Livingston Parish, Louisiana, 161, 163

Long, Earl, 19

Long, Huey, 103

Louisiana

and age calculation requirement, 172, 174

election of 1967, 169–71, 177

GDP for 1965, 20, 239n4

Louisiana Bar Association

criteria for admission, 147, 196

Ben Dawkins requirement for lawyer's membership in, 205

and Nils Douglas, 72

Lea Perez reporting Richard Sobol to, 103, 105, 251n3

and *Sobol v. Perez,* 190, 194

Louisiana Commission on Human Relations, 168

Louisiana constitution

right to jury trial, 84, 182–84

tests on, 171

Louisiana Department of Education, 139–40

Louisiana Education Commission for Needy Children, 207

Louisiana Financial Assistance Commission, 137–39

Louisiana law

death penalty cases in, 84

and NAACP, 109, 109n

punishment for misdemeanors in, 83–84

trial by jury in, 84, 86–87

on unlicensed legal practice, 186, 205

Louisiana Supreme Court

and Gary Duncan case, 95

impeachment case against Leander Perez, 22

and Richard Sobol's bond application, 113, 114

Louisiana Weekly, 37, 154

Lynch, Lincoln, 164–65

lynching, black workers in Bogalusa threatened with, 80

McBride, Rudy, 74

McBride Academy, 63, 140

McCarthy, Joseph, 58

McCarthyism, 51

McKeithen, John, 160, 163, 165, 168

McKinney, Westley, 44, 46, 46n, 244n12

Madison Parish, Louisiana, 105, 205, 206

Manta (yacht), 24, 104

March for Jobs and Justice, 160–66, 168

March on Washington (1964), 54

marshland, 9, 11, 13, 23

mass incarceration, 226

Mattice, Tony, 134, 136

Miranda v. Arizona (1966), 146, 225

Mississippi, 147

Mississippi River

basin of, 9

defining Gary Duncan's world, 9

levee system of, 8, 9, 10, 11, 12, 14–16, 20, 21, 24, 59, 74

mixed-race relationships, 40n, 243n6

Moncla, S. A., 32, 35

Mt. Olive Missionary Baptist Church, 174–75

NAACP
    Legal Defense Fund, 139, 146, 213
    New Orleans NAACP, 109, 109n
    Leander H. Perez on, 73
Nation, The, 80
National Guard, 161, 163
National Review, 201
Native Americans, Creoles identifying as, 40n
New Orleans, Louisiana
    desegregation of public schools in, 27
    and evacuation for Hurricane Betsy, 12, 16
    Leander H. Perez's opposition to Catholic Church's desegregation of schools, 29
    as "up the road" from Plaquemines Parish, 9n
New Orleans Item, 26
New Orleans NAACP, 109, 109n
New York Civil Liberties Union, 67
New York Times, 146–47
New York Times Magazine, 202
Nicholson, Jack, 216
Nixon, Richard, 168, 200, 205–6, 209, 223, 224

oil industry
    desegregation of, 215–16
    and Hurricane Betsy cleanup, 20
    and mineral leases, 23, 25–26
    offshore oil industry, 108
    in Plaquemines Parish, 10, 23, 23n
    and service contracts secured by black Americans, 117
originalism, legal theory of, 224
Orleans Parish, Louisiana, 102
Our Lady of Good Harbor school, 29–31, 34

Parish Fair and Orange Festival, 24
Parker, Carolyn, 38–39
Parker v. Gladden (1966), 85n
Patti, Frank, 35, 140

Perez, Agnes, 22, 121
Perez, Chalin, 59–61, 63, 105, 141–42, 215, 229
Perez, Leander H.
    and William F. Buckley Jr., 201–3
    on Citizens' Councils, 140–41
    on civil rights lawyers, 72
    conspiracy theories of, 75, 89, 101, 104, 117, 137, 155–56, 202–3, 251n1
    death of, 215
    and defamation suits, 22
    on "deplorable" situation, 22
    deposition in *Sobol v. Perez,* 149–57, 158, 160, 195
    and Armand Derfner, 187–88
    on desegregation of public schools, 26, 28, 31–37, 34n, 39, 59, 60, 62, 89, 91, 117, 120, 138–40, 154, 170, 192, 202
    as district attorney, 22–23, 25
    and Gary Duncan case, 106
    election fraud of, 26n
    fishing trips for political allies and lawyers, 104–5
    and forced labor of blacks after Hurricane Betsy, 18
    on Abe Fortas, 105
    graft of, 25, 151, 229
    and Hurricane Betsy, 19–21, 59, 141, 176
    and incident with Gary Duncan and Herman Landry, 70
    Glen Jeansonne's biography of, 251n1
    jobs provided by, 24
    as judge, 19, 22, 24–25, 239–40n16
    "Little War" of, 24, 24n
    mineral leases controlled by, 23, 25–26, 63
    and New Orleans NAACP raid, 109, 109n
    and Lea Perez's attempt to disqualify Richard Sobol, 105–6, 251n4
    personality of, 59, 60

physical appearance of, 91
as political boss, 23, 26, 35, 63,
    72–73, 74, 85, 107, 117–18, 135,
    151, 175, 182, 201
prison camp for "racial agitators" at
    Fort St. Philip, 71, 135, 153, 201
racist legislation written by, 28, 59
racist views of, 60, 73
and John Rarick, 170
restraining order on, 32, 34, 60, 61,
    63, 106, 140
role in Plaquemine Parish politics, 19,
    21–26
on segregation, 26–28, 27n, 29, 30,
    31, 33, 43, 59, 60, 243n6
shell development companies oper-
    ated by, 25, 240n18
and Richard Sobol's arrest, 116, 123,
    124, 144
Richard Sobol's lawsuit against, 127
state-managed land controlled by, 23, 25
"The Unconstitutionality of the 14th
    Amendment," 60–61, 170
voter-suppression techniques of,
    170–75, 176, 177–78, 260n23
and white segregation academies,
    32–35, 42, 61, 138–41, 206–7,
    262n1
and white voter registration drives, 176
Perez, Leander H., Jr. "Lea"
    conspiracy theories of, 75, 89, 101,
        104, 251n1
    deposition in *Sobol v. Perez,* 157
    on desegregation of public schools,
        60, 91, 101–2
    as district attorney, 59–60, 72, 91
    Gary Duncan prosecuted by, 208,
        211–12, 214–15, 224–25
    and Gary Duncan's arrest, 133
    at Gary Duncan trial, 91–94, 95, 96,
        97–98, 99, 101, 251n3
    end of political career, 229
    on father's fishing trips for political
        allies, 104–5

indictment for malfeasance, 248n13
and Eugene Leon, 75
on liberal media, 101–2
New Orleans private law practice of,
    105
and Leander H. Perez's deposition in
    Sobol v. Perez, 149
physical appearance of, 91
power struggle in 1980s, 251n1
racist views of, 60
restraining order on, 60
and Richard Sobol's arrest, 123, 124,
    133
and Richard Sobol's disqualification
    for Gary Duncan case, 102–6, 147,
    251nn3, 4
Richard Sobol's lawsuit against, 127
as witness in *Sobol v. Perez,* 197
Phoenix School, 117
phrenology, 27, 27n
Plaquemines Gazette
    advertisement for public school teach-
        ers, 118
    on Chalin Perez, 142
    on Leander H. Perez, 137
    and Leander H. Perez's "The Uncon-
        stitutionality of the 14th
        Amendment," 60–61
    on race mixing, 42
    on racial unrest, 102, 139
    racist op-eds in, 243n6
    on school desegregation, 120, 140
    on tuberculosis scare, 140
    on white segregated academies, 139
Plaquemines Parish, Louisiana
    bird-foot delta of, 9, 16
    Civil Rights Commission hearing of
        1961, 172
    Robert Collins on reputation of, 71,
        72
    as Gary Duncan's home, 8–9, 10
    FBI investigation of, 196
    federal election observers in, 176,
        177–78, 260n23

floods of, 11
hard work in culture of, 10
and Hurricane Betsy, 7, 12–16, 219
and Hurricane Camille, 218–22, 220n
hurricanes of, 11
infrastructure of, 24
and Martin Luther King Jr.'s death, 201
land between levees, 9, 9n
and mineral leases, 23–24
oil industry in, 10, 23, 23n
Leander H. Perez's political role in, 19, 21–26
Lea Perez's role in, 102
school desegregation in, 26, 28, 31–37, 34n, 39, 40, 45, 60, 61, 101, 117–20, 137, 215
voter registration in, 173–75
and white supremacy, 79
Plaquemines Parish Civic and Political Organization, 174, 175
Plaquemines Parish Commission Council, 63, 118, 142, 150
Plaquemines Parish School Board, 34–36, 34n, 60, 64n, 118
Poindexter v. Louisiana Financial Assistance Commission (II), 139
Pointe à la Hache, Louisiana, 69, 72, 74, 77, 104–5, 114, 125–26, 173
Pontchartrain Park, New Orleans, 40
Port Eads, Louisiana, 104
Porter, Paul, 53
Port of Plaquemines, 20
Port Sulphur, Louisiana, 24, 45
Port Sulphur High School, 36, 37, 38, 117, 119, 140, 215
Priest and the Politician, The (CBS special), 27n, 31
Prince Edward County, Virginia, 32–33, 32n
Prince Hall Grand Lodge, 252n8
private schools. *See* white segregation academies
Promised Land Academy, 63, 117
Provensal, Sidney

on closing of Belle Chasse High School, 61
and Robert Collins's testimony in *Sobol v. Perez,* 191
and Lolis Elie's testimony in *Sobol v. Perez,* 189
and Leander H. Perez's deposition in *Sobol v. Perez,* 149–50, 153, 156, 157, 158
Lea Perez's settlement offer for Richard Sobol, 147
and Lea Perez's testimony in *Sobol v. Perez,* 197
and Richard Sobol's testimony in *Sobol v. Perez,* 195, 196
and testimony of local white lawyers in *Sobol v. Perez,* 197–99
public schools
buses for, 35–36, 37, 39, 119, 119n
classroom materials stolen from, 120
desegregation of, 3, 4–5, 26, 32–33, 36–39, 40, 41
Leander H. Perez on desegregation of, 26, 28, 31–37, 34n, 39, 59, 60, 62, 89, 91, 117, 120, 138–40, 154, 170, 192, 202
and race-based redistricting, 194, 262n1
sports equipment stolen from, 119
tuberculosis scare in, 140
white students returning to, 215

race mixing, in Plaquemines Parish, 101, 117
race relations, in Plaquemines Parish, 4–5, 41, 42, 45, 60, 101–2, 110, 243n6
race war, 42, 60, 101, 160
Rachlin, Carl, 55
racial hygiene, 27
Ragas, Peggy, 37
Ramos v. Louisiana (2019), 226n
Rarick, John, 170, 188–89, 262n9
Rather, Dan, 31

Reagan, Ronald, 161, 200
Rehnquist, William, 224
Reston, Robert, 188
Rezneck, Daniel, 113–14
River Oaks Academy, 61–62, 117, 119, 142
Robert Hicks Foundation, 228
Roger Baldwin Foundation of the ACLU, 211
Rousselle, Lawrence, 156
Rousselle v. Perez, 251n1
Runyon v. McCrary (1976), 262n1
Ruth, Babe, 26n

St. Ann, Bernard
  and Gary Duncan's trial, 86, 89, 94, 96, 98
  and Hurricane Camille, 219
  and incident on Highway 23, 3, 4–5, 46, 70
St. Bernard High School, 36
St. Bernard Parish, Louisiana, 36
St. Tammany Parish, Louisiana, 161
Save Our Children campaign, 140–41
Scalia, Antonin, 224
Scanduro, Dominick, 240n16, 251n1
Scarabin, Randolph "Ruggie," 43–44, 46, 76, 77n, 86, 90–91, 94, 219
Scarabin, Wayne, 43–44, 46, 76, 77n, 86–90, 219
Schneider, Chris, 29–30
Schwarzschild, Henry
  and Anthony Amsterdam, 146, 257n8
  and Al Bronstein, 112
  and Capital Punishment Project, 229
  and *Duncan v. Louisiana,* 180
  and LCDC, 55–56, 57, 67, 211
  and Richard Sobol, 67–68, 159
  and *Sobol v. Perez,* 146–47, 187, 189
Schwerner, Michael, 56, 144
Scottville, School, 17, 117
seafood processing, 10
Sea Master (tugboat), 12, 13, 14, 15, 16
Seaway Academy, 42–43, 44, 63, 219

segregation
  of bars and restaurants, 215
  of businesses, 40
  in oil industry jobs, 10
  Leander H. Perez on, 26–28, 27n, 29, 30, 31, 33, 43, 59, 60, 243n6
  white segregation academies, 32–35, 42, 61–63, 117, 119–20, 137–42, 198n, 206–7, 215, 262n1
Selma, Alabama, 102
Shell Oil Company dock, 128
Shreve, Sara, 36n
Simmons, Charles, 120
Simple Battery statute, 77, 78, 83–84, 212
Sixth Amendment, 85, 85n, 182
Smith, F. J., 42–46, 69, 77, 128–31, 219, 244n12, 255n2
Sobol, Alfred, 51–52
Sobol, Anne Buxton, 223, 224, 229–30
Sobol, Barbara, 52, 57, 66–68, 114, 123–24, 159, 187, 213
Sobol, Joanna, 66–67, 159, 213, 224
Sobol, Marion, 51
Sobol, Richard
  and appeals court review of Gary Duncan case, 88, 95, 113
  arrest of, 116, 122–25, 143–44, 147, 191
  Bogalusa cases of, 79, 81–83
  bond for, 124, 126
  and Al Bronstein, 111
  as civil rights lawyer, 54, 113, 224, 225–26, 229
  and Collins, Douglas & Elie office, 48–49
  corporate law work of, 49, 52–53, 54, 56, 58, 64, 66–67, 73, 105, 159
  desegregation cases of, 49–50, 50n
  and Gary Duncan case, 71, 73, 74, 83, 107, 109, 179–82, 184
  and Gary Duncan case motion for delay, 99–100
  and Gary Duncan case motion for trial by jury, 85, 86–87, 93, 95, 115

and Gary Duncan case motion to quash, 74, 75, 76, 244n17, 248n16
and Gary Duncan's arraignment for battery, 78
and Gary Duncan's arraignment for Cruelty to Juveniles, 75–76, 248n16
and Gary Duncan's arrest, 133–34
Gary Duncan's initial meeting with, 69–70, 71
Mazie Duncan's phone call to, 68, 76
and *Duncan v. Perez,* 212–15
education of, 52
and election of 1967, 169, 259n2
family background of, 50–51
illness in Tallulah, 78–79
job offers of, 159
lawsuits filed by, 127, 159
as LCDC senior attorney, 159, 204
as LCDC staff attorney, 64, 66–68, 111, 247n14
as LCDC volunteer lawyer, 57–58, 64–65
and Mississippi election issues, 83
motorcycle trips of, 216–17, 223, 224
Lea Perez's attempt to disqualify from Gary Duncan case, 102–6, 147, 251nn3, 4
professorship at University of Michigan Law School, 211, 213
on school desegregation issue in Gary Duncan case, 88–91, 92, 98–99
and *Sobol v. Perez,* 146–48, 149, 187, 189
on technicalities in Gary Duncan case, 83
traffic stop of, 104, 105
and trial in Gary Duncan case, 86–91, 92, 93–94, 95, 96–100
and voting-rights cases, 169, 259n2
as witness in *Sobol v. Perez,* 194–95, 196
and A. Z. Young's march from Bogalusa to Baton Rouge, 160–66
Sobol, Zachary, 67, 213, 224

Sobol v. Perez (1968)
and Fred Cassibry, 214
Robert Collins as witness in, 191–92, 194
decision in, 205, 210
Gary Duncan as witness for, 179, 194, 195
Lolis Elie as witness in, 186–90, 191, 192, 194, 261–62n7, 262nn9, 13
federal government joining lawsuit, 185–86, 194
and Lea Perez's conspiracy theories, 251n1
Leander H. Perez's deposition in, 149–57, 158, 160, 195
and Lea Perez's settlement offer, 147, 257n12
Richard Sobol as witness in, 194–95, 196
team for, 146–48, 185, 192–93
A. Z. Young as witness in, 194
South
and desegregation of public schools, 26, 32–33
liberal media on, 102
risks of being black in, 107, 109–10
segregation academies in, 33
Southern Christian Leadership Conference (SCLC), 166–67
State v. Duncan (1967), 250n3
Student Nonviolent Coordinating Committee (SNCC), 55, 125, 166–67
Sugrue, Thomas, 258n4
Sunrise School, 38

Talley, Bascom, 188
Tallulah, Louisiana, Richard Sobol's cases in, 78–79
Tangipahoa Parish, Louisiana, 161–62
Taylor, Adrian, 108, 252n3
Taylor, Gregory Louis (Gary Duncan's son), 107–8, 131, 252nn3, 4
Taylor, Joe, 174
Taylor v. Louisiana (1975), 226

Temple, Ralph, 53–54, 57
Tenth Amendment, 171n
Terry, Ray, 64n
Times-Picayune, 143
Tinsley, Chick, 61–62, 119, 246n8
Title II of Civil Rights Act, 198
Title VII of Civil Rights Act, 82, 198, 214
Tureaud, A. P., 72–73, 139, 195
Turner, Theodore, 38, 237n7
Tuttle, Elbert, 143–44

Unauthorized Practice of Law Committee, 147, 196
US Civil Rights Commission, 172, 175
US Constitution, 84–85, 95, 171, 207
US Department of Health, Education, and Welfare, 140
US Department of Justice
  Civil Rights Division, 32, 33, 34–35, 62, 64n, 163, 175, 185, 223
  and Louisiana white segregated academies, 139, 140
  and voting rights, 170
US Supreme Court
  desegregation decision of, 26, 33
  and Gary Duncan case, 5, 95, 179–81, 192
  and incorporation doctrine, 84–85, 84n
  Richard Sobol's writ of certiorari to, 113, 114
United States v. Plaquemines Parish School Board (1967), 60, 64n, 118–19, 140

Venice, Louisiana, 9, 14, 16
Venice Marina, 12–15
Vietnam war, 164, 169, 205, 209
voter disenfranchisement laws, 28
Voting Rights Act, 120, 156, 169, 175–76, 198, 202, 205

Wallace, George, 169, 200, 202, 205
Warren, Earl, 183, 224, 225

Washington Parish, Louisiana, 104
Washington Research Project, 213, 216, 223
Wechsler, Herbert, 52
Weisbrod, Carol, 56
West, E. Gordon, 49–50
West Pointe à la Hache, ferry landing at, 74
wetlands, 9, 237n4
White, Byron, 208, 212
white segregation academies
  accreditation of, 139–40
  books donated by supporters, 140
  buses for, 119
  continued operation of, 215
  graduation ceremonies of, 141–42
  and grant-in-aid statutes, 138
  and Louisiana Financial Assistance Commission, 137–39
  and Leander H. Perez, 32–35, 42, 61, 117, 138–41, 206–7, 262n1
  and Save Our Children campaign, 140–41
  teachers raiding public school classrooms for supplies, 120
  and tuition vouchers, 33, 137–38, 198, 206–7
  and white solidarity, 33, 34, 61–63, 117, 198, 198n
white supremacy, 5, 79, 112, 140–41, 141n
Wisdom, John Minor, 139, 143–44, 175, 206–7
Wolbrette, Dorothy, 182–84
Woodlawn School, 35, 36, 36n, 117
workplace discrimination, 81–83, 82n, 159, 164
Wright, Marian, 213
Wyche, Zelma, 194

Young, A. Z., 159–60, 161, 162–65, 166, 168, 194

About the Author

Matthew Van Meter, raised a Quaker, has written for *The Atlantic*, the *New Republic, Longreads, The Awl*, and other publications. A graduate of Middlebury College and Columbia University, he reports on criminal justice, teaches at the College for Creative Studies, and works as assistant director of Shakespeare in Prison. He lives in Detroit.